Intimacy and Alienation

Lucidly written and trenchantly argued, *Intimacy and Alienation* proposes both a therapy and theory of human consciousness. Russell Meares posits a duplex self in the William James model of an 'I' and 'me', but extends it to include a third realm of being which manifests itself in a kind of intimate conversation, which is non-linear in form and brings into being an 'inner' life or self. When the fabric of such self is damaged by a traumatic experience, the resultant sense of an inner void leaves the individual without a voice other than one that is externalised and environmentally directed. The traumatic event is 'unconscious' both in the sense that it is not represented in an imaginative linguistic form and is recorded in a memory system not that of ordinary consciousness and not immediately accessible to patient or therapist.

It is the task of the therapist to foster the emergence of a form of conversation which shows elements of 'the stream of consciousness' and which will allow the integration of the traumatic memory into the patient's experience of self.

Russell Meares' unique exploration of the relationship between self and language bases itself on evidence from child development studies and memory research, while at the same time using illuminating clinical examples. At once invaluable to professionals in the field of psychiatry and psychotherapy, *Intimacy and Alienation* is an elegantly written work of wide interest to anyone interested in theories of memory, language and human consciousness.

Russell Meares is Professor of Psychiatry at the University of Sydney, and Director of Psychiatry at Westmead Hospital, Sydney.

Intimacy and Alienation

Memory, trauma and personal being

Russell Meares

With a foreword by Thomas Ogden

BRUNNER-ROUTLEDGE
ALERE FLAMMAM
Taylor & Francis Group

First published 2000
by Routledge
11 New Fetter Lane, London EC4P 4EE

Simultaneously published in the USA and Canada
by Taylor & Francis Inc., 325 Chestnut Street,
Philadelphia, PA 19106

Reprinted 2000 and 2001

First published in paperback 2001
by Brunner-Routledge
27 Church Road, Hove, East Sussex, BN3 2FA
29 West 35th Street, New York, NY 10001

Brunner-Routledge is an imprint of the Taylor & Francis Group

© 2000 Russell Meares

Typeset in Garamond by
Florence Production Ltd, Stoodleigh, Devon
Printed and bound in Great Britain by
Biddles Ltd, Guildford and King's Lynn

British Library Cataloguing in Publication Data
A catalogue record for this book is available from the British Library

ISBN 0-415-22030-0 (hbk)
ISBN 0-415-22031-9 (pbk)

Cover design by Leigh Hurlock
Cover illustration by Amanda Meares

In memory of Robert Hobson (1920–1999),
my teacher and great friend, with
affection and gratitude

Contents

PART 3
Integration

Epilogue

Foreword

If a book or an article is able to manage even once to create a feeling of surprising freshness of thought, I feel well rewarded for the time and effort that I have put into grappling with the ideas and the writing. That Russell Meares manages to achieve such freshness and originality on many occasions in this volume leads me to feel daunted by the task of doing justice to the energy of his work in this brief foreword.

For Meares, an understanding of human psychology in general, and the psychotherapeutic enterprise in particular, must be built upon an adequate conceptualisation of and way of speaking about what we mean by the experience of being 'myself'. He discusses this form of self experience in terms of an enormously complex interplay of such elements as language, memory, early cognitive and motor development, 'conversations' with ourselves and with others (which begin at or before birth), bodily sensations, the emergence of self-awareness, and the experiences of intimacy and alienation. In approaching this network of qualities of experience, Meares skilfully and creatively draws together in new ways aspects of the work of turn-of-the-century psychologists and psychiatrists including William James, James Mark Baldwin, and Pierre Janet; the neurologist Hughlings Jackson; early to mid-twentieth century philosophers such as Russell, Wittgenstein and Gilbert Ryle; a panoply of mid- to late twentieth century research psychologists including Trevarthen, Tulving, Schacter, Nelson and Bartlett; as well as aspects of the psychoanalytic work of Freud, Winnicott, Bion, Melanie Klein, Kohut, and others. Rarely will a reader find discussions of projective identification, the characteristics of various coexisting memory systems, and the outcomes of neuroimaging studies in the same volume. Meares is without peer in his ability to elaborate, integrate and significantly extend this rich and broad body of thinking.

One of the most original contributions of this book is contained in the elegantly executed discussion of what we mean when we speak of 'I' and 'me' and 'myself'. It is in this discussion that we have an opportunity to begin by listening to William James speaking of the experience of self which he thought of in terms of the experience of the continuous movement of the 'stream of consciousness'. James viewed all self-experience as 'partly known [me], partly knower [I], partly object and partly subject'. To this 'duplex structure' Meares adds a third term, a quality of self that comes to life in the space between self and other. In this space 'conversations' occur between two people that range from the earliest communications between mother and newborn to the most intimate (simultaneously self-revealing and self-creating) experiences of adults (which are to a large extent mediated by language). The three qualities of self are inseparable from one another and, in fact, have no meaning except in relation to one another. The themes developed in this discussion of the interdependent experiences of self are revisited from different vantage points throughout the book in a way that provides the volume its cohesiveness, a coherence that never lapses into ideological polemic and redundancy.

The fabric of the self as conceived by Meares is a delicate one, the integrity of which is damaged by traumatic experience, particularly when this occurs in infancy and early childhood. Instead of a feeling of personal 'me-ness', the individual is left with the experience of an internal void, an experience of being no one. Part of the medium through which early trauma makes its imprint on the psyche-soma is through the establishment of a dissociated memory system in which experiences of the disruption of self experience are stored in a form that cannot be processed as one's own past thoughts, feelings, perceptions, bodily sensations, and so on. Rather, these unthinkable thoughts and feelings that cannot be felt intrude into consciousness as unaccountable and often unnameable states of fear, despair, loneliness, dread and the like and intrude into the body as psychosomatic disorders. The psychotherapeutic enterprise as conceived of by Meares is directed at the recognition and naming of such self-alienating disruptions of self and the integration of these experiences with the rudiments of the patient's experience of 'I' and 'me' and 'myself' and 'you' and 'us'. I will not attempt to draw examples from the extensive clinical data discussed in this book. The pleasure of entering into that conversation with Russell Meares awaits the reader.

Thomas H. Ogden, M.D.
San Francisco, CA
March 1999

Acknowledgements

Two friendships have provided major contributions to the germinal background of this book. The first began in 1965. I was a trainee psychiatrist; Bob Hobson was in charge of the unit in Bethlem Royal Hospital, London, which specialised in severe disorders now called 'borderline'. At that time there was no suitable theoretical framework for treating people with this and related conditions. Although writers such as Melanie Klein, Harold Searles, and RD Laing provided valuable insights, this area of human experience was largely unmapped. As our conversations developed, and our friendship grew, in many settings, including the cricket field, in hard times and good, it seemed that, without expressing such a goal in an explicit way, we began to work towards a model, or a way of understanding and treating the problem of disrupted personality development. The first publications came out in the early seventies. By 1985, Hobson had named the project. He called it the Conversational Model. With characteristic generosity he called it a 'joint creation'. This book, which is dedicated to him, has grown out of our original endeavour.

The second friendship, with Bernard Brandchaft, began in 1983. Our immensely enjoyable and stimulating conversations have continued since then, on two continents. Bernard Brandchaft's focus upon 'minute particulars' of the therapeutic conversation and his sophisticated and original analysis of these moments played a large part in inspiring my exploration of the experience of trauma, which is the subject of the second main section of this book.

I would also like to thank Joseph Lichtenberg, President of the International Council for Psychoanalytic Self Psychology, not only for our collaborations and dialogue, but also for the opportunities he has provided for me to present my ideas at an international level.

I am grateful to my colleagues who are the faculty of Masters of Medicine (Psychotherapy) in Sydney University, at Westmead Hospital. Their enthusiasm and discussions have been important in the development of the ideas in this book. They are Mohan Gilhotra, Robert Towndrow, Joan Haliburn, George Lianos, Michael Williamson and Leo Van Biene. I particularly appreciate the help given me by Mohan Gilhotra. I also appreciate the support given by Eng Kong Tan in his leadership role with the Psychotherapy Section of the Australian and New Zealand College of Psychiatry and by Tessa Phillips, President of the Australian and New Zealand Association of Psychotherapy (ANZAP).

I am also grateful to the trainees in the Masters and ANZAP courses for the stimulus they have provided. There are now too many to thank individually. However, I wish to acknowledge the particular contribution of Jeff Yates.

The teaching programmes include a research component. Janine Stevenson, and more recently Anne Comerford, have been tenacious in their gathering of important outcome data. Evian Gordon, with whom I share the ambition to bring brain and mind together, has displayed amazing energy in developing ways of investigating brain function in our department. I thank him for his loyalty, enthusiasm and stimulation.

Many other people have been important in the creation of this book. Basil James, Professor of Psychiatry at James Cook University, Queensland, has given unfailing encouragement over a number of years. I have also been heartened by the interest taken in my project by Pierre Beumont, Professor of Psychiatry at Sydney University.

Thomas Ogden has been important in another way. We began to correspond, and to converse, in 1984 after each had published on the spatiality of human existence. His understanding of what I have been trying to do has given 'value' to my endeavour. I appreciate very much his foreword to this book.

The energy, dedication and good humour of my secretary, Rhonda Joel, was essential in bringing my endeavour to its fruition. I would like to thank my agent, Rose Cresswell, for the belief she has shown in my ideas.

Finally, and most importantly, I thank my wife, Susanne. She has acted as editor, and advised on neuropsychological and stylistic matters. Most essentially, as with my previous book, she has provided the creative environment in which it could grow.

Permissions

The author would like to thank those who have given permission for the following reproductions from other works to appear in this book; an extract from *Myth and Meaning* by Claude Lévi-Strauss, reproduced by permission of Pantheon Books; extracts from *Philosophical Investigations* by Ludwig Wittgenstein, reproduced with permission of Blackwell Publishers; an extract from 'Mind in Infancy' by Colwyn Trevarthen in R.L. Gregory (ed.) *The Oxford Companion to the Mind,* reproduced with permission of Oxford University Press; extracts from *Remembering* by Frederick Bartlett, reproduced by permission of Cambridge University Press; extracts from the

Standard Edition of Complete Psychological Works of Sigmund Freud, Vol. 12, 15, and 18, translated and edited by James Strachey, reproduced by permission of Sigmund Freud Copyrights, the Institute of Psychoanalysis and the Hogarth Press; extracts from 'The Nature and Function of Phantasy' by Susan Isaacs from *Developments in Psychoanalysis,* edited by Melanie Klein, published by Hogarth Press; extracts from *Remembrance of Things Past,* Vol. 12, by Marcel Proust, translated by S. Hudson, published by Chatto and Windus; extracts from *Ludwig Wittgenstein* by Ray Monk, published by Jonathan Cape; extracts from *The Grey Men: an Excperience* by Rebecca West, reprinted by permission of P.F.D. on behalf of the estate of Rebecca West; excerpts from *The Diary of Anais Nin,* Vols. 1 and 3, reprinted by permission of Harcourt Inc.; material from *The Fallacy of Understanding* by Edgar Levenson, reproduced with permission of Jason Aronson Inc.; extracts from *Structural Anthropology* by Claude Lévi-Strauss, translated by Clare Jacobson and Brooke Grundfest Schoepf, reproduced with the permission of Penguin Books; an extract from 'Trauma and Memory' by Bessel van der Kolk in B. van der Kolk, A. McFarlane, L. Weisaeth, *Traumatic Stress,* reproduced with permission of Guilford Press, New York; extracts from *Descartes' Error* by Antonio Damasio, reproduced with permission of MacMillan Publishers and Carlisle and Company, New York.

Some of the main ideas in this book have appeared in a somewhat different form in the following journal articles: 'The contribution of Hughlings Jackson to an understanding of dissociation', Meares R., *The American Journal of Psychiatry* 1999; 1561:1850–55. 'A Jacksonian and biopsychosocial hypothesis concerning borderline and related phenomena', Meares R., Stevenson J., Gordon E., *Australian and New Zealand Journal of Psychiatry* 1999; 33:831–40. 'Episodic memory, trauma, and the narrative of self', Meares R., *Contemporary Psychoanalysis* 1995; 31(4)541–56. 'The self in conversation: on narratives, chronicles, and scripts', Meares R., *Psychoanalytic Dialogues* 1999; 8(6)875–91. 'The "adualistic" representation of trauma: on malignant internalization', Meares R., *American Journal of Psychotherapy* 1999; 53(3)392–402. 'Value, trauma, and personal reality', Meares R., *Bulletin of Menninger Clinic* 1999; 63(4)443–58. 'Priming and projective identification; on being constructed', Meares R., *Bulletin of Menninger Clinic* 2000; 64(1).

I thank the editors of these journals who are respectively, Professor Nancy Andreason, Professor Sid Bloch, Dr Jay Greenberg, Dr Stephen Mitchell, Dr T. Bryam Karasu, Dr Kathryn Zerbe, for permission to reprint this material.

Chapter 1

The self in conversation

A man says 'I was not myself when you saw me last'. What does he mean? In logical terms, he makes no sense. How can one *not* be oneself? Yet what he says is understood. He speaks of a state which, in a general way, we know. It involves some fundamental shift in the ballast of personal being, an unpleasant disruption of the feeling of existence, in our sense of self.

Most people do not live entirely in the zone of self. From time to time, another system irrupts into psychic life, intruding into or, at times, knocking out the feeling and the kind of mental activity which underpins the sense of 'myself'. I am suggesting this system is composed of memories of past disruptions of the sense of self. These memories are 'unconscious' in that they are stored in a memory system which differs from that which underpins ordinary consciousness. They are not experienced as memories but are located in the present.

For many people, the intrusion of this disruptive system is transient and does not upset ordinary living. It passes, after a brief period of annoyance, anxiety, or desolation. For some people, however, it is an impediment. Its effect is damaging in relationships and debilitating in terms of coping. Moreover, it hinders personal growth. Disruptions of this kind are conceived, in this book, as traumatic. The intrusion of this system of traumatic memories is alienating. One feels somewhat estranged from others, and cut off from the basic feeling which is at the core of self. Management of traumatic memory systems, which can be conceived as dissociated, is a principal task of those working in the field of psychotherapy. This is the main subject of this book.

The first section concerns the nature of self and how it develops. The second section explores the form and feeling of one's experience when self is disrupted in a traumatic way. The third section focuses briefly on ways towards the restoration of self.

The first section, which explores the puzzle of self, uses the ideas of the great psychologist-philosopher William James to provide the germinal core of the argument. He conceived self as an awareness of the flow of inner life – the 'stream of consciousness' he called it. I enlarge his concept so that self is understood as a special form of conversation. This idea depends upon a distinction between two forms of human language and conversation. One of these conversations is seen as essential to the sense of self. It is non-linear, associative and apparently purposeless. The experience of self develops in a conversation which shows the 'shape' of this language, which has the form of the stream of consciousness and certain kinds of play.[1] It is the language of inner life.[2]

The second kind of language is logical, linear and clearly purposeful. It is directed, in the main, at the events of the world. It is the language of coping and adaption. The two main forms of human language are found in pure form only in unusual circumstances. The linear language of adaption is shown, undiluted, in legal and political documents. The other is found, relatively pristine, in certain kinds of poetry.

Most conversations involve a mingling of these two language forms. Embedded in the linear language built for coping with the outer world are elements of another kind of speech, which is related to inner life. An increasing amount of this latter language is associated with intimacy. Seen in this way, intimacy depends upon the development of inner experience, which can be shared with another.

Intimacy is not equivalent to confession or incontinent revelation. An intimate conversation has a peculiar warmth, a wandering form, which is associated with a feeling of well-being. The topics touched upon might seem, at first sight, banal. They might include, for example, a movie, horse-riding, a particular tree. Yet the way in which these things are spoken about resonates with something within us which is of high emotional value.

The other in this conversation is often a spouse or close friend. Yet it could be a stranger met once, for example on a plane. Neither attachment nor sexuality was involved. Yet this was an intimate conversation.

I argue that both self and intimacy depend upon a particular kind of memory. In the intimate conversation, one is aware of images from the past, particular episodes of one's life which can, for many people, be visualised in an almost cinematic way. As one talks about a movie, its scenes are held in the eyes of the mind. In the same way, horse-riding and the particular tree are spoken about not in terms of facts, such as the varieties of suitable horses, but in a way which is derived from and involves the immediate sensory alive-ness of past episodes in one's life (for example, riding towards the moon on an empty plain; wandering in a forest as a child). An intimate conversation is associated with a heightened feeling of being 'myself'.

The kind of memory upon which, I am suggesting, both self and inti-macy depend involves the recall of episodes of one's past. There is a 'doubleness' in this state. One lives in the immediate present, and at the same time is aware of a different domain of experience, which belongs to another time in one's life. In the case of the traumatic memory, double-ness is lost. One does not know the origin of its discomforting mood. No past can be recovered; the experience is located in the present. In another language, it is dissociated.

Stories of people suffering this kind of experience are given throughout the book. They include Jane, a woman in her forties, whose unpredictable moods were destroying her marriage. Her husband's apparently innocuous remarks, for example about her dress, the house, even the time of day, precipitated silence and dejection. More often her voice became high, shrill, and angry. Sometimes she threw things. The resolution of her difficulty is described in later chapters.

Since dissociation is an essential theme of the second section of the book, which concerns states in which self is disrupted, in which one is 'not myself', the section opens with an approach to the understanding of this somewhat mysterious phenomenon. The work of Hughlings Jackson, who has been called the father of British neurology, is used as a background for this understanding.[3]

Hughlings Jackson was considered a genius by his colleagues but his intriguing approach to mental illness has been largely neglected since his conceptions were beyond the comprehension of his time. He believed himself to be the first to use the term 'self' in the medical literature. His theoretical approach to 'self' is astonishingly close to current concepts, for example, that of Damasio, and resonates with attempts to model self in terms of non-linear mathematics.

I touch upon several forms of disruption of self. They include one kind neglected by major psychological theories. It involves a sense of damage to the peculiar feeling-tone which attaches to those ideas, behaviours and so forth which make up the core of self and gives them value. In the sphere of intimacy, we call it tenderness.

The memories of traumatic or disruptive experiences may be 'distorted' so that they do not represent what an objective observer might report. In this way they resemble 'false memories'. A Jacksonian model of dissociation is used to explain this phenomenon. The memories are seen as consistent with the emotion which accompanied the traumatic event and, in a sense, explain it.

Memories of a state in which one's feeling of personal existence are overthrown are registered implicitly as a stunted narrative, a 'script', which tells the individual he or she is bad, inferior, useless, and so on, confronting a traumatising other, who is critical, alienating, controlling, and so on. This system is triggered by contextual cues. It repeatedly enters and disturbs the conversations and relationships of ordinary life, determining conversations in which, in a subtle and particular way, the intimate is excluded. These conversations are relatively devoid of 'inner speech' and conducted in what might be called a language of alienation. They are linear, lacking in complexity.

A strange aspect of these conversations is that the other frequently takes on, without being aware of it, the characteristics of the original other who inflicted the trauma. The important phenomenon is understood in terms of modern memory research, in particular, by means of 'priming'. One's detection of the experience of being 'constructed' is a crucial aspect of the therapeutic conversation.

The final section of the book focuses on the therapeutic task. This is conceived in terms of the 'dissociation/integration'[4] model of Pierre Janet who was a major pioneer of the concept of the unconscious. Put at its simplest, the task involves the transformation of a conversation which is one of alienation into one which shows the form of the intimate. Emphasis is placed on the creation or re-creation of the doubleness of self through the resonance of the other. I also argue for the need to 'visualise' those aspects of experience, some of it traumatic, which, for the moment, lie beyond the reach of contemplation.

In summary, this book represents an attempt to build a psychotherapeutic theory about the idea of what it is to be 'myself'. An important background to this endeavour is the work of men who were giants in the fields of psychology and psychiatry in the era before the 'radical behaviourist purge' which was inflicted upon these disciplines early in this century. These men, William James, James Mark Baldwin, and Pierre Janet, can be seen as the founders of a psychology of self. James was the chief descriptor of self; Baldwin pioneered studies of its development; Janet explored the nature of its disruptions. I develop some of their ideas in my own way using data from memory research and studies of child development.

Although the main thesis of the book is based on work with people whose development has been severely disrupted,[5] its application is much more general. Traumatic memories, which are hedged about by protective systems, and which intermittently overthrow the ongoing sense of personal being, present in many guises, for example perverse sexual activity, suicidal behaviour, marital discord. Helping people integrate these 'unconscious' modes of experience into self as the stream of consciousness is the central objective of most psychotherapeutic work.

Part I

Self and development

Chapter 2

I, me, myself

A BACKGROUND

What we mean by the sense and feeling of personal being, or self, must be the starting point of a suitable theory of psychotherapy. Finding this starting point is no easy task. This is made clear by the experiences of Carl Gustav Jung and Heinz Kohut, the two main explorers, at least in the therapeutic sense, of the zone of self. Jung, towards the end of his life, said that his quest resembled 'a circumambulation of unknown factors'.[1] Kohut declared self to be 'not knowable'.[2]

The difficulty of grasping what self might be is compounded by the fact that the tradition of psychology and philosophy which was concerned with such matters was overthrown in what has been called the 'radical behaviorist purge',[3] which occurred about the time of World War I. As a consequence, those who struggle with the problem of grasping in words the evanescent sense of what it is to be humanly alive have no background on which to draw.

The kind of intellectual atmosphere which prevailed during the positivist–behaviourist era following World War I is illustrated by the work of the English philosopher, Gilbert Ryle. His highly influential book, *The Concept of Mind*, has been called a classic.

'With deliberate abusiveness',[4] using the tactic, as he said, of *reductio ad absurdum*,[5] Ryle set about destroying the notions of an inner life and of mind. Some of the contortions involved in asserting this view now seem almost risible. For example, Ryle concluded that it is permissible to talk about performing 'mental arithmetic' 'in the head',[6] but that it is not appropriate to speak of the same activity as going on 'in the mind'[7] despite the fact that the word 'mental', with which he was apparently content, means 'of or pertaining to the mind'.[8]

The implication is that the former expression is acceptable because the head is 'real', while the latter is unacceptable because mind is not. If this were so, how do I get into my head to perform mental arithmetic? Ryle anticipated this objection by pointing out that 'in the head' is a metaphor.

But then so is 'in the mind'. Are we to infer that there are 'good' and 'bad' metaphors, and so on?

Despite the frailty of this and similar arguments, Ryle's polemic[9] went almost uncontested in an era wedded to a curiously mechanical view of the human condition.

The positivist position depended upon throwing out these aspects of ordinary experience which did not conform to the rules of conventional logic.[10] That which remained had to be over-simplified,[11] or bent in order to make it conform. Russell, for example, wanted us to say 'It thinks in me', rather than 'I think', on the grounds that it was not logical to isolate the consciousness of mental states from the mental states themselves or, more precisely, to distinguish between the act of thinking and the thought itself.[12] However, Russell's use of the word 'in', the metaphor derided by Ryle, creates another dualism.

It came as a relief, analogous to the toppling of the Berlin Wall, when the hegemony of the behaviourist–positivist ideology was at last brought down. Although it continues to have a residual influence,[13] matters such as the nature of personal existence, once beyond the pale of scientific inquiry, can now be investigated. Indeed, the noted neuroscientist, Antonio Damasio,[14] has recently proposed a neural basis for self.

In this changed intellectual climate, interest has revived in major thinkers of the previous era who had been banished from the discourse of psychology, psychoanalysis and psychiatry during the half century or so domination of positivism and behaviourism. They include William James (1842–1910), James Mark Baldwin (1861–1934), and Pierre Janet (1859–1947).

These men were giants in their time. Their thought and writings were highly sophisticated. They were all professional philosophers. Janet was a philosopher before he turned to psychiatry in order better to study the phenomena which fascinated him. James' career had an opposite trajectory, beginning in physiology and moving towards philosophy.

James was considered the foremost psychologist of his era. Such was his eminence that at his death the *Boston Evening Transcript* lamented the passing of 'the greatest of contemporary Americans'.[15] His influence waned after his death.

The eclipse of Janet was even greater. The star of the Parisian school, he seemed likely to become the greatest psychiatrist of his time. By the 1960s he was almost forgotten, his name not mentioned in some standard texts of American psychiatry.[16] However, in recent years through the influence of such publications as that of Henri Ellenberger[17] and Bessel van der Kolk and Onno van der Hart,[18] the significance of his work is being rediscovered. Baldwin is now almost unknown.[19]

These three men form the core of what can be seen as a school of 'self'. James' career was devoted to the exploration of this experience; Baldwin was a pioneer in the understanding of its development; Janet, who remains the outstanding authority in the sphere of trauma, described the arrest of this development as a consequence of trauma.[20] Certain of their main ideas, somewhat elaborated, and woven together, make up my principal thesis.

Although, in retrospect, these men can be seen as the nucleus of a school, it had no institutional or formal basis. They were loosely linked together through personal friendship and the resonance of their ideas.

This group had few intellectual heirs. The most important was Jean Piaget, whose developmental studies were strongly influenced by Janet and Baldwin. He called Janet 'my professor' until the end of his life.[21] His work, together with that of LS Vygotsky working in Russia, who was also influenced by Janet and Baldwin,[22] provides essential input into my theoretical framework.

I, ME, MYSELF

What we mean by self must be based on accounts of personal experience rather than the dictates of logic. James brought to the study of self a refreshing sense of 'the open air of human nature'.[23] He was critical of those who wrote about philosophy and psychology but had 'no perception of the inward breath of life and health which blows through them'.[24] A key passage from his work is as follows:

> Whatever I may be thinking of, I am always at the same time more or less aware of *myself,* of my *personal existence.* At the same time, it is I who am aware; so that the total self of me, being as it were duplex, partly known and partly knower, partly object and partly subject, must have two aspects discriminated in it, of which for shortness we may call one the *Me* and the other the *I.* I call these 'discriminated aspects', and not separate things, because the identity of *I* with *me,* even in the very act of their discrimination, is perhaps the most ineradicable dictum of common sense and must not be undermined by our terminology here at the outset, whatever we may come to think of its validity at our inquiry's end.[25]

His self, then, is double. However, when we look again at this passage we find another word which refers to one's individual person. It is 'myself'. Where does it fit? Is it synonymous with 'me', as James implies, or is it something else. Since it is a different word, it may, like 'I' and 'me', involve a subtle but significant difference in meaning. Might 'myself' refer to a third term?

We can come to some kind of answer to this question if we reconsider the expression, 'I was not myself when you saw me last'. This person is saying something which, in logical terms, does not make sense. Nevertheless, in a general way, we know what he means. The speaker is referring to a state his hearers know. The expression implies a certain stability for 'I' and 'me' but a potential variability for 'myself'. In this case, 'myself' is not equivalent to 'I' and 'me'. Rather, it is a third term. This third term is necessary to the whole argument of this book. It emerges during development, is lost in trauma, and is recovered during successful treatment – the 'analytic third' of Thomas Ogden.[26]

I will argue that this third aspect of one's person develops extra-personally, in the outer world, as a form of activity, performed in the context of a particular relationship which is an early, or embryonic, form of intimacy. Following these ideas, it is necessary to modify the Jamesian conception. Personal existence becomes tripartite[27] rather than double.

The notion of a tripartite personal being belongs in a sphere of thinking which is different from that of experience, as will be seen in Chapter 4. We do not experience ourselves as either double or triple. Claude Lévi-Strauss described his own feeling of personal existence: 'I never had, and still do not have, the perception of feeling my personal identity. I appear to myself as the place where something is going on, but there is no "I" and no "me". Each of us is a kind of crossroads where things happen'.[28]

Lévi-Strauss is saying that there is no 'self' that he can make explicit, or describe. He can define it only as a sense of movement, of something happening. This intuition is fundamental.

The Lévi-Strauss description of self implies frailty. The sense of self depends upon things happening. The possibility arises that this 'happening' might stop. What would remain? Self, seen in this way, is nothing solid or substantial, not part of us like our bones and muscles. It is merely a constantly changing fabric of inner experience, a kind of gossamer or 'shimmer', to use a Wolffian word, which might vanish, leaving us with nothing. The sense of existence, then, goes on over a potential void.

The threat of this void hangs over those whose development of self has been damaged by a traumatic environment. The mental activity underpinning the stream of consciousness seems barely developed. Self is stunted and fragile. At times it may vanish, leaving a static, painful, even frightening, vacancy, often described as a 'black hole'.

James encapsulated much of this in a single, deceptively simple, sentence. He stated that: 'Thoughts connected as we feel them to be connected are *what we mean* by personal selves'.[29]

Although logicians may contend against it, it is *what we mean* by personal existence, or self. 'Thoughts', in this statement, should be understood as a shorthand term, referring to the stream of consciousness, to that drift of images, memories, ideas, imaginings, which are sensed during moments when our attention shifts away from our immediate surroundings. What is essential to this experience is a nonlinear 'shape', resembling that of play.[30] It has its basis in feeling which is characteristically one of 'warmth and intimacy'.[31]

Intermingled with, and at the bottom of the flow of inner life is the feeling of the body, which is with us all the time. To much of this body feeling we pay no attention at all, though it fluctuates with the state of self, which, in turn, is influenced by the form of our current interpersonal relationships.[32]

The Jamesian self is alive. It involves change and chance, freedom and variety. It is not static, not a thing, not a 'structure', to use common psychoanalytic parlance. It is a process.[33] Self is continuous but never the same. Its progressive and sequencing nature resembles the form of narrative. However, rather than a narrative the stream of consciousness is seen, in this book, as a special form of conversation (see Chapter 4).

Further exploration of James' statement, which is the germinal core of this book, leads to amplification of the tripartite model. In remarking that 'thoughts connected as we feel them to be connected are *what we mean* by personal selves', James equates the stream of consciousness with the 'me'. This creates a difficulty which depends upon the variability of the experience of the flow of inner life.

The fluctuations of self as the stream of consciousness are considerable. When one is alone, in a reflective state, musing, the stream of consciousness is prominent. Mostly, however, it is merely a background to the conversations of daily living.

This background provides a source for the conversational flow. In each case the source will be particular. A young woman, for example, talks to her child, her husband, her mother, her friends, the bus driver, and her colleagues at work, in different ways. She plays different 'language games'.[34] The 'self' who takes part in these conversations is, in a subtle way, various.

These ideas suggest that we live, so James believed, as a 'community of selves'.[35] Such a notion is problematic. It supposes that personal existence is potentially fragmented, discontinuous, or multiple. Such a supposition flies in the face of the common-sense view that personal being is unitary and unified.

The problem is resolved, to some extent, by the 'I'. 'I' is primarily a noun of 'position',[36] a metaphoric 'eye' from which attention is directed, so shaping an individual reality, which is in a state of ceaseless change.[37] The 'I' is a constant, offering a means of unifying personal existence. In this way one's person is conceived as a unified diversity.

This resolution of the problem of the potential multiplicity of self does not clear up the difficulty of equating the stream of consciousness with 'me'. The stream of consciousness is not only variable, it may be absent, as we have seen. This experience may be encountered in a state of terror. We are aware only of the source of threat, the intense affect, and the sensations of the body such as the beating heart, the constricting gut. In this situation we can say, following the Jamesian definition, that we are devoid of self. But the 'me' remains. There is always someone who we can view in a mirror or pick out in a photograph and say: 'That's me'.

James dealt with this difficulty by postulating different kinds of 'me'. He declared that: 'In its widest possible sense . . . a man's Me is the sum total of all that he can call his'.[38] It includes not only those experiences of inner life, which are an aspect of maturity, but also those aspects of the individual which appear in the world and which make up one's 'identity'. Most importantly, the 'me' is embodied. It is through the body that these fundamentally different aspects of the 'me' are united. This idea was developed, in some detail, by James Mark Baldwin.

Baldwin saw the body as in a sense Janus-faced, looking in two directions.[39] It is outer in the form recognised by others; yet it is also the place where an inner life is sensed as going on. This 'inner' experience, Baldwin remarked, 'is carried about'.[40] The two fundamental forms of 'me-ness' are integrated. 'The two partial contents, inner and outer, are together integrated in the larger whole of experience.'

We now distinguish three aspects of the individual person which can be called 'I', 'Me', and 'Self', the last being experienced as inner, though not entirely, as we shall discover in later chapters. This kind of distinction is an abstraction since these distinguishable elements of personal experience cannot be disconnected. There can be no 'me' without an 'I', no 'self' without a 'me'. It must be emphasised that although 'self' is distinguished in this schema from 'me', the stream of consciousness is invested with a sense of 'me-ness', of its being 'mine', which is the most fundamental of its attributes.[41] The kind of Jamesian 'me' which involves the inner life is sensed as a core, or nucleus, of personal existence. It is the 'self of all other selves'.[42] It has a feeling about it which gives it value. It is 'felt by all men as a sort of innermost centre within the circle, of sanctuary within the citadel'.[43]

This experience, however, is fragile. It can be damaged. Those who have been traumatised have a diminished sense of personal value and of the me-ness which is at the core of personal existence. Such an individual may now say: 'I'm nobody nowhere'.

CONSCIOUSNESS WITHOUT SELF

The foregoing discussion has been preparing the way for the notion that, for some people, consciousness is at times without self. This idea, when expressed to a lay person, is sometimes greeted with disbelief. The possibility that other people may have forms of personal existence which are very different to our own is somewhat startling. Because we assume that other people get hungry or tired, have memories and hopes, become happy or sad, we also assume that all experiences which make up being human resemble each other. This is not entirely so, as Francis Galton vividly demonstrated.

Galton was a cousin of Darwin and a pioneer psychologist whose work will be discussed further in Chapter 5. He produced two examples of very large differences in individual experience to which observers would have no access.

The first of these differences between people had not been suspected until 1794. In that year, John Dalton, a self-taught scientist who developed the atomic theory of matter, wrote a memoir concerning colour blindness. As Galton noted, individuals who suffer such 'peculiarities' of experience are unaware of the difference between their experience and that of others. Galton wrote:

> That one person out of twenty-nine or thereabouts should be unable to distinguish a red from green, without knowing that he had any deficiency of colour sense, and without betraying his deficiency to his friends, seems perfectly incredible to the other twenty-eight; yet as a matter of fact he rarely does either the one or the other.[44]

A second major difference between people, which Galton himself discovered, involves the capacity for mental imagery. He asked a series of people, including eminent scientists, to 'think of some definite object – suppose it is the breakfast table as you sat down to it this morning – and consider carefully the picture that rises before your mind's eye'. He asked further questions about the illumination, definition, and colouring of this scene. He was amazed by the results.

> To my astonishment, I found that the great majority of the men of science to whom I first applied protested that mental imagery was unknown to them, and they looked on me as fanciful and fantastic in supposing that the words 'mental imagery' really expressed what I believed everybody supposed them to mean. They had no more notion of its true nature than a colour-blind man, who has not discerned his defect, has of the nature of colour. They had a mental deficiency of which they were unaware, and naturally enough supposed that those who affirmed they possessed it, were romancing.[45]

Galton found 'an entirely different disposition to prevail' when speaking to those he met in general society. Many of these people 'declared that they habitually saw mental imagery, and that it was perfectly distinct to them and full of colour'.[46]

This remarkable study is consistent with the idea that others may have inner lives which differ in important respects from our own and that, furthermore, we may be unaware of these differences. It is counter-intuitive to suppose that others may not experience a stream of consciousness. Yet the data of John Flavell and his colleagues[47] suggest that this may be so.

As a forerunner to their studies on the discovery of the stream of consciousness in children, these researchers conducted a questionnaire study of 234 college students who were asked whether the following statement is 'probably true', or 'probably not true'. The statement read: 'Conscious mental events (ideas, percepts, images, feelings) normally follow one another more or less continuously in a person who is awake. They form a kind of "stream of consciousness", with first one conscious mental event happening, then another, then another'. Only 76 per cent of students checked the statement as 'probably true'; 12 per cent had no opinion, while another 12 per cent said that it was 'probably not true'.

Flavell and his colleagues had no explanation for these figures. Nevertheless, these findings support the possibility that for some people, a minority of the population, the experience of the self as the stream of consciousness is limited or stunted.

We are not born with a 'self'. It is a potentiality, to be realised in the context of a particular form of relationship with others. This relationship depends upon conversation and a form of mental activity manifest in some forms of play.

Chapter 3

Conversational play

The process of realisation of self through conversation begins soon after birth.

A young woman is shown her newborn baby for the first time. With a slow rising inflection she says 'Hello', as if the baby knew what she meant and as if they would talk with each other. She is playing a game.

Her behaviour, at first sight, may seem merely charming and, as such, not a vital part of her child's existence. This is far from the case. She is beginning an activity which is crucial to the child's development. Yet she is unaware of this. She is behaving naturally and the thought does not occur to her that what she has done in greeting her baby is what she should be doing. She is beginning to set up a form of conversational play, out of which will emerge the 'selfhood' of her child. This implies, as it is meant to imply, that self is both manifest in and created by words, but not mere words, but words used in a particular way, resembling the form of play.

This idea, that play is an essential part of adequate human development, has not been widely recognised, at least in the West. Play is for pleasure, amusement, diversion. Seen in this way, it is trivial, lacking the serious-ness of the 'real' world. It seems to be beyond the boundaries of respectable science and philosophy. Against this view I will be arguing in later chap-ters that the truth and reality of an individual human life is based in the kind of experience which is central to certain forms of play. No logic can discover this experience.

The principal concern of Anglo-American philosophy for much of the twentieth century, as remarked in the previous chapter, has not been the nature of human existence but the validity of formal propositions. Wittgenstein moved beyond the limitations of this approach. At first sight, his enterprise, conducted in the rarefied air of high philosophical inquiry, might seem unrelated to the scene of the young mother with her newborn baby. This is not so. Wittgenstein begins his philosophical investigations with an infant's experience of language, as described by Augustine. Wittgenstein remarks that we can think of the process of using words in the way Augustine described:

as one of those games by means of which children learn their native language. I will call these games 'language-games' and will sometimes speak of a primitive language as a language-game.[1]

The purpose of his notion of 'language games' was 'to free ourselves from the philosophical confusions that result from considering language in isolation from its place in the "stream of life"'.[2]

Let us return to the scene of the first 'language game'. The mother's game with her baby shows essential elements of the concept of play, which depends upon dualisms of the kind found in the polarity 'real/not real'.

Although she is pretending that the baby can understand her and knows who she is, there is part of her that thinks that this may be true. Like many mothers-to-be, she has talked to her baby as it grew inside her. She has a fantasy of who this person is to whom she talks.[3] She half-believes that her baby knows her voice. She is probably right. A number of studies have suggested that the baby, while in utero, is able to distinguish the mother's voice from those of other people. At birth, the baby prefers its own mother's voice.[4] Moreover, the mother's belief that her words will, in some way, be responded to by her infant is not entirely fanciful. Trevarthen, in an excellent review, notes that in the first few days of life the sounds of different syllables in speech, as well as their emotional tone are discriminated by the baby.[5]

Conversational play is not only 'real/unreal' but also 'serious/not-serious'. Although she is only playing, so that what she is doing is not serious, this play is accompanied by a feeling which is pleasurable, but larger than that. It gives value to the experience.

The mother's conversations with her baby have been studied by Kenneth Kaye.[6] He recorded 13,574 utterances from 36 mothers. He found that the mother's game, in which she pretends that an actual dialogue is going on with her baby, is a prominent feature of early life. For much of the time she takes both parts in this 'dialogue'. At six weeks of age, 16 per cent of the mother's utterances in Kaye's study were pure repetitions of the previous one. By the age of two years, only 3 per cent of utterances were of this kind.

The baby's responsiveness increases in the first weeks of life. There rapidly develops a characteristic interchange with the mother which, by the age of two months, has the form of a conversation. Trevarthen[7] has called it a 'proto-conversation'. It depends not only on vocalisations but also upon what Augustine called 'the natural language of all peoples', that is 'the expression of the face, the play of the eyes, the movement of other parts of the body, and the tone of voice'.[8] The movements, gestures, and expressive vocal tonings of the mother–baby dyad are finely co-ordinated so that the behaviour of one is dependent on the behaviour of the other. Although the interchange appears simple, it consists of a fluid and complex stream of behaviours which are interwoven and extremely difficult to code. Trevarthen describes it in the following way:

Microanalysis of ordinary face-to-face play between mothers and their two-month-old babies reveals a precise conversation-like timing in the way they address one another and reply. Babies stimulate gentle and questioning 'baby talk' which has a regular beat and characteristic expression of mood in its changing intonation, rhythm, and accompaniment of movements of head, eyebrows, eyes, and so forth. The infant watches the maternal display intently and then makes a reply, on the beat, with a smile, head and body movements, cooing, hand movements, and even lip-and-tongue movements which are called 'pre-speech'. Photographic records suggest they are developmental precursors of actual speech. These attempts at vocal expression are synchronised with hand gestures.[9]

This finely attuned interplay between the two partners creates a unified patterning, as if a single system were made of two main parts.[10] It is important that it brings pleasure to both partners. It is equally important that a break in the patterning, a failure of attunement, is quickly perceived by the baby, whose rapidly changing expressions are surprisingly subtle. These breaks have been artificially induced, in an experimental situation, by the mother adopting an expressionless face. The pleasure of the interchange, for both partners, is lost. The baby may show a depressed face. A larger break, where the baby is simply seated in a small chair next to her mother's chair, so that she cannot see her face, is very distressing for both partners.[11] The experience might be called 'disjunctional anxiety'.

These observations suggest that the proto-conversation is not mere to and fro. The resonance between the 'conversing' partners has a transformational effect which is beautifully intimated by Thomas Ogden,[12] in an exploration of a Robert Frost poem, which concerns Eve in the original garden and the effect of her voice upon the birds. It is as if the birds were children and she their mother. Her voice, heard throughout the day, gives something to the birds' song which causes it to be forever changed.

BABBLING AND 'DEEP STRUCTURE'

Conversational play arises as part of our evolutionary heritage. Although, as Darwin noted, the young chimpanzee shows remarkable similarities to the young human,[13] a major difference is found in the sphere of vocalisation. In her classic study, Susanne Langer[14] pointed out that whereas human infants babble, first making sounds that approximate speech at about three to four months,[15] infant chimpanzees show no tendency to spontaneously vocalise, coo, or babble.[16] She concluded that the higher primate has no instinctive tendency to play with sounds of his or her own making. However, the infant's solitary 'voice play', as Langer called it, is not the most important form of vocalising play. 'It is far more agreeable to carry on this play with others'.[17]

The kind of babbling produced by most infants develops, so that between seven and 10 months they begin to produce sounds resembling those used in spoken languages. This type of vocalisation is called 'reduplicated' or 'syllabic babbling'.[18] Progression to this stage of babbling depends, so it seems, on a resonance between the child's utterance and his or her hearing the sound created. On the other hand deprivation of babbling may profoundly disturb language development.

The latter effect was exemplified in the story of a child who had been tracheotomised. She was generally aphonic between the ages of 0.5 and 1.8 years. She was cognitively and socially normal, with near normal comprehension of language. Following the removal of the cannula from her trachea, her utterances revealed a tenth of the canonical syllables that might be expected in normally developing infants. In this way, she was like a congenitally deaf child. Two months later (1.10), she produced only a handful of different words.[19]

Chomsky proposed that language as it is spoken depends upon an innate system of language production, a 'deep structure' which is part of our genetic endowment. Babbling is presumably part of this endowment. In a very interesting study, this hypothesis was tested by studying manual babbling in deaf babies.[20]

Two babies who were profoundly deaf, born of deaf parents, were compared with three infants who had no hearing deficit. The deaf babies were being taught American sign language as a first language. The others were not. All babies were videotaped at 10, 12, and 14 months. Their manual activities were coded in a precise and detailed manner and entered into the computer database. In essence, the coding distinguished mere gestures from syllables expressed in sign language.

The results were intriguing. As expected, the infants who could hear were producing syllabic babbling sounds. The deaf infants were also exhibiting what might be called 'manual babbling' in syllables at the same age. 'Syllabic manual babbling' accounted for 32–71 per cent of manual activity in the deaf babies and 4–15 per cent of manual activity in the others. These results suggest that babbling, which is necessary to conversational play, is a manifestation of an inborn programme which underpins our communicative behaviour. It was expressed in these two deaf children by means of movements rather than vocally.

GAMES LIKE CONVERSATION

The mother and baby conversational game progresses so that physical objects begin to be included in their interplay. However, at first nothing else is as entrancing as the mother's face and the baby's attention is directed to it. As time goes on the baby is both more responsive to the mother and more spontaneous in greeting her. However, the baby also tends to spend less time attending to the mother and more on objects in the environment. For example, in one study,[21] mothers and babies were seated opposite each other with a tray of toys between them. At three months, the babies spent 12 per cent of their time looking at the toys. At six months, the same babies spent 60 per cent of their interaction attending to the toys. By this age, physical objects can become part of a game which has a reciprocal character resembling conversation. Jerome Bruner has studied such early games. He remarked that 'a game, in its way, is a little protoconversation'.[22]

Bruner studied two children playing the peek-a-boo game in which he charted the emergence of reciprocity, which is a central feature of conversation. When the game began at five months, the first child was little more than a smiling spectator.[23] The mother's language ('Where's he gone?') was an essential part of the game. Increasingly, the child also provided vocalisations in between those of the mother.[24] By seven months the child was responding to the game's predictable rhythm. By eight months the child began to take an active part, trying to make the clown-doll disappear and reappear by himself. During his twelfth month, the child initiated the game, hiding himself, and then reappearing. By 14 months there was a return to the clown-game, but now the child was an active agent, although allowing the mother to take turns. Roles had become completely interchangeable. The pattern of development of the second child's game-playing was similar. By 10 months, he became an 'agent', initiating the game half the time.

Finally, both the children understood the notion of 'turn taking'. Bruner calls it the 'handover principle'.[25] He noted that in the peek-a-boo game 'the mother would introduce a new procedure and gradually "hand it over to" the child'. He likened this procedure to Stern's[26] observations of 'attunement' and 'turn-taking' between mother and child, and Kaye and Charney's[27] study of how 'turnarounds' in early exchanges are scaffolded by the mother until the child can take his or her own part in them.

Both conversation and the peek-a-boo game depend on an appropriate sequencing of related components. This sequencing is essential to conversation and to the spontaneously developing games of early life. Bruner considered that the vocalisations that accompanied the games played between mother and child 'provide a skeletal or formal structure into which rich and more language-like variants can later be introduced'.[28]

He also stated that language 'begins when mother and infant create a predictable format of interaction that can serve as a microcosm for communicating and for constituting a shared reality'.[29] Put another way, Bruner was suggesting that the games of infancy are the precursors of conversation. I am proposing the reverse of this sequence. The reciprocal activity of conversational play is conceived here as the more fundamental and as the forerunner of the games between parent and child that are played in the first year of life. Like Bruner, I see these games as necessary to development and not mere amusement.

PRETENDING AND REALITY

Toward the end of the first year, the child has learnt the 'pretend' game, so that he or she might feign sleep[30] or pretend to drive a car.[31] Whereas, when conversational play began, only one partner was able to engage in pretence, now both partners have this capacity.[32] It is a curious paradox that the emergence of self, which is associated with such notions as genuineness and authenticity, depends in part upon the fakery which is involved in pretence. Does this imply that the normally developing child is, at times, a 'false self' to use a term which Winnicott made popular?[33] This expression implies pathology. James Mark Baldwin put his finger on a main difference between the child's pretending and a pathological situation.

Baldwin was a pioneer in the field of child psychology – a 'nursery psychologist', he called himself.[34] He was the first, after Schiller,[35] to develop a substantial argument which demonstrated the significance of play in human development. His argument implied that play was also the basis of culture, anticipating the main thesis of Huizinga's[36] classic study. Baldwin wrote:

> The play and art performer is a *poseur*, from start to finish. This becomes sublimated and obscured in developmental refinements in the art consciousness, but in the play-mode it stands out in all its naked frankness. It is not only exhibition of self – that is normal enough – but it is exhibition of a false self.[37]

What is healthy about this game is the child's sense of freedom. Baldwin expressed this view in the following way:

> Play is a swing of the pendulum toward control that has the psychic value of freedom. The self, the playing self, is not content with being its own self, with asserting *itself*, with denying all sorts of foreign control. It goes further, saying: 'I will prove this to you by being, according as I will, some other self, by choosing what sort of self I will to be. I will be a soldier, a wet-nurse, a hobby-horse. Yea, verily, I will perchance lose my life to find it; I will prove my self-hood by un-selfing self. I will be a mummy, a football, a door-mat, "any old thing" that even those who claim that I am, though a self, still under external control, would never in their wildest moments seriously take me to be!'[38]

The clinical presentation sometimes labelled 'false self' lacks this essential quality of freedom and vitality. It has its basis in the individual's *loss* of freedom. Bernard Brandchaft has argued[39] that the so-called 'false self' is the result of the child's 'accommodation' to the reality of the other. The child sacrifices his or her own experience in favour of another version which comes from 'outside'. The need to accommodate, to abandon one kind of personal freedom, is driven by an anxiety and a pathological form of attachment (see Chapter 11). It is associated with a feeling of 'deadness'.

Another essential element of the child's pretending, which also indicates health, might be called 'doubling'. Two models of reality are involved. In the example of the child pretending to sleep, there is a 'me' who is sleeping and 'me' who is not. 'Doubling' is also the basis of many forms of humour.

Humour depends upon the ability to hold two images in mind, one of which upsets the other. Towards the end of the first year of life babies begin to understand this kind of humour. For example, a child who is at the crawling stage, laughs when mother crawls towards the cot instead of walking. The rule, 'babies crawl, mothers walk', is overthrown by the unexpected image.[40]

The duality of consciousness which is involved in pretending is one of a number of dualities upon which the eventual appearance of self depends. However, by the end of the first year of life the duality which is necessary to the experience of the stream of consciousness is not yet established. This will depend upon further developments in the infant's conversational play. These will involve the use of words and the emergence of what might be called 'inner conversation'.

Chapter 4

Two forms of human conversation

The next major step in the development of self in conversation takes place after 18 months when the child starts to use words. The child begins to have a conversation with himself or herself. This, like the proto-conversation, also occurs in the context of play.

As remarked in the previous chapter, the child, as he or she grows older, shows an increasing interest in play-objects while in the vicinity of caregivers. This trajectory of interest culminates in the child playing and chattering, but appearing to pay no attention at all to the mother, father, or other caregivers. The emergence of this apparent monologue is illustrated by Bruner's observations.

At 21 months, one of Bruner's subjects began to play the 'peek-a-boo' game by himself. He

> filled a large kettle with pieces from a puzzle. He then greeted each piece with 'hello house!' when he spied it in the pot that he uncovered, sharing a smile with his mother as he did so. He repeated the routine again and again, each 'hello house' followed by 'bye-bye house' as he replaced the lid.[1]

The child in this episode is not, in any precise way, talking to himself. He is talking to a part of the external world, which he has imaginatively created. His behaviour is an aspect of the 'doubling' which is implicit in pretence. In this sense it is part of him just as the child who pretends to be asleep is experientially made up of two parts, a 'me' who sleeps and another 'me' who does not.

In Bruner's example, the child is not only talking to himself. His mother is involved. His sense of her presence is necessary to his playing. She shares the experience although she does not speak. This kind of play progresses to the point where the child behaves as if completely oblivious of mother or other people. He chatters as he plays with toys and other objects, totally absorbed, like an adult who is lost in thought. This is the scene of symbolic play.[2]

Although the child engaged in this kind of play *seems* oblivious of others, it would be a mistake to consider the child's experience is one of isolation. Jean Piaget[3] suggested that the sense of a presence of another, the care-giver, permeates the whole experience of symbolic play. This 'life of union', as he called it, is a necessary 'atmosphere' to the play going on.[4] The child is talking not only to himself or herself, but also to another who is experienced as part of the child's personal reality, whether or not he or she is speaking, responding in other ways, or even present. The child is conversing with an illusory person who is a condensation of the parent experienced in this way and a double of himself.[5] This is a pre-intimate relationship. (It is not yet intimate since the child at this age has not yet conceived the notion of 'innerness' which is essential to mature intimacy.)

The conversational form of the chattering which accompanies symbolic play is evident in the following example. A little boy is engaged in solitary play with a tinkertoy.

> The wheels go here, the wheels go here. Oh, we need to start it all over again. We need to close it up. See, it closes up. We're starting it all over again. Do you know why we wanted to do that? Because I needed it to go a different way. Isn't it going to be pretty clever, don't you think? But we have to cover up the motor just like a real car.[6]

These play-conversations may be quite complex, the child switching between two or more viewpoints.[7]

With the emergence of symbolic play we have the establishment of a third term. The field of what Piaget called symbolic play arises in a space, both real and metaphoric, between a 'me' and another who is sensed as part of the experience. This scene is conceived as the necessary precursor to self as the stream of consciousness.

An essential aspect of self as the stream of consciousness is 'ownership'. James wrote that 'It seems as if the elementary psychic fact were not *thought* or *this thought* or *that thought*, but *my thought*, every thought being owned.'[8] In symbolic play, the external world, that which is 'other', is transformed to become a world that is one's own. James Mark Baldwin, in a detailed and sophisticated study showing the emergence of self in play, described this process by which a world that is 'other' becomes that which is 'mine'.

During symbolic play the child takes the things of the world which are not his or her own and makes them into what he or she wishes them to be. 'Play is a way of making an object, for present and personal purposes, *what it might be*'.[9] This object now becomes a 'semblant object'. 'The selection of the object for play is a "personal" selection'.[10] In turning the object into what it wants it to be – the leaf into a boat, the stick into a man, the stone into a monster – the child makes a 'reconstruction of the real world'. This is a 'construction to be distinguished as within the inner world and as such to be brought into contrast with those objects, perhaps the same ones, which have their existence in the outer world'.[11] What is essential to the selection and to the play is freedom. The selection is not imposed and the play has about it what Baldwin called the 'don't-have-to-feeling'.[12]

In that the object is chosen and created according to the child's imagination, it has a quality of 'innerness'. Yet it is also the thing itself. 'The play object becomes not the inner or fancy object as such, nor yet the outer present object as such, *but both at once*, what we are calling the semblant object, itself the terminus of a sort of interest which later on develops into what is called "syntelic" or "contemplative"'.[13]

Baldwin's use of the word 'contemplative' suggests that the scene of symbolic play is the precursor of adult states of reflection or contemplation, conditions under which the stream of consciousness becomes prominent. He implies that symbolic play shows us the self in embryonic form. The same or similar laws govern each state.

In the play mode, then, the alien objects of the world are transformed into those things that are sensed as 'mine'. They have about them, as James remarked, 'a sort of warmth and intimacy'.[14]

Not all the things in the world can be touched and manipulated, yet certain of them are given the aura of ownership. The great anatomist, Frederic Wood Jones, spoke of the great 'delight' of this experience, describing his 'pleasure in admiring, with all the happy sense of absolute possession, my one peculiar chattel in Nature, my pathway to the moon'.[15] This sense of intimacy is created, I suggest, by the mental activity which underpins play, and which is manifest in language. This form of language seems likely to be an essential element of this transformational process.

The language of symbolic play which Vygotsky described can be called non-linear. It operates according to different rules from another language, which is linear and which the child uses while engaged with the world of objects, the social environment in general.[16] In this engagement, the child's language can be conceived as linear. It is relatively logical and has a goal.

For much of the time the child is in linear mode. His language is directed towards stimuli provided by the environment. It is a manifestation of 'directed thought'.[17] Some of the stimuli arise from the child's body, for example sensations of hunger or pain. The child's language has a purpose which is obvious and related to the stimulus. Characteristically it involves questions. The child asks for information, comfort, nurture. Why? What? How? When? are prominent in the child's expressions.

When engaged in symbolic play the child, rather than being outer-directed, is in a state which is embryonically 'inner'. The child's experience, as remarked previously, is equivalent to that of an adult who is lost in thought.

The chattering which accompanies the child's symbolic play is a language which is qualitatively different from that used for communication and for ordinary coping with the environment. 'Inner speech is not the interior aspect of external speech – it is a function of itself'.[18] It is often lacking the grammar of ordinary communicative language. It is condensed, makes jumps, and moves capriciously according to association and analogies. Indeed at times the condensations are such that both Piaget[19] and Vygotsky remark that it is incomprehensible. This led Vygotsky to conclude that its purpose was not communicative.

What is this language for, if it is not for communication? We can get some kind of answer to this if we examine what the child is chattering about. We find that he or she is characteristically telling a little story. It is of a peculiarly personal kind, having an imaginative quality. It is an embryonic narrative of self. We might suppose that this curious, non-linear form of language has the purpose of representing and so bringing into being, the sense of self.[20]

The child's use of words, like his or her selection and manipulation of toys and other things, is personal. A language is employed which is not the language for others but a language for oneself. We are led to the idea that a certain kind of mental activity manifest in play and a particular form of language, is necessary to the creation of the zone of the personal.

The two main forms of human language described here are found in pure form only in unusual circumstances. One, which might be called the language of adaption, is linear. It is shown, undiluted, in legal and political documents. The other, which concerns self, is non-linear and found, relatively pristine, in certain kinds of poetry. The habitual use of the language of adaption can be understood as a manifestation of alienation, whereas the sense of self is manifest in a language having something of the form of Vygotsky's 'inner speech'.

Before the age of about four, the child oscillates, often very rapidly, between two states. In the first, which depends upon a relationship of connectedness, attention is inwardly directed and the language non-linear; in the second, which involves a sense of disconnection between self and other, attention is towards the outer world and the language is linear. The child, then, has two languages and two kinds of conversation which occur in the context of different forms of relationship.[21]

CONVERSATION AND THE STREAM OF CONSCIOUSNESS

At about five, the non-linear form of language accompanying symbolic play begins to disappear. Vygotsky believed that it is internalised. At about this age, the concept of an inner world which is one's own and distinct from the outer world is achieved. This is evident in the child's gaining an understanding of secrecy.[22] It is also evident in the child's discovery of the experience of the stream of consciousness.[23] With this developmental step the child achieves the sense of self as defined by William James. The whole scene of symbolic play, which is the locus of the embryonic self, has become internalised. This includes the sense of the presence of the other, who is represented not as a single person but as a form of relatedness.[24] The non-linear form of language is now the language of inner life and can be seen as the language of self.

This developmental progression from 'outer' to 'inner' follows the famous principle put forward by Janet and Baldwin.[25] They proposed that those 'higher' functions, which the adult experiences as part of the inner world, were originally manifest in the outer world as actions conducted in the context of a particular relationship with others.

More specifically, Baldwin conceived the development of self as a process of doubling which is originally made up of 'ego' and 'alter'. The 'alter' is ultimately internalised in a reverberating process in which he or she is 'taken in' and then recreated, the process culminating in the formation of the 'bipolar self'.

At this new stage of development, the two languages become co-ordinated. Ordinary conversation now involves their intermingling. Embedded in the linear language of adaption is another, which is non-linear, and related to the world of self. The third term is no longer visible but it is now manifest in language. The play space is now very much a metaphoric field arising, as it were, *between* people. Self is not only 'inner' but is found, or at least manifest, in this metaphoric space. 'Myself', then, involves not only a sense of inner experience but also the movements of this experience going on between 'me' and other people. 'Myself' is 'in' and 'between'.[26]

Since that which is intimate pertains to one's 'inmost thoughts and feelings', 'one's inmost self',[27] conversations in which there is a large contribution from the non-linear form of 'inner speech' are more intimate than those in which it is relatively lacking.

The fluctuations, the waxing and waning of this kind of language in conversation, also show, as if in the world, the changing states of self. Seen in this way, 'self', which has long been regarded as beyond the reach of scientific investigation, becomes amenable to study. Words, or more particularly, words as they are arranged, are the markers of 'self'.

THE BINDING PROBLEM

The mental activity which is manifest in the language form Vygotsky described, has a purpose beyond transforming the alien objects of the world into a world that is one's own. These objects from the world of 'not-me' are disconnected from each other. The way in which they are brought together as aspects of a unified experience remains one of the great mysteries of neuroscience. This mystery has been called the 'binding problem'.[28] It seems likely, at least to me, that the transformational effect of the non-linear form of mental activity manifest in certain forms of play and language includes a unification of the potentially discrete and separate sensory data which impinge upon us every moment.[29]

The discontinuities and fragmentation of the child's experience are great. Ingenious studies conducted by Tom Bower[30] show that the infant's existence is made up of a multiplicity of spaces. He tested, and seemed to confirm, Piaget's postulate that, for the child, the identity of objects is created either by their position or by their movement. For example, a chair if first placed before a bookcase and then moved in front of a blank wall, becomes a different chair since it occupies a new position. There are now two chairs. For the infant there is a multiplicity of objects where for the adult there are few.[31]

A brokenness of personal existence is also evident in children's conversation. What is true seems to be true only for that moment. Such a truth may have no connection with circumstances a few minutes later. Piaget described the situation in the following way.

> Up till the age of 7 or 8 children make no effort to stick to one opinion on any given subject. They do not indeed believe what is self-contradictory, but they adopt successively opinions, which if they were compared would contradict one another.[32]

The way in which the diverse bits of personal experience are woven together into a coherent whole includes the use of a form of narrative, which was first evident in the child's symbolic play with the world-to-be-manipulated. An example of such a narrative comes from William James.

The case concerned a deaf mute who became a professor. The following is extracted from his recollections concerning the moon.

> He asked himself with astonishment why the moon appeared regularly. He thought it must have come out just in order to see him. He began to speak to it then and imagined he could see it smile or frown. Finally, he made the discovery that he had been beaten much more often when the moon was visible. It was as if it watched him and reported his misdemeanours to his governess (he was an orphan). He often asked himself who it could be. At last he decided that it was his mother, because whilst his mother had been alive he had never seen the moon. He went to church on Sunday imagining that the moon wanted him to go, as he had been accustomed to go with his mother. His conscience developed, thanks above all to the moon's influence (it was a full moon on the evening when he discovered that some money he had pilfered had disappeared from where he had hidden it).[33]

This boy's story provides explanations of several mysteries of his existence. They include the nature of the moon and the whereabouts of his mother. His story also links together, or integrates, a number of aspects of his ordinary living. His mother, his governess, the moon, morality, and religion are bound together in a single narrative.

His story, in creating meaning out of a series of mysterious and disconnected events, helps to build a personal reality. Stories, used in this way, are 'acts of meaning'.[34]

This kind of narrative is lacking in the conversations of those whose development has been disrupted. Janet, who observed a large number of people whose lives had been scarred by traumata,[35] found that these people were unable to bring together adequately the various experiential 'atoms', to use his word.[36] Their principal deficiency, as he saw it, was a failure in 'personal synthesis'. 'They show the want of mental unity.'[37] Moreover, his patients conversed in the manner of a 'chronicle'. 'They live from day to day' 'without images of the future' or 'remembrances of the past.'[38] They told the 'same monotonous story',[39] full of complaints, day after day.

These observations suggest that the fundamental therapeutic task is to foster the emergence of the non-linear form of mental activity which will allow some unification, and so enlargement, of a personal reality. However, this process of unification will not involve the non-linear mental function alone. The reflective processes must also be activated, as briefly intimated in the Jamesian conception of the 'I' and again in Chapter 6.

TWO SPHERES OF EXISTENCE

We have now identified the two main conversations of childhood, which are underpinned by different kinds of mental activity. Bruner called these modes of thought narrative thinking and propositional thinking.[40] However, it is important that these modes of thinking are not viewed in isolation. They are central features of two scenes of personal existence.

The child's two different languages are related to two different orientations. The language of adaption is directed outwards, whereas that of symbolic play is directed to that which is embryonically inner. They are also related to two differing aspects of interpersonal existence. In the zone of adaption, the child is who he or she is in relation to others as objects. Facial expression, gender, demeanour, and other aspects of appearance, which are first known at about eighteen months,[41] make up this sense of who-one-is. The child can now look at a photo of himself or herself and say 'That's me'. The zone of adaption might also be called that of 'identity'.

On the other hand, the relationship in the zone of the self is with a part of oneself which is related to an intimate or pre-intimate experience of another.

In ordinary adult human living these 'two spheres of existence'[42] are seamlessly united, linked and contained by the body, so that to talk of them in terms of separateness is something of an abstraction. Personal being involves the co-ordination of these two domains, and of the different forms of mental activity which underpin them.

Despite this caveat, the co-ordination takes different forms in different situations. In some circumstances the linear logical mode of thought will prevail, while at others, during reverie for example, the wandering, associative drift of non-linear thinking becomes more prominent. The way people view their existence and shape their lives is influenced by the manner of this co-ordination. James identified two contrasting forms of orientation towards the world which in certain individuals become habitual, and which are expressed in contrasting philosophies. In an essay on 'Types of thinking', he distinguished between 'intimacy and foreignness'.[43]

The attitude of 'foreignness', which treats the world as object, emphasises logic and tends towards monism. 'Intimacy', on the other hand, involves an empathic attitude, in which one stands within that which is to be understood. This attitude admits to pluralism, sees the world as multifarious and multitudinous, consistent with the notion that we live as a 'community of selves'.

The forms of experiencing the world which James identified replicate, on a grander scale, the three-year-old child's oscillation between the zones of self and adaption.

INTIMACY, ATTACHMENT, AND AFFILIATION

The domain of self, which depends upon intimate relating, is more fragile than that of adaption. It must come into being through the child's developing secure attachments to his or her caregivers, who have provided appropriate responsiveness. He or she develops the feeling of trust. This feeling allows the child eventually to use symbols and exercise the narrative function, as Jeremy Holmes[44] has pointed out.

On the other hand, the child who has not been given the necessary caregiving environment of pre-intimate relatedness is wary, vigilant, outerdirected, with a diminished ability to play. James noted that 'the difference between living against a background of foreignness and one of intimacy means the difference between a general habit of wariness and one of trust'.[45]

These observations show that attachment and intimacy are not equivalent and must be distinguished in order adequately to understand development. Affiliation is different again. It refers to companionship between peers and 'the desire to do things in company with others'.[46]

It is necessary, also, to distinguish intimacy from sexuality. Many sexual relationships are non-intimate; many intimate relationships are non-sexual. Attachment behaviour, which emerges during the first year of life, takes some time to develop, whereas an intimate conversation can occur with a stranger, who may never be seen again.

These different forms of pair-bonding, one supposes, have different evolutionary purposes. Intimacy is the most fragile. People whose development has been disrupted may show competent attachment behaviour with their children, affiliation with friends, but have a failure in the sphere of intimacy, living out a relationship of alienation and isolation with a marital partner with whom, nevertheless, sexual relations are maintained. They live in relationships characterised by non-intimate attachment.[47]

LANGUAGE GAMES

We live within two realities, neither of which contradicts the other, and neither of which is either 'correct' or 'incorrect'. Henri Bergson, the great philosopher who was admired by James and who was Janet's school-fellow and friend, described these two realities in a way which resonates with the Jamesian distinction but uses different language. One reality is that of consciousness, the other that of science. 'No philosophical doctrine denies that the same images can enter at the same time into these two distinct systems'.[48] The distinction between experiential and scientific realities allows apparently opposing or contradictory statements to stand as valid within the appropriate system. For example, 'The sun is setting in the west' is valid within the former. 'The sun is not setting in the west', in referring to the same event, is valid for the latter. To learn of the second or objective reality is not to abolish the first.

Not only is it necessary to distinguish between scientific and experiential realities, it must also be recognised that they depend upon different languages. This idea might be inferred from Wittgenstein.

Wittgenstein's most famous work is the *Tractatus-Logico-Philosophicus*. It concerned his attempts to discover the limits of what can be expressed in terms of factual propositions. He concluded that a great deal lay outside these limits. Some of it was nonsense and some of it of great importance. His initial strategy, on contemplation of this dilemma, was expressed in the famous words which concluded his work: 'Whereof one cannot speak, thereof one must be silent'.[49]

However, another strategy is possible. Although the language of scientific reality is that of factual propositions, and that of the 'deep truths' of our existence is not, silence is not a necessary response to the latter kind of experience. A more useful response might be to search for a different form of language by which it could be expressed. This indeed seemed to be Wittgenstein's quest when he returned to philosophy after a long period away from it. His return was accompanied by the recognition that he had made 'grave mistakes' in the 'Tractatus'.[50]

Since we are various, we use and need multiple language-games, a range of conversational styles which lead to a sense of connectedness and which help to depict, and so bring into being, a personal reality.[51] This kind of language must have certain characteristics of 'inner speech'.[52] Something of its 'shape' is intimated in the style of Keats' last letter,[53] in which he tells his friend, Charles Brown, of his imminent death and of his love for him. He does this without drama or self-pity. The relevant sentences are interspersed in an apparent meander through topics such as symptoms, incidents in the past, friends, or the health of others. Bit by bit, the work is done, so that in the end it may not seem to be done. Keats, having quietly completed the task of farewell, concludes, 'I can scarcely bid you good-bye even in a letter'.

Chapter 5

Memory

By the age of about five, the two main spheres of existence inhabited by a younger child are linked up. Their co-ordination can be demonstrated in the child's conversation.[1] Although we are supposing that this unification is likely to be due, at least in part, to the non-linear form of mental activity underpinning play, it cannot explain the related phenomenon of the emergence of the stream of consciousness out of what I am assuming to be its precursor, that is, the field of symbolic play.

Some other factor must be involved which brings the child from a state of earlier consciousness to that state in which is sensed the 'flow' of inner life. Why should the stream of consciousness not appear until about the age of four, five, or some time after? One of the first to consider this question was the great German physiologist, Ewald Hering (1834–1918).[2]

Freud called Hering's most famous essay a 'masterpiece'.[3] It was given as an address to the Vienna Academy of Sciences in 1870. During the course of this speech he said:

> It seems, then, that we owe to memory almost all that we either have or are; that our ideas and conceptions are its work, and that our everyday perception, thought, and movement are derived from this source. Memory collects the countless phenomena of our existence into a single whole; and, as our bodies would be scattered into the dust of their component atoms if they were not held together by the attractors of matter, so our consciousness would be broken up into as many fragments as we have lived seconds but for the binding and unifying force of memory.[4]

These important remarks suggest that memory, or at least a certain kind of memory, unifies the multitudinous atoms of experienced data, past and present, that make up the flow of inner life.

What is this form of memory? Perhaps the first to study it was Francis Galton.

GALTON'S WALK

Galton conducted some experiments upon himself. The first is described in the following way.

> I walked leisurely along Pall Mall, a distance of 450 yards, during which time I scrutinised with attention every successive object that caught my eyes, and I allowed my attention to rest on it until one or two thoughts had arisen through direct association with that object; then I took very brief mental note of them, and passed on to the next object. I never allowed my mind to ramble. The number of objects viewed was, I think, about 300, for I had subsequently repeated the same walk under similar conditions and endeavoured to estimate their number, with that result. It was impossible for me to recall in other than the vaguest way the numerous ideas that had passed through my mind; but of this, at least, I am sure, that samples of my whole life had passed before me, that many bygone incidents, which I never suspected to have formed part of my stock of thoughts, had been glanced at as objects too familiar to awaken the attention.[5]

Galton was 'perfectly amazed at the unexpected width of the field' of the everyday operations of the brain. He found that his walk had triggered memories of events 'about which I had never consciously occupied myself of late years'.[6]

He repeated the walk and found that certain memories were repeated. 'The roadways of our minds are worn into deep ruts' he remarked.[7] He then refined his experiment creating a list of 75 words. He carefully, and in a standardised way, recorded his associations to these words.

The notion of unconscious mental activity was implied in Galton's study. He supposed that a subject must have 'a continued living interest in order to retain an abiding place in the memory. The mind must refer to it frequently, but whether it does so consciously or unconsciously is not perhaps a matter of much importance'. Otherwise, 'the recollection sinks'. He found that some memories, which were rare, 'had lain *absolutely* dormant for many years'.[6]

Galton attempted to establish the period in life from which his memories came. Thirty-nine per cent came from boyhood and youth; 46 per cent from subsequent manhood; and 15 per cent from quite recent events. The early memories showed the greatest recurrence, suggesting a greater fixity.[8]

Galton's 75 cue words were of three different kinds. The first group consisted of physical objects (for example, 'abbey') which could be visualised; the second group consisted of activities (for example, 'abasement') which admitted of 'histrionic representation'; and more abstract words (for example, 'afternoon'). The last group was more likely than the others to trigger purely verbal associations.

Galton published neither the actual list of words nor his associations to them. He wrote: 'They lay bare the foundations of a man's thoughts with curious distinctness, and exhibit his mental anatomy with more vividness and truth than he would probably care to publish to the world'.[9]

Galton's study led him to conclude that conscious mental life is able to call up from another zone of mental function a large number of related ideas, imaginings, feelings, memories, and so on. He called this the 'ante-chamber of consciousness', which he described in the following way:

> There seems to be a presence-chamber in my mind where full conscious-ness holds court, and where two or three ideas are at the same time in audience, and an antechamber full of more or less allied ideas, which is situated just beyond the full ken of consciousness. Out of this antechamber the ideas most nearly allied to those in the presence-chamber appear to be summoned in a mechanically logical way, and to have their turn of audience.

Galton became aware that the contents and organisation of this metaphoric antechamber was beyond his control. 'If the ideas do not appear, I cannot create them, nor compel them to come.'[10]

Galton considered that his experiments supported the possibility 'of still deeper strata of mental operations, sunk wholly below the level of conscious-ness, which may account for such mental phenomena as cannot otherwise be explained'.[11]

Galton's walk serves as a metaphor of self as the stream of consciousness. In the case of the walk each feature of the progression triggers an associa-tion. In the case of the flux of inner life which emerges during reverie, the associations themselves trigger subsequent associations. In both cases, organ-ised collections of memories, which are not conscious or barely conscious, are the sources of these successive associative elements of the experiential stream. The most important of these organisations of memory relates to who-one-is in relation to another.[12]

THE DOUBLENESS OF MEMORY

William James is the next main figure in the elaboration of the memory system implied by Galton's walk. James identified several essential elements of this kind of memory. First of all, it involves a 'doubling' of conscious-ness. Memory is not simply 'the revival in the mind or copy of the original event'. It involves 'the additional consciousness that we have thought or experienced it before'.[13]

This 'doubling' of memory had been described some years earlier by Hughlings Jackson.[14] As an example, he told of entering a room which smelt of roses. The perfume brought back to him the memory of another room in which he had spent much of his time as a child. His mind now held together two models of experience, one, a room in the past, and the other, a room in the present.

James identified a second feature of what he was calling 'secondary memory'. He wrote:

> Memory requires more than a mere dating of a fact in the past. It must be dated in *my* past. In other words, I must think that I directly experienced its occurrence. It must have that 'warmth and intimacy' which were so often spoken of in the chapter of the self, as characterising all experiences 'appropriated' by the thinker as his own.[15]

In this passage, James distinguishes between a memory that concerns knowledge and another kind of memory consisting of personal experience, which involves the feeling of intimacy. In autobiographical terms, the first kind of memory provides a series of facts. These facts might include, for example, the schools one has attended, the years of that attendance, and the names of the teachers. This knowledge of facts is different from a personal experience of one's school years. The second kind of memory is made up of episodes of personal experience that have a sensory aliveness. The stereotypic episode has oneself at its centre and is made up of sights, sounds, smells, and the feeling of one's body. One conjures up a scene, perhaps of the schoolyard.

TULVING'S EPISODIC MEMORY

The Jamesian description of memory was, for a long time, disregarded in memory research. However, Endel Tulving reintroduced the notion of a personal memory system in a seminal paper published in 1972. He distinguished between a memory concerning knowledge of the world, which he called semantic, and another system of personal memories, which he called episodic.[16] Although exciting some controversy,[17] Tulving's conceptions have been widely influential. So far as I am aware, however, they have not been incorporated into psychotherapeutic theory.

Tulving's reintroduction of a system of personal memories into the field of memory research has been paralleled by the rediscovery of Galton. A modification of Galton's method is now being used in order to study episodic memory in the clinical setting. Herbert Crovitz published a book entitled *Galton's Walk* in 1970.[18]

Tulving[19] distinguishes five kinds of memory systems that, at the moment, can be distinguished. They are (1) episodic, (2) semantic, (3) procedural,

(4) perceptual representation, and (5) short-term memory (that is, working memory). Semantic and episodic memories can be expressed in language. Consequently, they are termed 'declarative'.[20] They are also termed explicit.[21] On the other hand, 'procedural' memory, which concerns memory for motor skills and repertoires, is nonverbal or preverbal.

An important enlargement of Tulving's nomenclature has emerged in recent years. The new categorisation separates episodic memories which are recent and those that are remote in time. Katharine Nelson has been important in introducing this elaboration of Tulving's distinction.

Nelson distinguished, in adult memory, between memories for recent events which can be described as episodes but which are relatively short lived. It is possible, for example, to describe unremarkable events such as the journey to work, or what occurred at lunch, for some days after they have occurred. However, they fade and are lost. It will not be possible to describe that particular journey and that lunch a year later unless one or other has been unusually significant. These episodic memories do not become part of the remote episodic memory system which she is calling 'autobiographical'. These are the memories which Galton's method was recovering, which James described, and which Tulving was calling episodic. Following Nelson, I shall call this form of memory 'autobiographical' and will distinguish it from those memories of the quotidian which, perhaps, concern last week's events, which fade from memory, but which for a time can be described as episodes.

Each kind of memory system is seen as a 'module'[22] of the larger memory system. Lesions of the central nervous system can cause the function of one module of neural organisation to be lost, whereas the function of others is largely retained. For example, patients with Korsakoff's syndrome, who are amnesic, retain motor skills. Moreover, they can learn to use novel tools or to perform new tasks involving repertoires of movement.[23] A strange feature of this learning is that the patient may be unable to remember having come across such a task before, but performs it nevertheless.[24]

It is important, in terms of the argument about the effect of trauma, which will be put forward in Chapter 6, that the autobiographical and episodic memory systems can fail while semantic memory continues to function.

The loss of episodic memory is illustrated in the following anecdote.[25] It concerns a patient Tulving calls K.C., who had suffered a head injury. K.C. is in Dr Tulving's room. Tulving takes an object from a drawer and asks K.C. to identify it. 'It's a stapler,' he replies. He is told that the stapler will now be hidden and that he should remember the place in which it is hidden, because he will be asked about it in the future. Dr Tulving then hides the stapler behind the bookcase. About a week later, K.C. is again in Dr Tulving's room. He is asked if he remembers their previous conversation in this room. He denies any memory of the episode. He is told that the conversation certainly took place. While K.C. was in the room, he is told, a stapler was hidden. He is now asked to find it. Without hesitation, he retrieves it from behind the bookcase.

Although this man had lost his capacity for personal memories, he had retained the ability to record from these episodes certain 'facts'. These facts might include attributes of self and others which are a consequence of the unremembered episodes and events. This idea is essential to the concept of the traumatic memory system.

DEVELOPMENT

The modules of memory do not develop simultaneously, but sequentially. Developmentalists distinguish between recognition memory and recall memory.[26] Recognition memory is evident soon after birth. The baby of less than two weeks is able to recognise as familiar certain stimuli emanating from the mother – her eyes,[27] the smell of her milk,[28] the sound of her voice.[29] Recognition memory is presumably the first manifestation of the perceptual representation system, which is nonverbal and not connected to ordinary consciousness. It is an aspect of implicit memory,[30] that is, memory which does not involve any conscious or explicit recollection of a prior episode. (The perceptual representation system is discussed further in Chapter 12.)

Recall memory, in contrast to recognition memory, depends upon the capacity to bring to mind stimuli that are not present at that moment. It involves knowledge of the world and is, in this sense, semantic. It begins to appear during the last half of the first year,[31] when the baby might crawl to a cupboard to find something he or she knows is kept there. This early semantic memory becomes declarative during the last part of the second year of life, when words are first used.

Episodic memory appears during the third year of life. By the age of three, children have the capacity to recount specific episodes concerning everyday happenings of the recent past.[32] However, these stories are generally not remembered months later, even if the story has been recounted several times.[33] Episodic memories occurring before about three and a half are brief and not remembered later in childhood or during adulthood. They are lost in 'infantile amnesia', the inability to remember events before this age, or thereabouts.[34]

Autobiographical memory which, as previously remarked, concerns episodes in the remote past, emerges in the fifth year of life.[35]

SPECIFIC AND GENERIC MEMORIES

Katherine Nelson not only distinguishes between episodic memory and autobiographical memory, but also between specific and generic forms of memory. (The significance of this distinction in terms of the main thesis of the book will become apparent in Chapter 7).

A generic memory system can be seen as the resultant of collapsing together in memory, in the manner of averaging, a number of similar events or experiences (for example, 'We used to go to the beach in summer. Each day we'd walk down a cliff path . . .'). Generic memory is a schema which helps the individual with ordinary coping by providing a model for behaviour when the typical event, which is encoded in the schema, recurs. The schema is made up of roles of self and other, emotional states, response sequences, and at times, locations. The more frequently an event has been experienced, the more script-like the child's account becomes.[36]

Nelson found that three-year-olds were quite good at describing, in general, a recurring event such as having lunch at preschool.[37] They were much less competent at remembering specific episodes. From an evolutionary point of view the early emergence of generic memory makes sense. Generic memory is more useful in terms of personal function than a series of unconnected memories of individual events, unless of course those events were life-threatening. Indeed, at first sight, a memory for specific, often insignificant, events seems to have little value, in an evolutionary sense.

Generic memories are obviously important from the point of view of survival. They provide general rules about suitable responses to the environment. But what can be the value, for example, of remembering a picnic on a riverbank when one was eight, or of sitting on some steps with one's mother at the age of four, watching the sunset. These memories, unlike generic memories, seem to offer no biological advantage to the human primate. However, when we think of how these memories are used we begin to sense their significance. These memories are the basis of stories, and of stories which link up groups of people. When one family member asks 'Do you remember that picnic . . .' and another replies with a linking memory, a moment of a form of bonding has occurred. Stories help to hold families together but they also do more than this, as Bartlett intimated in his classic work. He wrote that:

> In all well-established modern communities, every family has its own characteristic mental life; its memories which it alone cherishes; its secrets which are revealed to none but its own members. Moreover, these memories, like the religious traditions of the family group of earlier days, are no mere series of individualised images of the past. They may be this, but they are also models, examples, a kind of basis for education and development. In them is expressed the general attitude of the group, so that they do more than reproduce its history, they define its nature, its strength and its weakness.[38]

More widely shared memories contribute to the stories which bind together large and diverse groups of people. These stories are frequently of a religious or mythological kind. Such storytelling also holds together the sense and feeling of an individual life. William James' account of the boy's personal story of the moon is an example. Stories which come from the zone of the personal are essential aspects of intimate relating.

AUTOBIOGRAPHICAL MEMORY AND REFLECTION

The emergence of autobiographical memory at about four is presumably related to the child's discovery of the stream of consciousness, at about the same age. Hering had supposed that the establishment of memory allowed us to experience a unified flow of mental life. Put another way, he saw the memory function as a necessary pre-condition to the experience of this state. There is, however, another way of looking at it.

Since both involve the doubleness of consciousness which James had deemed essential to not only the sense of self, but also autobiographical memory, it may be that they are different but related aspects of the same developmental progression. Both depend on the reflective capacity, which allows one to say to oneself 'This is a memory', or 'These are my thoughts'. The appearance of these capabilities represents a change from what Edelman[39] called primary consciousness to higher order consciousness. This enlargement of consciousness must coincide with a stage of cerebral maturation in which new neural connections, creating a notional feedback loop, come into operation.[40] They add to older systems of monitoring and evaluating individual functions which can now be demonstrated by means of neuroimaging.[41]

It must not be supposed, however, that the capacity to reflect upon inner states is simply the manifestation of maturation of certain aspects of brain function. Although this will be necessary to its emergence it is unlikely to be sufficient to it. A sense of self as the stream of consciousness, and the related phenomenon of autobiographical memory, presumably depend upon not only a genetically encoded programme of 'biogenesis' but also suitable social environment which allows it to evolve. This idea follows the views of the great Russian psychologists, Lev Vygotsky and Alexander Luria,[42] who saw child development, particularly in terms of the late developing functions, as reflecting the interweaving of 'biogenesis' and 'sociogenesis'.

Part II

The trauma system

Chapter 6

Uncoupled consciousness

One's sense of personal being is upset from time to time. The stream of consciousness is taken over by a different form of mental life, shown by a negative emotional shift and a different kind of conversation. Such occurrences, for many people, have a minor effect on ordinary living. These people are called 'sensitive', 'moody', 'prickly', 'aggressive', 'easily offended', and so on. For some people, the disruptions are more severe, damaging close relationships and impeding personal growth. The changes of behaviour which accompany the altered form of psychic life are seen by others as part of the individual's personality. However, these incursions into the ongoing sense of existence are manifestations of traumatic memories which are outside, that is, not integrated into, the prevailing personality structure. They can be seen as dissociated, a term which implies the sequestration from ordinary consciousness of a particular complex of mental life, which operates almost autonomously.[1] Since this book concerns a 'dissociation/ integration' model of psychotherapy, it is necessary to come to some understanding of what is meant by the term dissociation. The next two chapters are mainly devoted to this task.

The notion of self and its development, outlined in previous chapters, provides our starting point. Self, as an awareness of the stream of consciousness, is double, and so also is that form of memory which is part of it. Trauma has the effect of overthrowing the doubleness of self. It causes 'dedoubling' or 'uncoupling' of consciousness. This is most importantly manifest in the sphere of memory. This 'dedoubled' state, I am suggesting, is that of dissociation. This very simplified explanation requires elaboration. It is provided by a consideration of the theories of Hughlings Jackson. However, before turning to Jackson, a more detailed description of dissociation is needed.

JANET AND DISSOCIATION

Dissociation is a word freely used in psychiatric and psychologic circles yet its meaning is by no means clear. Pierre Janet is the originator of the concept, although he did not, at first, use the term dissociation, using instead the words *désagrégation* and *dédoublement*.[2] The latter conveys the idea of a compartmentalisation of a certain segment of psychic life. However, the state is more complicated than splitting.[3] *Désagrégation* suggests a sense of falling apart, a disintegration. This notion is central to Janet's understanding of dissociation.

Janet repeatedly remarked upon the 'pathological incapacity to collect the elementary sensations in a general perception'[4] in his patients. He explained this idea by talking of the 'atoms' of experience of which our consciousness is composed, which are held together in a way which is still not understood. A failure of 'personal synthesis', as he called it, is a fundamental difficulty of people who suffer major dissociative experiences and who were once given the diagnosis of 'hysteria'. Although Janet was the star of Parisian psychiatry at the beginning of the twentieth century, a man who seemed likely to found his own school, his fall from influence, like that of Baldwin, was spectacular.[5] As a consequence, Janet's work was largely lost, much of it remaining untranslated. His major conceptions have been widely misunderstood, at least until quite recently. In the clinical realm, the phenomenon of dissociation has been quite neglected.[6]

The recent interest in psychological trauma has caused attention to be focused, once again, on the concept of dissociation. However, authorities differ in their understanding of it. It is sometimes considered equivalent to states such as day-dreaming or absorption in creative activity.[7] This is unlike the conception of Janet, who saw the phenomenon as pathological and equivalent to a hypnotic state.[8]

Most people have experienced a state which is like dissociation. Following some catastrophe or terrible event, one may feel strange, detached, somewhat disconnected from things. The world around one may seem a little unreal. Even one's body may feel different. The sense of time passing is changed. This state resembles that of extreme exhaustion.

Dissociation is often seen as a defence against the feelings, which may be overwhelming, engendered by catastrophe. The problem about this view is that people who dissociate are more vulnerable to post-traumatic stress disorder following a traumatic event than those who do not dissociate.[9] Seen in this way, dissociation is the opposite of protective.

An alternative view, which is also my own, sees dissociation, at its first appearance, as the manifestation of a subtle disorganisation of cerebral function brought about by the overpowering effect of the emotions associated with the traumatic event. It is not, on this occasion, a defence. However, somebody who has once experienced dissociation may be able subsequently to reproduce the experience for protective purposes. This voluntary or quasi-voluntary replication of the experience is analogous to the behaviour of a child with a certain kind of epilepsy who is able to bring on a fit when the circumstances of his or her life become difficult or unpleasant. On the other hand, it cannot be said that all recurrences of dissociation are defensive. It may be that the previous experience of trauma creates a vulnerability which leads to the recurrences. This is consistent with a large amount of evidence showing that those who have been traumatised are more likely to dissociate than people who have not.[10]

The episodes of dissociation which Janet described, and for which he is known, had an extravagant form. This included fugue states in which the subject wandered for long periods, sometimes for months at a time, without subsequent memory of where he or she had been. One of these accounts concerned a young man of seventeen. This example is chosen because Janet notes that the fugues, in this case, followed 'some fatigue or fit of drunkenness'. The relevance of this observation will become clear in the following section on Hughlings Jackson's theories.

> At thirteen he often went to a small public house, visited by old sailors. They would urge him to drink, and, when he was somewhat flustered, they would fill his imagination with beautiful tales in which deserts, palm trees, lions, camels, and Negroes were pictured in a most wonderful and alluring way. The young boy was very much struck by those pictures, particularly as he was half tipsy. However, when his drunkenness was over, the stories seemed to be quite forgotten; he never spoke of travels, and, on the contrary, led a very sedentary life, for he had chosen the placid occupation of a grocer's boy, and he only sought to rise in that honourable career.
>
> Now there come on quite unforeseen accidents, almost always on the occasion of some fatigue or a fit of drunkenness. He then felt transformed, forgot to return home, and thought no more of his family. He would leave Paris, walking straight ahead, and go to a more or less great distance through the forest of St. Germaine, or as far as the department of the Orne. Sometimes he walked alone; at other times he rambled with some tramps, begging along the roads; he had but one idea left in his head; namely, to get to the sea, enlist in a ship and sail away towards those enchanting countries of Africa. His journeys ended rather badly; he would awake suddenly, drenched, half starving, either on the highroad or in an asylum, without ever being able to understand what had happened, without any memory of his journey, and with the most ardent wish to go back to his family and his grocery.[11]

The most prominent element of this state is the disturbance of memory. However, dissociation also involves changes in attention, amongst them what Janet called a 'contraction of the field of consciousness'. This, like memory disturbance, is a cardinal feature of the phenomenon. Other cardinal features are depersonalisation–derealisation, discontinuity of personal existence, and hallucinosis. They will be touched upon in the following chapter.

THE UNCOUPLING OF CONSCIOUSNESS

Hughlings Jackson (1835–1911) believed himself to be the first to use the word 'self' in medical literature.[12] Intriguingly, his model of self, derived from neurological observations and couched in neurophysiological terminology, depends upon doubling and upon reverberating systems of representation. In this way, it resonates with the duplex self and its development, described so far.

It seems not unlikely that James was influenced by Jackson who, although only seven years his senior, was already an authority while James was working towards his great work of 1890. He corresponded with Jackson and visited him in London.[13] Jackson was, at this point, on his way to becoming the 'father of British neurology'.

Jackson is remembered for his neurological work. However, such was his brilliance that a number of his innovations were not comprehended by his colleagues. The most neglected part of his opus concerns mind and self. He was a pioneer in the sphere of mental illness, believing that detailed observations of minute changes in cerebral function might lead to an understanding of psychological disorder.

Jackson was greatly impressed by the evolutionary theory of Darwin, particularly as it was expressed by Herbert Spencer (1820–1903). He developed the idea of a hierarchial arrangement of the central nervous system, the highest centres being the last to evolve and the last to appear in human development. In principle, this hierarchial assembly was similar to that proposed by Janet.

It seems likely that Janet was influenced indirectly by Jackson via Théodule Ribot, who Janet recognised as one of his two 'masters', the other being Charcot.[14] Ribot had introduced into France the fundamentals of Jackson's evolution-based theories.[15]

Jackson's approach to mental illness was highly logical. It begins with fundamentals. He wrote that: 'What we call the scientific investigation of insanity is really an experimental investigation of mind'.[16] This being so, we must start with a working model of 'mind'.

In formulating such a model, Jackson stated that: 'We must be thoroughly materialistic in our method'. At the same time he warned against a confusion of 'psychical states with nervous states',[17] of mind with brain. Nevertheless, one rises out of the other so that there emerges a 'concomitant parallelism',[18] a concept which Freud found particularly useful and which he quoted in English in his paper on aphasia.[19]

Anticipating philosophical argument, Jackson asked 'that the doctrine of concomitance be provisionally accepted as an artifice, in order that we can study the most complex diseases of the nervous system more easily. There can be no difficulty in understanding the *statement*'.[20] The next step in his argument concerns an adequate description of mind. Jackson conceived it as double, consisting of subject and object, or as he put it, of 'subject consciousness' and 'object consciousness'. Like James, Jackson emphasised that this discrimination is an abstraction. 'Each is only half itself'.[21] Subjective consciousness, the I, is comparatively unchanging. 'It is thus a constant to object consciousness which is continually changing.'

Jackson's conception resembled the 'duplex self' of William James, since it depended upon the 'introspection of consciousness'.[22] Like the Jamesian self, it was made up of a pole of awareness (the 'I') and another of the objects of awareness (the 'me'). However, Jackson's description of the 'me' is limited and James' elaboration of it, as the stream of consciousness, is a necessary one.

How does self arise, or as Jackson was trying to understand it, how did it evolve? Once again, he began with fundamentals. Jackson conceived of the central nervous system in terms of what he saw as its simplest functional unit. This basic unit was reflexive, the most fundamental element of sensori-motor function. Each of these units is a representing system. The brain, in his view, evolves and develops through an increasingly complex co-ordination of these units. As the organism evolves to a higher stage of function, it is not as if something new were being tacked on, which provides new representations. Rather, there is a re-representation. At a higher stage still, there is a re-re-representation,[23] so that the most recently evolved part of the brain, the cerebral cortex, is 'universally representing'.[24] 'The whole nervous system is a sensori-motor mechanism, a co-ordinating system from top to bottom'.[25]

How does mind or self arise out of this co-ordinating system? Jackson rejected the idea that any special new form of neural function had been built into the human brain during evolution. He noted that it would be rather odd if, during the course of building a structure, there was a change in the primary material of which it was composed. Freud quoted with approval Jackson's remark that with evolution nothing new or even supernatural was introduced into the system.[26] Jackson wrote: 'We must be on our guard against the fallacy that what are psychical states in lower centres fine away into psychical states in higher centres'. He asked: 'Of what "substance" can the organ of mind be composed unless of processes representing movements and impressions?'[27]

The emergence of self does not represent another new module of function stacked on top of older ones. Jackson wrote that 'There is no autocratic mind at the top to receive sensations as a sort of raw material, out of which to manufacture ideas, etc., and then to associate these ideas'.[28] The appearance of self is the manifestation of a more complex co-ordination than previously. What is new, then, is a new, or higher, system of unification of the whole organism 'whereby the organism as a whole is adjusted to the environment'. He quoted approvingly from Ribot: 'Le moi est une co-ordination'.[29] This new co-ordination came about, he believed, through the evolutionary emergence of pre-frontal cortical activity. In this sense, the pre-frontal cortex could be called the 'organ of mind'.[30] However, this is not to say that self *resides* in the pre-frontal cortex. Rather, the new structure allows a more complex co-ordination of what is 'anatomically a sensori-motor machine'.[31]

When seen against work that is going on at the present time, Jackson's achievement is extraordinary. Although Jackson was writing when knowledge about brain function was very limited, his conception of self is compatible with the most recent authoritative formulations. One of the most impressive of these comes from the noted neuroscientist, Antonio Damasio. Damasio believes his may be the first contemporary attempt to make 'a specific proposal for a neural basis of subjectivity'.[32]

Two of Jackson's ideas are central to Damasio's thesis. First, representations of all parts of the body are involved in the nervous activity which results in the experience of self. Second, this experience depends on co-ordination of all parts of the brain. Even now these ideas seem new. Damasio remarks that 'the idea that mind derives from the entire organism as an ensemble may sound counterintuitive at first'.[33]

In accord with Jackson, Damasio considers that the particular kind of neural activity which underpins mind or self depends on the pre-frontal cortex. This is not to say that it resides there. Rather, self is a process continuously going on and, at the same time, fragile. 'At each moment the state of self is constructed, from the ground up. It is an evanescent reference state, so continuously and consistently re-constructed that the owner never knows it is being remade unless something goes wrong with the remaking'.[34]

Damasio, of course, goes beyond Jackson. His principal advance on Jackson's model concerns the significance of feelings in human life and human cognition.

DISSOLUTION

Jackson's main postulate, based not only on evolutionary theory but also on his own meticulous observations of neurological patients, was that those mental functions which have evolved last and which are the slowest to develop are the most fragile, the most vulnerable to assaults upon the brain–mind system. The greater the assault the further will be the retreat down the developmental and evolutionary pathway. He called the process, the reverse of evolution, dissolution.

Jackson saw self as a manifestation of the evolutionary passage towards greater complexity and specialisation, and greater voluntary control over a particular function. The latest functions are also the least completely developed, and the most dependent on the environment for maturation.[35] Jackson's theory predicts that where environmental circumstances are unfavourable, self will be manifest in stunted and impoverished forms, showing diminished complexity and lessened voluntary control over its movements. His theory also predicts that insults to the brain–mind system will result in memory function failing in hierarchial manner. The greater the perturbation of the system, the earlier will be the form of memory which operates within it. Moderate trauma will eliminate autobiographical and episodic memories, leaving the semantic and other systems intact. Severe trauma leaves only the earliest, most primitive, preverbal memory systems functional.

Jackson considered that the investigation of mental illness should not be confined to psychiatric patients. It should begin with studies of 'the slightest departures from a person's standard of mental health'.[36] He was particularly intrigued by the mental condition in which an electrical discharge causes a subtle disruption of cerebral function, a disturbance often so slight that it would not be apparent to the uninterested observer. There is a change in consciousness which he called the 'dreamy state'.[37] This state, which resembles dissociation, follows only the 'slightest fits'. The person so afflicted is defectively conscious. The patient reports, for example, becoming 'dim to his surroundings', or that 'although he hears people talking he does not know what they say'.[38]

Jackson noticed that people performed complicated actions after one of these states but the individual was barely conscious of what he or she was doing. Furthermore, there was an impaired memory for the period of these actions. Jackson called these behaviours 'automatisms'. He emphasised that they were not a direct consequence of the epileptic discharge. Rather, the automatisms followed the discharge, as if neuronal 'exhaustion' had caused a temporary cessation of certain fragile aspects of cerebral function.[39] These automatisms resemble those described by Janet, which have a psychological basis. It is of interest that some fugue-like wanderings occur in people with a history of epilepsy.[40]

These observations showing that the exhaustion following epileptic discharge may produce behaviours and symptoms which are like those which have a psychological basis, lead to the idea that an assault upon the brain–mind system has similar results whether this assault is upon the 'brain' or the 'mind'. This indeed is an important implication of Jackson's 'parallel concomitance'. The idea is also in accord with the view of Lenore Terr, one of the major figures in trauma research. She makes a comparison between states induced by psychological trauma and those produced by physical trauma, drugs, or alcohol.[41] Janet's case of the boy who suffered fugue states supports her viewpoint. His fugues were usually preceded by fatigue or by alcoholic intoxication.

Harry Stack Sullivan had a view similar to that of Terr. He remarked that a psychological trauma was equivalent to a blow on the head, leaving a lacuna in the psychic system, an interruption in a personal existence. 'About the most the person can remember in retrospect is a somewhat fenestrated account of the event's immediate neighbourhood'.[42] And again: 'the effect of severe anxiety reminds one in some ways of a blow on the head, in that it simply wipes out what is immediately proximal to its occurrence. If you have a severe blow on the head, you are quite apt later to have an incurable, absolute amnesia covering the few moments before your head was struck. Anxiety has a similar effect'.[43]

The comparisons between psychologically and physically induced states made by Terr and Sullivan suggest that study of slight disturbances of cerebral function of the kind, for example, associated with epilepsy, might lead to a greater understanding of the effects of psychological trauma. In particular, Jackson's 'dreamy state' may provide a model for understanding the concept of dissociation. A consideration of the essential features of Jackson's description begins with an extremely interesting case report. It involves a doctor who gave Jackson written accounts of his attacks.

On one occasion he was called to see a patient who had something wrong with her respiratory system. While beginning his examination he became aware that he was going to have a slight fit and he turned away from the people in the room so that they would not notice. He 'came to' some time later. He was sitting at a table writing out the diagnosis of pneumonia of the left base. The patient was no longer in the room and had presumably been sent to bed. Nobody seemed to have noticed anything strange about the doctor's behaviour. He felt that he needed to check on his diagnosis made during this period. He found that his diagnosis was perfectly correct on re-examination of his patient.[44]

This is a remarkable incident. A man is able to perform complex tasks of data-gathering and reasoning while he is apparently unconscious of them. He is functioning in this way by means of a memory system which is of a sophisticated kind. It includes the facts of his medical training, his knowledge of symptoms, signs and how to discover them. This is semantic memory. Another kind of memory, which emerges relatively late in development has been lost. This is episodic memory. He can remember nothing of the examination. The story is lost to him. Yet those around him apparently noticed nothing amiss while he was going about his business of doctoring.

The story of the doctor provides a background for an understanding of the phenomena of dissociation. His mental state can be seen as 'dedoubled' or 'uncoupled' using the Jackson–James notion of the duplex self made up of an 'I' and a 'me'. As he goes about his task of doctoring in an automatic way, this doubleness is lost and he is without reflective awareness.

PSYCHOGENIC MEMORY DISTURBANCE

Following the implications of 'parallel concomitance', and observations such as those of Terr and Sullivan, I am suggesting that the effect of a severe psychological shock or overwhelming emotion is like a blow on the head or the after effects of a slight epileptic discharge. It produces a mild cerebral disorganisation which, according to Jacksonian theory, will have its main effects upon late maturing systems rather than upon those which develop earlier and which are older in an evolutionary sense.

The doctor had suffered a disruption which is larger than that which occurs following most psychological trauma in that he suffered what seemed to be a total loss of the reflective capacity. Both the stream of consciousness and episodic memory were inoperative. Nevertheless, total amnesia for psychologically traumatic events is increasingly reported.[45] Jacksonian theory predicts that the loss of memory will involve the episodic and autobiographical forms of memory rather than semantic or more primitive modes of remembering. This prediction was supported by the study of a case of dissociation involving a fugue state reported upon by Schacter et al.[46] Episodic memory, which is dependent upon pre-frontal activity, was absent. On the other hand, semantic memory was retained.

The fact that dissociative amnesias are more common where the brain–mind system has been made vulnerable by previous disruption such as head injury[47] or psychological trauma during the maturational period[48] is also consistent with the hypothesis expressed here.

The memory of the catastrophic event will be recorded, according to the dissolution hypothesis, in a hierarchial way. Those events which do not cause severe disorganisation will be recorded in memory systems, such as the semantic, which are nearer to ordinary consciousness and which are not evident very early in life. More extreme traumatic experiences will cause these memory systems to become inactive. In this case, the traumatic experiences are recorded in more primitive forms of memory, that is, in the perceptual representation of procedural systems. Memories of events which occur before the emergence of the reflective capacity at about the age of four will also be registered in these systems. Since these memories are beyond the reach of ordinary consciousness there is an amnesia for the period of life before the age of three-and-a-half or four, or thereabouts.

Lenore Terr has given striking evidence that trauma in infancy is recorded in the procedural memory system, which concerns motor repertoires. She found that traumatised children for whom she was caring, from time to time performed the actions they had to go through during the traumatic event. The children were aged between 28 and 36 months at the time of the trauma, but when she saw them at an older age they were unable to describe these events in words.

Some of the children had been sexually abused. In these cases, the abuse had, at times, been photographed for pornographic purposes. Terr had access to these photographs and was able to correlate the behaviours she observed in the children with the form of sexual abuse which was inflicted upon them. The repetition of these traumatic events was evident not only in bodily movements but also represented in play.

In addition to the accounts of the actions of her traumatised children, Lenore Terr also provides evidence consistent with the idea that trauma occurring in the pre-reflective period is recorded in the perceptual representation system. This memory system is very accurate, highly specific but atomised and inflexible.

Terr writes: 'When a trauma or series of extreme stresses strikes well before the age of 28 to 36 months, the child "burns-in" a visual memory of it'.[49] The event is registered as a sensory imprint. This 'burning-in' is also evident in terms of skin sensation. One of our patients, for example, had been raped by one man while being pinned down by the forearms by another. From time to time, particularly when she was anxious, she could feel the skin in her forearms twisting laterally. It was as if an aspect of the trauma had been 'burnt in' or imprinted on her body.

Another patient had a strange facial sensation, also when she was anxious, which at first she could not link to any past event. She felt as if a silken cord wavered obliquely across her face. It turned out that some years previously she had been in a car accident. In the brief moment before the accident, she could see that it was about to occur and believed she would die. However, she was unhurt apart from a scalp wound. As she lay on the side of the road, a stream of blood trickled obliquely across her face.

In his valuable review of memory and trauma, Bessel van der Kolk notes that 'memories of the trauma tend, at least initially, to be experienced as fragments of the sensory components of the event: as visual images, olfactory, auditory, or kinesthetic sensations; or intense waves of feelings that patients usually claim to be representations of elements of the original traumatic event. What is intriguing is that patients consistently claim that their perceptions are exact representations at the time of the trauma'.[50] Janet considered that his patients suffered 'an ensemble of maladies through representation'.[51]

RECURRENT DISSOCIATIONS

A traumatic event, if it occurs once, is generally remembered. However, if the traumatic event recurs, the likelihood is greatly increased that it will not be remembered. In many cases it might be supposed that the traumatic experience is recorded in semantic memory. This is a memory for facts, which include the attributes of self and other during the traumatic event. (The development of attributions is explored in Chapter 9.) This kind of memory does not allow access to the episodes during which these 'facts' were created. In this sense, the traumatic memory is 'unconscious' although certain aspects of it can be expressed in words.

I am calling the collection of memories concerning similar traumatic events, which is stored in a memory system beyond the reach of reflective awareness, a traumatic memory system. It is triggered by contextual cues which resemble, in some way, the original trauma. These cues may be external, produced, for example, by particular circumstances of a conversation.

The cues may also be internal. An emotional state, for example, may trigger the traumatic memory system which now takes over the field of consciousness.

The traumatic memory system is organised as a complex of cognitions, emotions and tendencies to respond. It corresponds to Janet's subconscious fixed idea. The system may be large and make up a kind of subpersonality in an extreme case. My focus is upon small, even miniature, traumatic memory systems. I am supposing that a series of events, such as being ridiculed or criticised, are stored in a memory system which is not that of ordinary consciousness. In this sense they are 'unconscious'. They are triggered when particular circumstances of the present moment resemble, however slightly, the original traumatic experience. The story of Jane, mentioned in Chapter 1, exemplified this state of affairs.

Jane's marriage was falling apart because she and her husband were having frequent rows which seemed to come out of nowhere. She was becoming depressed; he had started to drink.

The origins of their fights seemed trivial. They were of the kind illustrated by another case, described by Michael Lewis.[52] A husband and wife take turns in cooking and in setting the table. On the first night, she is cooking and he is setting the table. 'Why don't we use the other knives?' she asks. 'O.K.' he replies, and changes the knives.

The next night their roles are reversed and she is setting the table. 'Why don't we use the new tablecloth?' he asks. She erupts: 'Am I so stupid I can't even set a table?' Her voice is shrill and strident. He feels attacked and retaliates. Neither partner understands what is happening to them.

This woman's behaviour has its origins in a past of being shamed. I am suggesting that her sudden anger is an expression of a miniature form of dissociation. She is in an altered state of consciousness. The future and past are virtually absent. Furthermore, there is a disturbance of memory. Her husband's remark evokes the memories of past experiences of shame, but since these are 'unconscious' neither she nor her husband know that she is in the grip of a traumatic memory system. The experience is located in the present. The attributes of the original figure who shamed her are now given, or 'transferred', to her husband.

In the case of Jane, the traumatic system can be conceived as semantic. Other traumata, however, will be stored in earlier or more primitive memory systems. Their activation will be manifest in a way which differs from that of Jane. An important instance involves a traumatic memory system which is largely procedural, that is, concerned with motor repertoires. When this system is triggered by contextual cues so that the subject is now, as it were, 'within' it, he or she plays out the traumatic script. In this dissociated state, in which the individual is unaware that he or she is in the midst of memory, the individual 'acts out' the circumstances of traumatic memory.

Seen in this way, a theory of dissociation offers a way of understanding the somewhat mysterious behaviour of traumatised individuals, who frequently find themselves in situations in which the trauma is inflicted upon them once again. Freud explored the nature of this repetition in his classic paper of 1914. He wrote:

> We may say that the patient does not *remember* anything of what he has forgotten and repressed, but *acts* it out. He reproduces it not as a memory but as an action; he *repeats* it, without, of course, knowing that he is repeating it.[53]

IMPLICATIONS

The notion of recurrent dissociations has two important implications. First, it predicts that in some people, at least, changes in conscious state, of a minor kind, will be repeatedly triggered during the course of ordinary living. In many cases, the individual will be unaware of the origins of this change in state. Second, these disruptions of the ongoing sense of personal being by traumatic memory systems will act as impediments to personal growth. Janet remarked of certain of his patients:

> Unable to integrate traumatic memories, they seem to have lost their capacity to assimilate new experiences as well. It is . . . as if their personality has definitively stopped at a certain point, and cannot enlarge any more by the addition and assimilation of new elements.[54]

The following chapter touches upon aspects of this state.

Chapter 7

Disrupted maturation: the dissolution hypothesis

Hughlings Jackson's hierarchial model of psychic function depends upon the notion of a reverberating system of representations, in which a representation is re-represented, after which the new representation is re-re-represented. The highest level of these reverberations allows 'self' to emerge. Since he was writing when little neurophysiological evidence was available, his model was a conceptual one. Nevertheless, it resembles modern attempts to create a neural model of mind or self. It also anticipates models based on non-linear mathematics (see Chapter 14). Most intriguingly, it resonates with the development of self outlined in previous chapters. This view of child development sees the other, the caregiver, as performing the task of the re-representation on behalf of the child. The reverberation is going on in the outer world. Eventually, it becomes part of the child's personal system. Put another way, it is 'internalised'.

These ideas provide a metaphor for conceiving disturbances in the maturation of self. This is the metaphor of 'dedoubling' or 'uncoupling', introduced in the previous chapter. This uncoupling, however, is of a larger kind than implied by the Jacksonian model. It depends upon the view that the human being is not an isolated system but part of a larger organism which includes the social environment. Maturational failure must be conceived not only in terms of brain function but also in terms of the individual in relation to others. As Luria and Vygotsky put it, 'biogenesis' and 'sociogenesis' are interwoven.

A model of the emergence of self which depends upon a series of reverberating representations leads to predictions about how this process may be disturbed. First, it may be disturbed through traumatic 'uncouplings' as described in the previous chapter. Second, the caregivers may fail, through their own egocentricity and lack of empathy, to provide the resonating representations, based on feeling, which show the child who is 'me'.

Seen in this way, and following the argument of the previous chapter, disruption in the maturation of self is a consequence of an environmentally induced impediment to the activity of aspects of a late developing cascade of descending neuronal loops, of largely pre-frontal origin, which create the higher form of 'coupling' of brain function necessary to the emergence of the stream of consciousness.

The literature concerning borderline personality disorder, which is frequently seen as a consequence of a developmental arrest in the sphere of self, supports the predictions concerning failures of the caregiving environment. People suffering borderline personality disorder in the typical case, endured a traumatic early life.[1] When they were children most of them were abused, either physically, sexually, or emotionally. Second, the parents of these people have been shown to be deficient in another way. Golomb and colleagues found that mothers of borderline subjects treated their children egocentrically, as need-gratifying objects.[2]

If, however, the 'uncoupling' metaphor is to have any validity as a way of approaching disturbances in the development of self, some continuity must be shown between the phenomena found in a single and transient dissociative episode and the more enduring features of borderline personality disorder. This is the subject of this chapter.

EMPTINESS AND ALIENATION

Those suffering borderline personality disorder are afflicted with a pervasive sense of emptiness which, at times, has a painful intensity. The individual often makes desperate attempts to 'fill' the emptiness by means of stimulus seeking behaviours such as reckless sexuality, substance abuse, gambling, even theft. It is as if there is 'nothing inside', no inner life. What happens is going on in the environment and in the body. There is no stream of consciousness.

Such a state exists when one is overwhelmed by the effect of trauma and in a state of fear. One is conscious only of the source of the fear, the emotion itself, and the immediate surroundings. Should the traumatic state lead to dissociation, the individual typically experiences a sense of alienation which is technically termed depersonalisation–derealisation. There is a sense of unreality about one's surroundings (derealisation) and also an estrangement from one's person, which includes the experience of the body (depersonalisation).[3]

The origins of depersonalisation are not yet understood. The phenomenon can be approached in terms of Claparède's famous paper of 1911, which is entitled 'Recognition and "Me-ness"'. He wrote: 'The propensity of states of consciousness to cluster round a *me* which persists and remains the same in the course of time, is a postulate of psychology, as space is a postulate of geometry'.[4] With increasing intensity of trauma, and a contraction of consciousness, there is a diminution in the sense of 'me-ness' and also of 'warmth and intimacy' of self. The more severe the trauma, the greater the diminution of the fundamental 'me-ness' and the 'ownership' of those experiences which are sensed as part of the personal rather than the collective reality.

As the sense of well-being, which is part of the 'warmth and intimacy' of self, is lost, it is replaced by a negative affect. This unpleasant feeling results in a negative personal evaluation (see Chapters 8 and 9).

These experiences are felt in the totality of self, which includes the body. In a state of alienation and disconnectedness, body feeling may change so that alterations occur in its rhythms, its 'smoothness', its density and shape.[5] The individual may feel so insubstantial that he or she could be blown away by the wind.

Depersonalisation is usually accompanied by a sense of the strangeness and unreality of one's surroundings. The derealisation of dissociation can be explained in terms of another of Jackson's doublings which he considered fundamental. It involves a constant matching between models of the world formed in the past and those appearing in the present. Jackson wrote that 'what is most fundamental in mental operations' is 'the double process of tracing relations of likeness and unlikeness'.[6] Derealisation can be understood as a consequence of mismatching between the models of memory and those of immediate experience.[7]

The 'myself' who is part of this scene feels altered and different − 'not myself'. This experience does not match the experience of 'myself' which is stored in memory. One inhabits a landscape which is unfamiliar and alien.

The alienation of a single dissociative episode resembles the more enduring, although less marked, disturbance of the sense of self in a patient with borderline personality features who may say such things as 'I don't have a clear feeling of who I really am', or 'I'm nobody nowhere'.

DISCONTINUITY OF PERSONAL EXISTENCE

A discontinuity of personal existence is characteristic not only of dissociation but also of borderline personality disorder in which 'splitting' is authoritatively seen as a central issue. The individual shows rapid changes of state, particularly of an emotional kind. Discontinuity of personal existence can, like the experiences of emptiness and a stunted feeling of 'me-ness', be understood in terms of a failure of the satisfactory emergence of the stream of consciousness.

Jacksonian theory predicts a fragmentation of psychic life and, in particular, of self, when an assault is made upon the brain–mind system. Self, as a manifestation of the highest level of co-ordination of the fundamental elements of brain function, is not only a result of co-ordination, but is also a unifying factor. A failure of the systems underpinning self will result in the sense of personal discontinuity of dis-co-ordination. Since the co-ordination underpinning self is at the highest level in Jackson's hierarchy, it will fail first in the face of severe trauma. 'Personal synthesis', to use Janet's term, will be deficient.

How such fragmentation might come about in neurophysiological terms is not yet known. However, as noted in Chapter 4, I am supposing that it involves both the reflective function and that associative non-linear form of mental activity which underpins the stream of consciousness. Both are impaired or lost during the experience of trauma.

That the drift of images, feelings, memories, ideas, imaginings, and so forth, of which the steam of consciousness is composed, is lost during trauma is obvious. It is less easy to describe the impairment of the reflective function. This description involves a consideration of the spatiality of personal existence.[8]

The highest levels of consciousness suggest a sense of space or distance between the awareness of mental events and those events themselves. An example is provided by famous descriptions by Jules Poincaré (1859–1912) of his state of mind during mathematical creativity.[9] At times, he could 'view' the symbols with which he played almost as if he were in a theatre. This high level of reflective functioning – we might say of the 'I', using Jamesian language – is lost when one is terrified. The object of the terror is, as it were, pressed up against one. The 'view' is lost. The function of the 'I', in unifying the potential diversity and disconnectedness of personal experience, is diminished.

The breaking-up of personal experience following a noxious insult to the brain–mind system was described by Rebecca West. She had suffered a severe febrile illness. While recovering in a nursing home she 'fell into a curious state'.

> I lost my power of suppressing irrelevant impressions and co-ordinating those that remained. I felt obliged to watch the trees outside my window and their behaviour in the sunshine and wind, to note the characteristics of every person who spoke to me, with a quite disagreeable intensity, and I was so fatigued by this constant effort of apprehension that there was no continuity in the working of my brain. Every moment of consciousness was distinct and unrelated to any other. Instead of being a stream, my mental life was a string of disparate beads.[10]

Just before her discharge, presumably in order to foster her rehabilitation, she was sent out on a walk. She walked to the top of the hill just outside the small town where she was recuperating. When she got to the top, she realised that she could not see the view, in any proper sense.

> I could not see the view. I could see it in bits, but not as a whole. It was like trying to take a photograph of a view with a non-panoramic camera. And what I saw seemed like a meaningless painting on glass. The patchwork of colours carried no suggestion of textures and contours. I had to work hard to interpret it; to see, for example, that spattered rhomboid patch was cornfield.[11]

Just as her mental life was a 'disparate string of beads', she could not integrate what she saw. The view appeared only as bits.

It is important that Rebecca West's 'curious state' appears in the period
of exhaustion following her severe illness. It is not a direct consequence of
the toxic condition, just as Jackson's doctor's state was not directly due to
a discharge of cerebral electrical activity.[12]

Rebecca West realised that her 'mechanism was hopelessly out of gear'.
She was painfully aware that the stream of consciousness had gone. The
sense of continuity, which is a cardinal feature of self, had been lost. As a
consequence, her mental life was not a stream but 'a string of disparate
beads'.[13]

For those with borderline personality disorder, personal existence is also
like 'a string of disparate beads'. Mental life lacks both continuity and
cohesion.

STIMULUS ENTRAPMENT AND CONTRACTION
OF THE FIELD OF CONSCIOUSNESS

Those with borderline personality disorder suffer what might be called a
'stimulus entrapment'. They seem to be at the mercy of their environments,
as if unable to 'turn off' the stimuli impinging upon them. As a consequence, their conversations are frequently a reading off of their immediate
circumstances. They give a catalogue of recent events, of the sensations of
their body, of their problems at work and at home. They speak in the
manner of a 'chronicle' (Chapter 14).

Such people live within a narrowed temporal horizon in which there is
little apparent awareness of a future or a past. The conversations of our
patients at Westmead Hospital have been studied by the linguist, Michael
Garbutt.[14] He coded all utterances recorded in randomly chosen audiotapes
of 15 sessions with different borderline patients. The codings identified the
temporal domains with which the utterances were concerned. Those domains
included the recent past (last few days), the remote past, and the world of
the therapeutic relationship (that is, the present). Whereas the therapists
focused on the last of these domains, the great majority of the patients'
conversation (57.8 per cent) was about the previous few days. The remote
past of childhood was rarely referred to (3.9 per cent).

The state of stimulus entrapment resembles a cardinal feature of
dissociation, which is what Janet called 'a contraction of the field of consciousness'.[15] This state can be understood in terms of memory, in this
case, working memory. This was mentioned in the chapter on 'Memory' as
one of the five forms of memory which Tulving considers can be distinguished on the evidence currently available. Since it depends upon pre-frontal
activity, Jacksonian theory predicts that it will be among the first functions

lost following an assault upon the brain–mind system. It is necessary at this point briefly to consider the nature of working memory.

Working memory refers to the mental activity which gets us through our ordinary day. A relatively large number of pieces of information are held in short-term memory and co-ordinated, selected, and used, by means of a flexible attentional system. Patricia Goldman-Rakic,[16] a major figure in research in this field, defines working memory as 'the ability to keep an item of information in mind in the absence of an external cue and utilize that information to direct an impending response'. Baddeley[17] conceives working memory as 'an alliance of temporary storage systems co-ordinated by an attentional component'.

The attentional component depends upon pre-frontal activity which holds representations of stimulus information 'on-line'.[18] Put another way, this activity allows a number of channels of information to remain open at the one time. An example of this capacity is driving while conversing with a passenger, at the same time listening to music on the car radio. At least five systems of mental processing are going on simultaneously. In addition to his or her engagement in the conversation while being aware of the music as a background, the driver manipulates the controls, is monitoring the traffic, and is holding in mind a plan, or mental map, which directs the journey. Working memory is clearly linked up to episodic and auto-biographical memory. The conversation, the music, and the surroundings the car is passing through will trigger memories from a more remote past than that which is used in working memory.

Should the system of working memory fail, the number of channels of information kept open is diminished. The driver is aware only of the tail light ahead. There is, to return to Janet's concept, a constriction of consciousness.

The notion of working memory is remarkably like Janet's *fonction du réel*, the failure of which results in a contraction of the field of consciousness. Ellenberger, in describing the 'function of reality', remarks that Janet 'equated it to what Bergson had called the "attention to present life,"' but gave a more detailed analysis of it.[19] Ellenberger goes on to say that: 'The function of reality implies attention, which is the act of perceiving outside reality as well as our own ideas and thoughts. These two operations, voluntary action and attention, are combined into a synthetic operation, *présentification*, that is, the formation in the mind of the present moment.' As Janet put it: 'The real present for us is an act of a certain complexity which we grasp as one single state of consciousness in spite of this complexity, and in spite of its real duration which can be of greater or lesser extent . . . *Présentification* consists of making present a state of mind and a group of phenomena'.[20] This state, however, is fragile. Janet believed that 'the most difficult mental operation, since it is the one which disappears first and most frequently, is the *fonction du réel*'.[21]

As far as I am aware, there are no studies of working memory, which involves a co-ordination of attention and remembering, in those with borderline personality and related disorders. However, there is evidence concerning attentional disturbance. (Some data suggesting subtle deficiencies in the related forms of memory, the episodic and autobiographical, are only indirect.[22])

The conversations studied by Michael Garbutt suggested that the individual was forced unduly to attend to environmental events. This state resembles that of Rebecca West when she found herself 'obliged to watch the trees outside my window and their behaviour in the sunshine and wind, to note the characteristics of every person who spoke to me, with a quite disagreeable intensity'.

In a series of papers, we have shown that the people suffering the spectrum of disorders which made up Janet's syndrome of hysteria, including borderline personality disorder,[23] have severe attentional deficits. Janet himself had commented upon this difficulty. He wrote: 'With hystericals, attention is altogether the most difficult thing to fix, and that but a few can succeed in directing it'.[24]

People suffering these disorders are as if unable to inattend to, or 'turn off', ordinary meaningless stimuli which come from their environment. Their bodily responses continue to show an orientation to those stimuli long after other subjects have habituated to them. Those given the diagnosis of hysteria[25] and borderline personality[26] disorder show an inability to 'screen out' irrelevant and redundant sensory events.[27] These findings provide a partial explanation of the pre-occupation with bodily discomfort and distress which is a feature of these disorders. For these people, sensation is unusually salient[28] and so may become 'amplified'. A stimulus which in most people is merely uncomfortable may excite pain in the person whose development has been disturbed.[29]

THE POSITIVE SYMPTOMS: AFFECT DYSREGULATION AND HALLUCINOSIS

The dissolution hypothesis predicts the disturbance of affect regulation and the impulsivity which are among the more prominent features of borderline personality. An individual afflicted with this disorder typically shows marked and sudden shifts in emotional state, particularly of a negative kind. He or she is volatile, likely to flare into anger.

An explanation of affect dysregulation depends upon an aspect of the dissolution hypothesis not mentioned so far. Jackson distinguished between negative and positive effects of dissolution. The negative symptoms were those produced by the failure of higher order function; positive symptoms referred to behaviours which were essentially release phenomena. He conceived higher order co-ordinations of brain function as also having some controlling or modifying effect on earlier developing functions. When the higher order co-ordinating, controlling and modulating activity is lost, there is an exaggeration and increased prominence of the earlier functions, which include affects.[30]

The notion of positive symptoms is also useful in attempting to understand the hallucinosis which is a feature of both recurrent dissociation and traumatically impaired maturation.

Jackson considered hallucinosis in terms of the 'faces in the fire' phenomenon.[31] We all have the capacity to see shapes in the flames of a fire, in clouds, and in rocks. They are often faces. However, a higher order monitoring and evaluating function results in these experiences being judged illusory. Loss of this function, which might correspond to Janet's *fonction du réel*, leads to the reality of these illusory perceptions remaining unquestioned. This approach to the origin of hallucinosis has recently been explored in brain imaging studies.[32]

Hallucinosis is a little remarked upon aspect of the spectrum of disorders which made up the syndrome studied by Janet. It is extremely common in dissociative identity disorder and not infrequent, in our experience, in borderline personality disorder. Unfortunately, however, since the phenomenon is not generally described, people admitting to these hallucinatory experiences, which are often of an auditory kind, are sometimes given the mis-diagnosis of schizophrenia.

CONCLUSION

The complexity of Hughlings Jackson's thinking was often beyond the comprehension of his contemporaries.[33] It was 'particularly modern – so much so, in fact, that his ideas are receiving more serious consideration today than they did in his own time'.[34] Jacksonian theory has been little used to understand mental illness. However, it may become more relevant as these disorders are increasingly viewed as brain–mind problems, rather than as either 'organic' or 'psychological'.[35]

In this chapter I have attempted to show that Jackson's dissolution hypothesis not only predicts the features of an immediate psychological shock leading to the disturbance of self found in dissociation, but also the phenomena found in those who have suffered a more enduring, though perhaps less florid, impediment to the appearance of self.[36] This failure helps to explain the sense of emptiness, the disturbances in the continuity of personal existence, and the deficiencies in the spheres of attention and memory found in this group of people. These disturbances can be conceived as a manifestation of impeded maturation of a cascade[37] of neuronal loops linking various areas and elements of brain function which are the last to emerge in both evolutionary and developmental terms.[38] Since the maturation of this late coupling is seen as 'experience-dependent',[39] its relative failure is potentially mutable, at least to some degree, and amenable to a psychotherapeutic approach.

Chapter 8

A theory of value

The disruption of personal being involves not only an uncoupling of consciousness, but also the loss of a sense of its value. This is a matter of central significance. How value arises, or is diminished, in the sphere of the personal is the main theme of this chapter.

How is value to be conceived? Once again, William James leads us towards an understanding of this notion.

Following his statement that: 'Thoughts connected as we feel them to be connected are *what we mean* by personal selves', he wrote: 'The worst a psychology can do is so to interpret the nature of these selves as to rob them of their *worth*'.[1] Although this remark was directed at psychological theorists, it has more profound implications. James is implying the possibility of a fundamental form of trauma which comes about through a destruction of the feeling of worth which is central to a sense of an inner life.

This approach to trauma is not elaborated to any great extent in James' work, but he does develop the notion of the value of the stream of consciousness. He wrote:

> If the stream as a whole is identified with the Self far more than any outward thing, a certain portion of the stream abstracted from the rest is so identified in an altogether peculiar degree, and is felt by all men as a sort of innermost centre within the circle, a sanctuary within the citadel, constituted by the subjective life as a whole.[2]

The use of the word 'sanctuary' is evocative. It implies the metaphor of sacred ground, a highly valued area which will be protected as a certain set of ideas will be protected in a religious movement. These ideas are central to that religious system. Core aspects of these ideas may be known only to initiates. Any devaluation of those ideas will be responded to with vehemence, perhaps hatred, and with thoughts of revenge. This notion of the sanctuary resonates with the concept of the intimate and the idea that for all of us there is a core of experience, of images, memories, fantasies, and so on, which is felt as the centre of our personal life and which is given value.[3]

This notion of value being given to this core experience is crucial. Yet our major psychological theories neglect it. However, James' writing implicitly directs us towards a way of understanding it. He wrote that a personal reality, which he calls individuality in the following passage, is based on feeling.

> Individuality is founded in feeling; and the recesses of feeling, the darker, blinder, strata of character, are the only places in the world in which we catch real fact in the making, and directly perceive how events happen, and how work is actually done. Compared with this world of living individualised feelings, the world of generalised objects which intellect contemplates is without solidity or life.[4]

James is saying that we cannot reach or understand an individual's personal existence simply through the cognitive processes. However, he does not quite arrive at the origins of value. It was Carl Gustav Jung who made the next link.

Jung wrote: 'The function of value – feeling – is an integral part of our conscious orientation and ought not to be missing in a psychological judgement of any scope, otherwise the model we are trying to build of the real process will be incomplete. Every psychic process has a value quality attached to it, namely its feeling tone'.[5] And again: 'Feeling informs you through its feeling-tones of the values of *things*'.[6] This is the main point of this chapter.

I am suggesting that it is the feeling tone which is always part of personal reality which gives the individual his or her sense of his or her value. A feeling of well-being, of feeling good, is the source of self-esteem. This feeling, which is a particular kind of pleasure, is often only a background experience. It arises through a resonance between one's core experience, the essence of one's immediate personal reality, and the responses of others.[7]

PHILOSOPHICAL BACKGROUND TO THE NOTION OF VALUE

Although value is a central aspect of personal existence, it is relatively neglected not only by psychological theory but also in philosophical discussion. James, with his emphasis on the significance of feeling, was out of step, both as a philosopher and a psychologist, with the prevailing atmosphere of the twentieth century. The following section is a brief review of the philosophical approach to the concept of value over this period.

We begin with Passmore's extensive, thorough, and highly acclaimed, account of the philosophical ideas of the last hundred years. It has no entry for 'feeling' or 'affect' in its extensive index. 'Emotions' are given a dismissive footnote, in a discussion of Sartre, as 'debasement of consciousness'.[8]

The mainstream philosophical stance was epitomised by AJ Ayer's positivism.[9] He considered that significant propositions were of two kinds. First, there were statements which could be confirmed by observation. The second class of propositions was made up of mathematical and similar scientific propositions which were deemed to be tautologies. Anything which did not belong to these two classes was considered metaphysical, and so nonsensical. In this climate of austere rationalism, an idea as tenuous as that of 'value' could not flourish. Despite this difficulty, there have been attempts to found 'axiology', that is, a theory of value.

Although the study of value was initially economic, certain German philosophers of the nineteenth century began to consider the concept in the sphere of the personal. They included Rudolf Lotze (1817–81). The works of the Austrian philosophers, Alexius Meinong (1853–1920) and Christian Freiherr von Ehrenfels (1859–1932), were particularly significant. Their ideas, and the term 'axiology', were introduced to an Anglo-American audience by Wilbur Marshall Urban (1873–1952) in 1909.

Urban's *Valuation: Its Nature and Laws* was well received by other philosophers of his time, but is now almost forgotten, despite his subsequent eminence as the Chair of Philosophy at Yale, from which he retired in 1941. Urban's quest was to understand 'the feeling of value attached to the idea of my friend'.[10]

Despite his complicated language, reminiscent of his mentor James Mark Baldwin, Urban's thesis is clear. Value is based in feeling. 'The psychological equivalent of the worth predicate is always a feeling'.[11] Making abstractions to emphasise his point, he wrote: 'Existence is perceived; truth is thought; value is felt'.[12]

Urban distinguished his position from that of Meinong and Ehrenfels. Although he agreed with Meinong who 'makes feeling the worth-fundamental'[13] he was critical of his 'intellectualised approach'.[14] This is implied in Meinong's view that 'feelings of worth are exclusively judgement feelings'.[15]

Urban's disagreement with Ehrenfels was greater. Ehrenfels conceived value in terms of desire. Using Ehrenfels' own statements, Urban was able satisfactorily to demonstrate that another feeling is primary. Not only may value be sensed in the absence of desire, where desire exists the feeling of pleasure is more fundamental to the valuation.

> Feeling is, therefore, after all primary. The worth of an object is directly proportional to the strength of the desire, but this strength of desire is determined by the difference of the place of the object in the hedonic scale.[16]

Pleasure alone, however, is not the basis of value. Drug induced states, for example, do not lead to the judgement of value. Urban worked towards a view which saw the basis of value as feeling-in-relation.

A fundamental distinction seems to exist between feeling which is a mere feeling-tone, accompaniment or effect of a sensation or revived image, and feeling-attitude which is characterised by the direction of the feeling toward the object. Feeling attitudes alone seem to contain the worth-moment.[17]

The notion of feeling-in-relation is a difficult one. It was pursued in different ways by other major contributors to the theory of value. Ralph Barton Perry (1876–1957) argued in *A General Theory of Value*[18] that an object acquires value when an interest is taken in it. His compatriot, John Dewey (1859–1952), considered that value arises as a result of the pleasure which accompanies the consequences of intelligent action.[19] In terms of a current jargon, he was talking of 'mastery'.

Urban realised that feeling-in-relation went beyond these conceptions. In the final pages of his treatise, he returned to the work of Lotze who saw value as depending upon 'the feeling or consciousness of harmony . . . of unity and continuity'.

Although considering that Lotze's thesis needed 'decided modification', Urban sensed that his formulation was important. Of particular significance is Lotze's notion that value arises as a consequence of 'those special forms of continuity, between inner and outer existence'.[20] This idea is fundamental and forms the basis of a developmental approach to the origins of value touched upon later in this chapter.

Value and Meaning

Although the positivists wished to distinguish between the sphere of value and another domain of meaning and fact,[21] in his later work Wittgenstein moved away from this position. He seemed to be saying that the feeling is actually the meaning.

Wittgenstein implied that the dictionary does not give us total access to meaning. Rather, it is the way the words are used, including the emotional tone which accompanies their expression, which gives meaning. In this way, 'understanding a sentence is much more akin to understanding a theme in music than one may think'.[22] For example: When longing makes me cry "Oh, if only he would come!" the feeling gives the words "meaning". But does it give the individual words their meanings? But here one could also say that the feeling gave the words truth.'[23] Although the word is not used here, it implied that value is attached to the individual for whom the longing is felt.

Wittgenstein's example suggests that feeling underpins not only value but also meaning. His views must have seemed strange in a philosophical climate in which, as Heidegger put it, 'affects and emotions' 'sink to the level of accompanying phenomena'.[24]

Heidegger, for his main part, argued that feeling, or 'mood', is central to a personal reality. The world about us, in his view, is never encountered as a series of neutral percepts, experienced devoid of emotional tone. Rather, a personal reality is inevitably related to a mood. Our world is always valued, not valued, or even despised.[25]

Urban had anticipated the main gist of these theses, at the same time expressing himself with considerably greater clarity. He wrote:

> It is only by reason of the very fact, that they are valued, that the mechanically determined elements of reality in any sense have meaning for us. Far from being a mere fact among other facts, that which we mean by our evaluation of objects is something independent of this world, and so little merely a part of it that it is rather the whole world seen from a special point of view. Over against a world of facts is set a world of values.[26]

In essence these ideas lead to the conclusion that the feeling which gives value also gives meaning. Extending this idea, we can say that this meaning is an elaboration of personal worth, of one's goodness or badness. The feeling creates a personal reality (see Chapter 9). This proposal has fundamental implications in developmental terms. The child who feels good, attaches meaning to this feeling and to this valuation, so that other people who are part of him or her, share this goodness and are idealised. On the other hand, experiences which are essentially traumatic involve a negative valuation. The traumatised child senses himself or herself as bad, even though the trauma was not his or her fault. The other people who are part of the experience are also bad, persecutory, and so on.

RESONANCE (OR 'FIT') AND THE ORIGINS OF VALUE

The preceding ideas provide a background for considering the child's development of value, particularly of a personal kind. The most important of these ideas came from Lotze, as Urban understood him. The pleasure which generates a sense of value comes from a harmony, or resonance, between inner states and the outer world. This kind of relatedness, which is more than mere congruence, is essential to satisfactory development.

This kind of resonance is central to the proto-conversation between the mother and her infant. It involves a fine co-ordination between the facial expressions, vocalisations and body movements of mother and child such that they can be conceived as a single system made up of two people.

The particular form of pleasure upon which value depends arises as a consequence of caregivers' responses which create a feeling of 'fit' with the immediate experience of the baby. For example, a baby is lying on the bed surrounded by young, smiling, women. The baby becomes more and more excited and pleased, wriggles and beams, showing in its body, face and voice a feeling of joy. This pleasure was not just 'there'. It was engendered by the harmonious connectedness between the baby's state and this state as it was represented in the faces and voices of the equally pleased young women.

More complex forms of this kind of response will be necessary in the continuing development of this child. As the child grows older, his or her core experiences will require more sensitive and imaginative resonance particularly when the child begins to develop a sense of an inner life. The caregivers' responses, in that they represent in the outer world the essentials of the child's experience, are a re-knowing, a re-cognition of the child's experience.

The experience of pleasure which results from this recognition depends, I have suggested,[27] upon a matching process which is essential to our ordinary coping with the environment. It goes on continually, although largely out of awareness. Constantly, events of the outer world are matched against models of the past, including the very recent past. Out of these matchings, feelings are generated. The most fundamental of these feelings is the sense of familiarity.

The matching system judges most of our surroundings as previously known but not relevant to the task at hand. They form a background to which we do not attend. These surroundings, in their familiarity, have attached to them a feeling of security, however low level or out of awareness this feeling might be.

Changes in surroundings, however small, cause a change in the matching judgement from familiar to non-familiar. We pick up cups, turn door handles, walk up stairs, taking little notice of what we do. If, however, the cup seems unusually heavy, the door handle turns too far, or our footfall on one of the stairs sounds different from the rest, our attention is aroused. An increasing lack of familiarity is associated with a growing feeling of insecurity and anxiety. Indeed it is often supposed that the infant's 'stranger anxiety' is generated by a mismatch between previous models of a face and the new, unexpected one.

More complex matchings produce other affects. For example, laughter results when an event in the environment turns on its head the model of such events stored in memory. The baby laughs when mother crawls towards her. The rule is upset which says that 'babies crawl, mothers walk'.[28]

The pleasure which generates value comes from events in the environment which match or are concordant with models of the individual's ongoing personal experience. This matching, or concordance, is of a very particular kind. It involves a resonation with what is known of oneself, however dim or tenuously formed this knowing may be. Pleasure arises when the responses of the other show a re-cognition of our personal reality. This may not be the 'reality' shown to the world. The concordance, resonance, or re-presentation is with that complex of feelings, imaginings, memories, which is sensed as the core of an individual existence. The resultant affect may be extremely powerful, as is evident in Bertrand Russell's extraordinary description of his first meeting with Joseph Conrad.[29]

It is important to note that pleasure is not necessarily generated by admiration or the pride shown by others in the developing individual's achievement, behaviours, or expressions. Such responses may, at times, be sensed as coercive.

The pleasure which comes with the sense of harmony between inner and outer does not only involve people, but also other elements of the environment. This idea leads to John Dewey's theory about the origins of value.

Pleasure follows when one creates in one's mind a plan, or model of some kind, and sees its fulfilment in the world. On the other hand, the failure of the plan, the lack of the validation in the external environment, results in negative affect. This can be demonstrated, at least in a limited way, very early in life.

Michael Lewis, a major figure in the field of affect development research, together with his colleagues, performed intriguing experiments on babies as young as two months of age.[30] Each baby had a string attached to his or her wrist. This string was connected to a screen. The children learnt that, by their arm movements, they could make something happen on the screen. The string was then disconnected from the screen mechanism so that when the babies moved their arms they failed to achieve the expected change in the environment. With this failure, the babies acted as if angry or depressed. They either banged their arms harder, in frustration, or gave up, looking downcast.

The opposite effect is shown more clearly in older children. Kagan studied children in the second year of life. He observed what he called *mastery smiles*, which reflect the child's pleasure in accomplishing planned tasks. The smile 'follows prolonged investment of goal-directed effort – which serves a previously generated plan'.[31] Lewis remarks that by the age of three pride is added to the joy of accomplishment.[32] Valuation has become more clearly evident.

The relationship between value and a sense of mastery or power is a crucial one and implicit in the origins of the word 'value'. It is derived from an ancient Indo-European word which means power or strength, and also those who have it, for example, princes.[33] 'Value' is related to words such as 'invalid', in which power is lost, and 'convalesce' which is to grow strong again. Something which is 'valid' 'possesses legal authority or force'.[34]

The relationship between power and value is implicit in James' image of the sanctuary, which evokes the concept of the sacred.[35] The power of a sacred object rests not in the object itself but in the feeling invested in it.

TRAUMA, OR, ATTACKS UPON VALUE

Attacks upon the positive feeling, the sense of well-being, which is at the core of a personal reality which has developed under 'good-enough' conditions are major but neglected traumata.

Attacks upon value may not seem, to an observer, to be attacks at all. Although certain of these responses of the social environment, for example those involving ridicule or shame, are obviously hurtful, others appear quite benign. To an observer, the caregiver might be behaving 'sensibly' (for example, 'Don't do it like that.'). The kind of trauma which is the main focus of this book can be conceived in terms of 'invalidation'.

'Validation' occurs when the answer of the world resonates with the more personal elements of an individual expression. There arises a sense of pleasure which gives value to that part of the personal which has been given re-cognition. On the other hand, failure of re-cognition leads to a sense of 'invalidation' and personal devaluation.

This conception of trauma is implicit in the formulations of those authorities who, using a variety of terms, put forward the notion that responses of the other which, in some way, present again (re-present) the immediate experience of the child, are necessary to development.

Enid Balint,[36] for example, described the child's need of 'an echo or feedback' from the caregivers who must 'recognise'[37] their child. Winnicott, in various places, expressed a similar view.[38] Where such recognition is not habitually given, or when it is, repeatedly, a misrecognition, the child suffers developmental damage. Michael Balint wrote of the deleterious consequences of a mismatch between the baby's experience and the mother's perception of it.[39] However, more than these writers, Kohut saw the need for empathic resonance as central to human development. Moreover, he considered that consistent failure of such resonance was a main cause of disrupted development.[40]

The main emphasis of a number of writings upon the malign effect of chronic mismatching is upon the central organisation of experiences concerning self, that is upon 'structuralisation'. A lesser emphasis is given to the feeling engendered by matching and mismatching. It is important that the proto-conversation is fun, a 'dance', pleasurable to both partners. The feeling of being joined up with another person in this way is immensely enjoyable.

In my view, this feeling is primary, at least in clinical terms. Children who have not sufficiently encountered the feeling-based responses of others, which connects with their own immediate experience, are left with a persisting dysphoria, involving emptiness and deadness.[41] Out of these negative emotional states emerges a negative judgement of value, of low self-worth.

The value which is attached to the positive feelings at the core of self is damaged not only through repetitive mismatching but also through direct attacks upon these feelings. Sullivan called them the 'tender emotions'. When their expression meets with a devaluing response such as ridicule, the developing person 'may be literally hurt'.[42] A threat of damage is sensed not only through the revelation of peculiarly personal and intimate feelings but also through the expression of ideas, memories, imaginings, which are highly valued, and felt as part of a personal core. Exposure risks the experience of shame. In extreme circumstances, shame is devastation, associated with a loss of personal worth.

Sullivan's description leads to the idea that the core of personal meaning and value is not just about the individual, but is also about another person who is part of that feeling, and who is idealised. The tender emotions include feelings for another, feelings such as love and affection. Sullivan saw an attack on these emotions, through such responses as mockery or ridicule, as amongst the worst disasters that can befall the developing individual. The result might be what he called the 'malevolent transformation'.[43]

Sullivan's ideas are helpful in understanding the effect of sexual abuse. Although much of what we know about trauma is based on studies of disaster and of physical and sexual abuse, the effect of trauma cannot be defined by or deduced from the event itself since the evidence shows that potentially terrifying situations, such as exposure to high intensity combat, may lead to only low levels of post-traumatic stress disorder.[44] On the other hand, sexual abuse, which may not involve threats to life or involve physical damage, frequently has severe effects. The evidence suggests that it has more pathogenic potential than physical abuse, in which the bodily harm inflicted may be greater. These findings lead to the idea that psychological trauma involves an assault on that which is peculiarly personal, the system of self.

The 'tender emotions', so fundamental to human existence, have, for a long time, been excluded from the discourse of psychology, psychiatry, and psychoanalysis as scientific disciplines. In 1935, Ian Suttie pointed out that 'in our anxiety to avoid the intrusion of sentiment into our scientific formulations' we have 'gone to the length of excluding it altogether from our field of observation'.[45] Consequently, his pioneering book on the subject was largely ignored.

Suttie, like Sullivan, was concerned about damage to the tender emotions. However, his concern had a wider scope. He saw that such harm can be culturally determined. He pointed out that in certain societies there may be a 'taboo on tenderness'.[46] Traumata inflicted as a consequence of a cultural imperative are transgenerationally transmitted.

Traumata, whether they come about through failure of validation, through invalidation, or through direct attacks on the personal, are stored in a memory system which is different to that which underpins ordinary unconsciousness, as outlined in the previous chapters. Typically they are recorded not as episodes, but as facts.

The 'facts' of the trauma concern, in particular, value-attributions. How these attributions are formed is considered in Chapter 9. They tell the individual that he or she is bad, useless, ugly, incompetent, stupid, in relation to an other who is critical, controlling, devaluing. Since this memory does not include the event, the subject does not know it is being remembered. Rather, when it is triggered by contextual cues, it is experienced as belonging in the present. In a typical clinical situation, this half-known system of value-attribution colours the whole of the encounter, in a way which may be barely discernible.

TWO ILLUSTRATIVE EPISODES

The patient was a man in his thirties, Robin C. He had presented with frightening suicidal ideation. These ideas had appeared quite suddenly. He could not find any reason for them. He was treated at first with anti-depressants although his depression was atypical. After failure to gain an adequate response he was referred for psychotherapy.

Robin was an isolated, withdrawn, shy, scholar. He had never formed a close relationship. His liaisons were always, in the end, impossible. He chose women who were already married, or women he could not view as suitable partners nor to whom he could make an emotional commitment.

He was the son of English immigrants to Australia who maintained pretensions of superior status in their new country. They belonged to that culture, described by Suttie, which implicitly imposes a 'taboo on tenderness'. Their son was expected to achieve according to their notions of superiority. His father frequently beat him; his mother was singularly unresponsive. They lived on a farm in Victoria, in the foothills of the Great Dividing Range. He gained some solace through his interest in the flora of the neighbouring forest. He discovered nearly 20 varieties of native orchids, some of which had not previously been described. This childhood interest led him to a career in botany.

This particular session begins characteristically. He has a flat voice and talks politely, as if to fill in the time. He talks about 'sensible' things. Then he passes on to describe brunch in a curious place, a cafe-restaurant in a junk yard. People sit around on broken bits of furniture, under large trees, and are served by young people with Californian and Swedish accents. It seems he likes the anti-establishment atmosphere. He picks up some second-hand books and is pleased to find this attitude in these books, of which he has never heard. Their style – the combination of irony, despair and negativism – appeals to him. He chuckles as he tells this story. Very quickly, however, the voice fades and he begins to mumble. Then, after a short pause, he begins again, in a new voice, quiet, matter of fact. He mentions some tasks which he must complete. 'It's like I was before'. Soon he is talking about his anger and depression at the beginning of treatment. Then he tells, in his flat voice, of a very recent feeling of wanting to kill people. (In a later session, he remarked that he could understand the feelings, the mind, of a man who had committed a massacre in a Sydney shopping mall.)

In this session, the traumatic system has been reactivated, even to the extent of its violent imagery. Yet the trigger is very slight. The books he discovered had a personal significance which his casual demeanour and perfunctory description belied. The therapist's failure to respond to the story of the books resonated with his parents' failure to respond to his personal reality and to give it value.

This tiny, and barely perceptible, failure on the part of the therapist resembled, in its form, much larger traumata, so precipitating the system. An understanding of his original presentation now emerged. It followed a publisher's neutral response to his proposal about a book on orchids.

The problem for the therapist in a case such as this, is that the patient wishes to be understood but fears being known. His flat voice hides the significance of his words. He is like a man previously described.

> Highly valued thoughts turned over in his mind, as he said, like a series of beautiful and highly coloured constellations. In order to express them properly, he required emotive language. He avoided this, however, so that when he presented his ideas to others, the ideas as it were, paraded in disguise. Any attack on the grey prose with which he expressed them was deflected, since he could reassure himself that what others saw was not the *real* idea.[47]

When the therapist understood this system she was able to connect with those parts of his conversation which disguised that which was emotionally laden and personally significant. Through these connections, he led her into a zone of experiencing made up of dreams and fantasies and which represented an undeveloped and unresponded to core of self.

Such highly valued experience which is at the core of self is often kept secret, as it was in the case of Robin C. Its imaginative and sensitive elaboration is a principal therapeutic goal. Since it is the potentially germinal centre out of which grows a creative life, it might be called a 'generative secret'.[48]

Memories of attacks upon value are not only reactivated by the social environment, which in many cases is 'constructed' to resemble the original trauma, but also internally. This system of internally triggered disparagement has been described by Brandchaft.[49]

Internal cues triggered the system of devaluation in the case of Jane, the married woman in her forties whose story has been previously mentioned. Whenever she described an event or activity in which she felt pride or well-being, sooner or later the description would change to one of self-depreciation and devaluation. For example, she spoke of setting up a room in which she was going to make tapestries. There was pleasure in her voice. Then her face fell, her eyes looked down, and she said it was a stupid thing to do, she would be no good at it. When what had occurred was pointed out to her, she commented that she had never been any good at things like that.

The therapist caused her to reflect upon the change in feeling-tone as she told this story and upon the subsequent telling of personal stories in a similar way. Eventually she came to the spontaneous realisation that although she was sure her parents felt they were acting in her best interests they repeatedly made her 'feel like an idiot'. Any good feeling which arose from her own activities was crushed. Internalisation of these experiences left her with a fear of the pleasure which is at the core of self and which gives it value.

CONCLUDING REMARKS

It is often said that psychoanalysis is a science of meaning. Most importantly, however, it also concerns value. Although value is a central aspect of personal existence, it is relatively neglected in traditional theory. The illustrative examples given here suggest that a therapeutic approach which focuses on 'meaning' will differ from that which gives priority to 'value'. In the past, 'meaning' has seemed the more important objective. I am suggesting that the emphasis be reversed. Privilege must be given to feeling-tones and how they arise in particular forms of relatedness. For people such as Jane or Robin C., interventions of the meaning kind are often interpreted in terms of the template of the trauma system. They tell the patient, for example, that he or she is stupid, weak, incompetent, rude. Unwittingly, what is uttered with benign intent becomes a form of derogation.[50]

The central theme of this chapter concerns the feeling of well-being which arises when the responses of the other resonate with that which is sensed as the most personal of one's experience. Out of this positive feeling arises valuation which produces a judgement of self worth. Another class of responses is felt as attacks upon value. They are recorded as a traumatic memory system. Its repeated evocation, by both internal and external triggers, constantly interrupts any emergent sense of well-being. In order to achieve an integration of this system into that of self, there must develop a focus upon the 'minute particulars'[51] of the therapeutic conversation, such as the change of state shown by Robin C. This focus will not, at least at first, concern meaning. It will involve exploration of the shifts in the feeling-tones upon which depend the valuation of personal existence.

Chapter 9

Feeling creates reality

The basis of a particular personal reality in feeling is starkly evident in the traumatic system. The construction of this reality goes beyond judgements of personal worth, of goodness and badness. Memory of the whole event, including the attributes, and even the appearance of the other, is influenced by the basic emotional state. This dreadful feeling also colours and shapes the story of the event. This story, like the little boy's story of the moon, gives a meaning to what had happened. The story is unidimensional, stunted and without the progressive, sequencing quality of the narrative of the stream of consciousness. Although unsatisfactory, it is adaptive in the manner, in some cases, of a delusion, organising current and subsequent experience.

An example of such a story is provided by an incident during the therapy of a young woman, Lavinia T., who had a severe borderline condition which was complicated by an eating disorder. She was intelligent and had read fairly widely about the latter disorder.

The therapist was also a young woman, named Dr Lucy Brook. She was soon to go on vacation. Her patient's developmental history involved severe separation anxiety which was related to her mother's repeated use of threats of abandonment as a means of exerting control over her child. Sensitive to this background as the core of a traumatic system, Dr Brook began to prepare her patient for the problem of separation during her vacation by giving her the dates of its occurrence. Although the therapist tried to explore the response, her patient merely shrugged off the news as if it were inconsequential.

Following the session, the patient wandered for hours. She told the therapist about it in the next session. She was not clear where precisely she had gone. However, she did remember walking through a large cemetery some miles from the hospital. There she made a curious discovery. She found the gravestone of Lucy Brook who was buried next to her mother, Hilda.

After this session, the therapist, out of interest, telephoned the custodians of the cemetery to inquire about these gravestones. They did not exist. No people of that name had been buried in the cemetery. Yet it seemed the patient was not lying. There was no point in such a lie. A plausible explanation of her story is as follows.

The revelation of the therapist's imminent departure triggered a traumatic memory system, based on the severe anxiety engendered by threats of abandonment during Lavinia's childhood. This memory system now overthrows the previous state of consciousness. In this state, consciousness is 'uncoupled'. The reflective process is almost lost, impairing the function of episodic memory and along with it the monitoring and evaluating systems which are part of the function of the 'I'.[1]

These systems match perceptions of present experience against memories of similar situations and events which have occurred in the past. Where their function is weak, the powerful effect of an immediate emotion creates, unencumbered, the psychic reality. Out of this reality a story is created.

In her changed state of consciousness, Lavinia T. could not, as it were, view her experience. She was sunk within it, precipitated into the traumatic system by the news of what felt like abandonment. This was her reality. Perhaps, in this state, it seemed the therapist was actually dead, since the child tends to equate death with abandonment.[2]

Alternatively, the news of the impending separation may have precipitated a rage of a murderous kind. In such a condition, the gap between wishes and their fulfilment is greatly narrowed. A revengeful wish that someone should die may produce the thought that this death has already occurred. In her undoubled state, the fantasy of her therapist's death is now a reality, and constructed in terms of a memory of her gravestone.

The therapist, however, is not only hated but also idealised. This is manifest in the name of her mother, which resembles that of Hilde Bruch, the famous therapist, best known for her work on eating disorders.

Lenore Terr gives an example of a similar creation of an individual reality on the basis of feeling. This arose in a traumatic situation. Terr[3] interviewed 25 children who had been kidnapped from their school in a small town called Chowchilla and kept captive while their kidnappers sought a ransom. One of the girls had argued with her mother before the kidnapping. She gave a description of one of her kidnappers which matched that of her mother.[4] However, her kidnappers were male.

There is no reason for this girl giving an incorrect description. A speculative understanding of this strange behaviour is similar to that for Lavinia T. and the gravestones. This child was presumably extremely upset by the fight with her mother who was more powerful than she, controlling, and frightening. The same feelings, magnified, are associated with the kidnappers. However, she is now in a state of terror. This has a disorganising effect upon consciousness, the doubleness of which is impaired and with it the higher order monitoring system which matches current experience against models of the past in memory. A coarser matching system is now dominant, lacking the fine discrimination of the later evolved mechanisms. Since the feelings relating to the kidnapper match those recently felt for her mother, they are aggregated within the same miniature complex of meaning. The features of the mother are 'transferred' to one of the kidnappers.

These anecdotes suggest that the contents of a traumatic system, as judged by disinterested observers, will include 'distortions' of those who inflicted the traumata. Moreover, these constructions of the other based in feeling are transferred to other people and situations whose features, in some way, resemble those of the original traumatic system. Although the word 'trauma' does not appear in the index of Klein's works, this system resembles what the Kleinian school call 'phantasy'. Susan Isaacs' authoritative paper on this subject remarks upon this curious phenomenon of misperception. She wrote:

> The personality, the attitudes, and intentions, even the external characteristics and the sex of the analyst, as seen and felt in the patient's mind, change from day to day (even from moment to moment), according to changes in the inner life of the patient (whether these are brought about by the analyst's comments or by outside happenings). That is to say, the patient's relation to his analyst is almost entirely one of unconscious phantasy.[5]

Although the 'phantasy' can be called a distortion, it is also a reality, and a powerfully held one. Attempts to alter it through reasoned efforts and systematic work on the faulty cognitions, are largely unsuccessful. They have a power analogous to certain kinds of religious belief, forged in an atmosphere of high emotional intensity. Reason, as James pointed out, is a feeble fabricator of a personal reality compared with that which has a basis in affect. He wrote witheringly of those who understood religious belief as intellectually derived.[6]

CONFABULATION

The stories of Lavinia T. and the girl from Chowchilla resemble the confabulations which are produced by patients with neuropsychological disorders. Morris Moscovitch has given an intriguing account of this phenomenon.

The false stories which these patients tell are not lies in that they are not told with the purpose of deception. In the past, their false story telling was seen as a strategy for filling in gaps in memory. In Moscovitch's view they are more than this. They reflect the patient's 'attempt to relate to his or her experiences'.[7] Furthermore, they are not merely an incorrect reassembly of memories. The tales that are told, at least in some cases, are 'true inventions'.[8]

Essential to confabulation is a disruption of 'one or more of the normal mechanisms of remembering'.[9] The phenomenon is typically associated with damage to the ventro-medial pre-frontal region,[10] which Damasio suggests

is essential to the emergence of self. Damage to this and related structures is likely to cause 'deficient retrieval processes at output that are involved
in monitoring, evaluating and verifying recorded memory traces, and placing
them in proper historical context'.[11]

These deficiencies are very like those we have supposed, on theoretical
grounds, to be necessary to the production of stories created in a state
induced by trauma. In the latter case, the disruption of the monitoring
functions is not due to structural damage. Rather, it is an aspect of dissociation, a term which is appropriately applied to Lavinia T.'s state of mind
as she wandered. The state of dissociation is replicated by hypnosis and
auto-hypnosis. It is reversible.[12] Similarly, in the case of Lavinia T., the
failure of operation of the higher order system of evaluation and retrieval,
which is part of the reflective process, is temporary. It might be hypothe-
sised, however, that in those who have been traumatised this system is more
unstable, since such people show an increased tendency to dissociate. This
altered state of consciousness can be triggered, as a passive process, by
contextual cues or actively induced in the manner of auto-hypnosis.

Since the reflective processes are immature in childhood, children's stories,
at least at times, resemble confabulation. Traumatic anxiety in the pre-
reflective period will be organised in the child's mind according to a story,
which does conform to what the adult sees as 'reality'.

The earliest experiences of trauma will be recorded in the earliest forms of
memory system which are beyond reflection, without words, or true symbolisation. This conglomerate of 'unreal' experience will presumably be composed
of bits of bodies, faces, visceral and muscular sensation, etc., and organised
around the primitive rage and terror which is associated with trauma. This
primitive organisation is reminiscent of Melanie Klein's 'unconscious fantasy'.

The constructions which the child makes of his or her experience before
the establishment of the reflective capacity at about the age of four will
not be remembered. They will be lost in the period of infantile amnesia.
Nevertheless, they will continue to affect the child's life as systems of unconscious memory.

UNCONSCIOUS KNOWLEDGE

Unconscious memory is not necessarily confined to the pre-reflective period.
Those traumatic experiences which cause uncoupling of consciousness will
also involve the creation of quasi-narratives which give these experiences
meaning, and which are recorded in memory systems earlier than those of
autobiographical and episodic memory.

Lenore Terr's evidence suggests that a traumatic memory system is likely
to be formed through repeated, or cumulative traumata, rather than as a
consequence of a single event. An isolated trauma is typically remembered

fairly accurately while multiple personally damaging incidents are remembered poorly.[13] Terr calls singly occurring trauma, Type I, and the multiple kind, Type II.

Most repeated traumata are, of course, not of the severity experienced by the children at Chowchilla. Nevertheless, the way in which repeated traumata are recorded in memory resembles the structuring of her experience made by the girl who remembered the male kidnapper as a woman.

Few people can escape small kinds of traumatisation. The experiences of shame and of the fear of abandonment must be almost universal. Where these traumata are sufficient to disorganise and to disrupt the effectiveness of the reflective processes, the traumatic memory will be stored in a different memory system to that related to ordinary consciousness, that is, not in the episodic memory system but in a memory system that, although usually verbal, is earlier or more primitive than the episodic system. The traumata are not recorded as incidents, but as a form of 'knowledge' of negative self-characteristics. The individual is as though unconscious of the origins of these attributions, which convey the feeling that he or she is, for example, bad, stupid, ugly, incompetent, or a failure. This possibility receives some support from the case of K.C., described by Endel Tulving, and mentioned in Chapter 5.

K.C. received a severe head injury at the age of thirty. Following the injury, K.C. was unable to remember a single thing that had ever happened to him. However, apart from this massive deficit, of which he generally seemed unaware, his cognitive functioning was relatively intact. His IQ and language comprehension was normal, and his short-term memory was also intact. After the accident, his personality changed. 'Whereas he used to be outgoing, adventurous, and gregarious, he is now passive, cautious and reticent'.[14] His demeanour is 'attentive and polite'.

K.C. and his mother were asked to rate themselves and each other in terms of 72 personality traits. The ratings concerned not only his current personality, but also his premorbid personality. The results showed that he had a fairly realistic knowledge of his personality features, but only as they concerned the present. Since his injury, K.C. had relearned the traits which were characteristic of him. Tulving[15] writes:

> He had done so despite the fact that his episodic memory system is severely impaired and that as a consequence, and as far as we know, he has no access to any behavioural instances from which the traits can be inferred. The facts of the case suggest that K.C.'s self knowledge is represented in a memory system other than episodic memory. This other system is presumably semantic memory.

The traumatic memory system resembles K.C.'s unconscious knowledge. In addition, it consists of negative affect and negative self attributes, which are linked to attributes of the other.[16] The patient experiences himself or herself as weak, bad, helpless, stupid. In extreme cases he or she may feel monstrous, repulsive, vermin-like. The images are yoked to those of another who is controlling, critical, humiliating, etc. At its worst, the image is of a monster, devil, or witch with hideous destructive powers. These images are not the products of dream, but arise in waking life. They may be taken into the session as actual perception, so that the face of the therapist is changed and terrifying, as previously remarked.

Different traumatic memory systems are likely to be organised about different feeling states. These states might involve a mingling of emotions. The central affect is anxiety. Sometimes it is felt merely as a dull and pervasive tension, a feeling of unsafety and unease. At an extreme, there is terror. Shame is common and expressed as humiliation, or utter exposure. Anger is often intense and felt not only towards the other but towards oneself, so that revengeful hate is linked to destructive and suicidal ideas.

The patient may confess, with shame, that in the midst of these fantasies involving hateful and terrifying images, he or she might wish the raping, abusive, and destructive scenes to be acted out upon him/her. At the same time the thought is utterly horrifying, repellent, and rejected. Mixed up in all this are mutilated parts of bodies. The traumatic memory system is embodied.

THE GUILT GAME

Each of these systems is, in its own way, entire. It involves a form of relationship with its own laws, its own language, its own 'game'. An example is the guilt game.

Guilt does not have a single pathway. It arises in several ways. The best known scenario finds its basis in feelings of destructiveness which are sensed as having caused damage to the other, in a quasi-magical way. The subject is now involved in efforts to save the other, upon whom existence depends, by repeated acts of reparation.[17] Another system, less remarked upon, involves the sense of indebtedness. It is a form of stiflement which is reflected clinically in the patient's remarks which intimate that he or she is, to a profound degree, a burden.

The word guilt, Partridge[18] tells us, is derived from the old English *gylt*, which is of obscure origin. It may be akin to the old English *scyld*, the old Norse *skuld*, meaning sin or guilt, and the approximate synonym of the old High German *scult*, Middle High German *schult*, *schulde*, and the German *schuld*, and therefore ultimately, to the English *shall* and *should*. If this were so, the original meaning of the word guilt involves an imperative injunction, or prescription. It can be either positive or negative, 'should' or 'should not'. In the former case, guilt arises where what should be done is not done. This is different from the guilt which is the consequence of what *has* been done.

The system of guilt developed through indebtedness is elaborated in the classic study of *The Gift* by Marcel Mauss first published in 1925. In a brilliant and wide ranging essay he scanned the custom of gift-giving in a diversity of cultures, including the Melanesian, Polynesian, North American Indian, Early Scandinavian, Indian, and Imperial Roman. It seemed to him that in those societies there was as if a 'force in the thing given which compels the recipient to make a return'.[19]

As Mauss saw it, the gifts given in this system were more than 'inert objects'. They were related to the person who gave them and in this way were personalised. Since this gift is conceived as if a part of one person had been given to another, it implies a relationship, evoking the requirement for reciprocity and a sense of indebtedness. Now 'the recipient becomes dependent on the donor'.[20] As a consequence it is dangerous to receive a gift. 'The sanction for the obligation to repay is enslavement for debt'.[21] An analogous system of enslavement operates in those families in which one or both parents make clear what they have given or given up for the sake of their children. The child's efforts at repayment are never quite enough. An example of the guilt game in operation was given by Anaïs Nin.

In her diaries, Nin describes the linked polarity of the guilty child and the sacrificial mother.

> She became all Mother, sexless, all maternity, a devouring maternity enveloping us; heroic, yet, battling for her children, working, sacrificing. Accumulating in us a sense of debt, a sense that she had given her life to us, in contrast to the selfishness of my father.[22]

Later, she identifies with her mother, taking in some of her characteristics, and becoming a second mother to her brother. 'I felt as if I were not myself any more, but my mother, with a body tired with giving and serving, rebelling at his selfishness and irresponsibility. I felt my mother's anger and despair.'[23]

Nin was not able to be free of this system. As an adult she repeatedly assumed a sacrificial role in relation to men. This is particularly evident in the relationship with Henry Miller. She spent her money not on herself but on Miller and others, as if they were her children:

> My concept of love was sacrifice. All that I needed I gave away. For years I did not even have a fountain pen, but Henry had one and Gonzalo. I had no records, but they did. When I was alone, I ate badly, to save money. I didn't have money to take all my diaries out of France. This winter, I had no gloves in freezing weather. Gonzalo buys books, and I take mine out of the public library and they are filled with bedbugs.[24]

She is eventually stifled by both roles. The guilty child and the self-sacrificial mother combine to quell her creativity. A friend writes to her:

> When you are driven by scruples or guilt to retrogress in order to help others live, and when they try to crystallise you in one role, you lose your ability to maintain and sustain the flow, you arrest the turning of the bigger wheels, you get caught in the spokes.[25]

THE TRAUMATIC SCRIPT

The various memory systems organised around particular feeling states are shown in subtle shifts of emotional tone which occur throughout a conversation. They are associated with slight changes in tone of voice, in the form of language, and in bodily movements.

They are the markers, in many cases, of unknown areas of psychic life, which have not been linked up in conversation with the world of another.

I am suggesting that these unknown areas of psychic life are the result of the high anxiety accompanying trauma. This state has a noxious effect on central nervous system function. It causes those functions that have evolved most recently and developed latest to be diminished or lost, in accord with the Hughlings Jackson hypothesis. Episodic memory will be impaired or cease to function. Abstract information about the anxiety-provoking incident will be stored in earlier forms of memory, without knowledge of its origins.

People construct stories in states of trauma which have the effect of making form and meaning out of an inchoate emotional and perceptual state. The story of trauma is like a script. It is made in isolation and shut off from the domain of discourse. No discrepant information can enter into it. It is a system of 'facts'. These facts do not have the progressive, sequencing, changing, and open features of the narrative of self. The facts are retold in a repetitive, changeless way. It is a recital governed, as Brandchaft has said, by 'invariant organising principles'. Although I have called it 'the impinging narrative',[26] its stunted form is not really a narrative at all. A new and more comprehensive story must be told.

Chapter 10

Malignant internalisation

To be caught as the other in the traumatic system is an estranging experience. These words imply a depersonalisation which is felt by both partners.

There is a curious paradox in this experience. You, as the other, feel as if you are not there, that you do not exist as a person. The patient in the grip of the traumatic memories, which are not recognised as such but as a current reality, stares past you, to the side of you, always in the same direction, or straight ahead, as if you were not in the room. This can go on for months. One woman, who had been in therapy for a year, remarked that she realised, with a shock, that she hardly knew what I looked like. This realisation came to her after seeing my photo on the cover of a book.

Simultaneously with this sense of alienation and disconnection is another which is its opposite. The patient shows an extreme sensitivity, akin to hyper-vigilance, which involves an awareness of the smallest changes in the therapist, such as slight alterations in posture or variations of respiration.

It is as if the dyad were fused, two people living the same life. The patient seems to experience the other as part of himself or herself. This is also conveyed in the patient's language, which is often a virtual monologue, apparently uninfluenced by the therapist's contributions. Remarks are made which suggest the therapist is aware of all the patient's inner states, as if there were no boundary between them.

This experience of the other represents, I believe, a relationship with the traumatising other in which is lost one of the major dualisms upon which, both Jackson and Baldwin insisted, mature human consciousness depends. This results in a form of pathological identification or internalisation.[1]

DUALISM AND IMITATION

The doubleness of personal existence starts up soon after birth. It is provided by another. At this stage of life the baby cannot view his or her experience, in the manner of the stream of consciousness. The child, to use Baldwin's term, is adualistic. The mother, however, shows the baby what he or she feels like. Her responses to the baby, although they do not precisely imitate the baby's facial and vocal expressions, closely resemble them, adding to them, showing them in a somewhat elaborated form.[2] The face and voice of the mother is where the baby's existence as the 'me' resides. Together, the mother and baby play out an embryonic stream of consciousness. She enacts a germinal 'me' in relation to baby's rudimentary 'I'.[3]

The baby, at first, is not imitative in the manner of the mother. Early imitation is almost echopraxic.[4] Infants of 21 days will mimic facial gestures made by an adult (for example, lip protrusion, tongue protrusion, and mouth opening). Piaget called this earliest form of imitation, reflexive.[5] The mimicry is done without freedom, as if imposed on the child, as if the adult's gestures are experienced as the baby's own.

Imitation which has the freedom of play appears towards the end of the first year of life. At this age children imitate actions which have a social meaning, such as waving 'bye'.[6] This is a game, quite different from the reflexive mimicry of early infancy. Imitation as play is clearly evident at about 12 months, for example, the child 'drives' a toy car. In the second year of life the child performs what Piaget called 'deferred imitations'. This term indicates that the imitation takes place when the model is no longer there.

Deferred imitation and symbolic play are related behaviours.

In early chapters, it was suggested that the language and activity of symbolic play had the purpose of representing, and so bringing into being, a personal reality. It depends upon a special form of conversation, in which the child, absorbed in the play, talks to a part of himself or herself who is related to someone else who is sensed as part of the child's personal system. This condensation is only partly illusory since the other is an actual person.

Imitation is also both play and a representing activity. The image in this case is of a different kind, composed by the body, whereas in symbolic play it is made by words and the things in the world.

Like symbolic play, the imitation involves choice. The child freely takes an aspect of someone else's behaviour and represents it in the movements of his or her body. The child tries out this behaviour as an experience, coming to know through his or her own actions, how the other feels. It now becomes, like the objects of symbolic play which belong in the outer world, part of the personal world which is developing a sense of 'innerness' and 'ownership'.

The child's imitation (for example, she is trying to walk in her mother's high-heels) is dualistic. The imitation is 'detached from the original copy-object'.[7] The direction of this dualistic behaviour might be seen as the reverse of that which occurs in symbolic play. In the latter case, the child takes an experience from his or her personal world and makes an image of it in the outer zone. While imitating, the child borrows a model from the outer world and literally incorporates it into the personal, that is, into a bodily state.

Oscillations between the poles of this dualism are an essential aspect of development, as Baldwin understood it. The child's beginning to develop a sense of self, the feeling of being a subject, leads to the child understanding that others also have a personal world. 'My sense of myself grows by imitation of you, and my sense of yourself grows in terms of my sense of myself'.[8]

The child's imitative behaviour has a feeling basis. It is playful, without anxiety, and freely chosen. It is pleasurable, and this pleasure is related to the idealisation of the person who is imitated, who has been part of, and made possible, the child's ongoing sense of well-being. Seen in this way, imitative behaviour is an aspect of 'pre-intimate relatedness'.

The idea that one takes in, in the manner of incorporation, certain aspects of the idealised other in an intimate relationship can be described even in adult life. Jean Genet, for example, describes his experience of his lover, Stilitano.

> Stilitano would subtly insinuate himself into me; he would fill out my muscles, loosen my gait, thicken my gestures, he would almost colour me. He was in action. I felt, in my footsteps on the sidewalk, his crocodile leather shoes creaking with the ponderous body of that monarch of the slums.[9]

Idealisation of another can arise, after the early period of childhood is passed, when no actual relationship exists. Adolescents, for example, idealise movie stars, singers, and athletes, adopting their mannerisms and dress. This is not, in the usual case, merely fashionable behaviour. The idealised figure portrays, in some way, a manner of living which resonates with essential aspects of the young person's sense of personal existence.

These identifications, together with more primitive incorporations illustrated by Genet's account, are taken into the personal system as a form of 'aliment', to use Piaget's word, which is 'assimilated' into the structures of the personal world which accordingly 'accommodate' by reorganisation and expansion. In this way, they contribute to the growth of self representation. The original behaviours, borrowed from another, become transformed and made part of the developing individual's personal system. Traces of the original model are hardly to be found. The integration presumably depends, at least in part, on the non-linear form of mental activity underpinning play.

TRAUMA AND ADUALISM

The scene which is the forerunner of 'normal' internalisation is exemplified by the little boy, maybe he's two, who swaggers around with his hands in his pockets just like his dad. His sisters giggle in delight while they watch him. He is playing a double game. He knows he is *not* his father, but pretends he is. There are two models in his mind, one of himself and another of his father. His imitation involves an idealisation of his father. He feels that he is like him.

The traumatic situation involves the opposite experience to that of playful imitation. In particular, dualism is lost.

The trauma, whatever its kind, has the effect of impacting upon the psychic system like a loud noise. The sense of inner life is knocked out. There is an outward orientation toward the other who is now far from being experienced as an intimate. Mental activity is linear. Rather than feeling at one with the other person, the subject senses him or her as not merely object, as a neutral figure, but as disconnected and alien. He or she, the traumatised, is alienated and fearful.

As the inner life is obliterated so also is the sense of 'me-ness' which is at its core. The feeling of 'me' shrinks as a function of the intensity of the trauma.

Since self and body are a dual unity, the shrinking of the 'me' is associated with bodily changes. The individual may feel tiny and match-like, insubstantial, or deformed.

As the high anxiety aroused by the traumatic situation wipes out all sense of a world going on within, there remains nothing else but the figure of the traumatiser, the terror, and the bodily sensations, such as a beating heart, a sense of constriction. In severe states, since there is no sense of self left, the only experience of a person is of the other. In this adualistic state, the other comes to inhabit the victim. Since the space between self and other is lost, self and the traumatiser are represented as fused.

The traumatic form of relatedness is not assimilated, so that when the memory of it is triggered, perhaps by a state of high anxiety, it is sensed as not-me, coming from outside the sense of self. During these states, the subject may experience themselves as the other who is alien. The 'it', one patient called it. The experience may be of being demonised. Another patient described it:

> It was if it were subconscious, like I was being controlled by something out of my power. It was like being demonised. Like having someone in your body making you speak and making you act, even though you're fighting it the whole time. Like your body's not your own. You don't have control of your body or your speech.

This representation of self fused with the alien other produces oscillations in selfstate, in which, at times, the individual appears as the frightened and helpless victim and at others, perhaps a few seconds later, as the traumatising other. One woman was able to describe these switches or 'reversals'.[10]

At times she seems to be taken over, or inhabited, by a colonising voice, which she feels is not her own.

This woman, Patricia K., periodically finds herself talking in a voice which is cruel – 'pissed off', in her own words – and diminishing. She recognises this voice as her mother's. This recognition occurs soon after she has spoken. She realises that the mother could be extremely cruel, particularly towards her father for whom she displayed open contempt. She was dismissive of his more tender feelings, and was repeatedly calling him 'pathetic'. When her mother was in this mood, nobody could measure up.

The patient realised that the mother's voice speaks within her at moments of insecurity and anxiety. Moments when, as she put it, the inner ballast is not right, and things are out of kilter.

Patricia K. was able to distinguish between states when she was taken over by the traumatic system and when she is more truly herself. There was an automatic quality to her outbursts which were compared to a different kind of experience in which she felt as if she had room, a spatiality, and in which she felt more generosity. In the latter state she was calm, in the first she was not.

MONSTROUS ATTRIBUTIONS

A series of negative self attributes form part of the organisation of the traumatic memory system. They are mingled with negative attributes of the other. These attributes are formed by a process described in the previous chapter.

Images are created which arise from and are consistent with the underlying feeling. These images reflect the terror, alienation, and sense of personal disintegration which form the core of memories of severe trauma. They frequently have a monstrous form and may be depicted as dismembered or deformed. Since this experience arises in a state when higher order evaluating processes are inactive they remain relatively unmodified. Like the 'faces in the fire' phenomenon, which might underpin visual hallucinations in traumatised people, they are experienced in the absence of that monitoring system which constantly matches between present events in the outer world and models of similar events stored in memory.[11]

Since monstrous attributions are created in a state in which the reflective process is inoperative, as in early childhood, they are likely to be recorded in a memory system which is unconscious. This nightmare world of powerful and frightening feelings, revengeful and forbidden wishes, mingled with bodily and facial representations is portrayed in myth, fairy story, and religious imagery. It has been explored, most notably, by Melanie Klein and her followers who call this region of experience that of 'unconscious phantasy'.

UNCONSCIOUS PHANTASY

Klein's glimpse into the frightening world of infantile fantasy is an intuition of a strange kind of genius. In my view, she was describing the representations of trauma.

The representations of trauma, to summarise previous chapters, can be understood, according to Jacksonian theory, as having an organisation of a hierarchial kind. The lesser traumata, occurring later in life, will be recorded in memory systems which are closer to ordinary consciousness than those which are more severe and/or experienced earlier in life. They will reflect the work of more mature processing systems than severe/early trauma. Put in terms of Tulving's categorisation the lesser traumata will be recorded in semantic memory; the more severe traumata will be represented in the perceptual representation and procedural systems.

The traumata suffered by Jane, who erupted over the tablecloth incident, are recorded in a memory system which, although not recognised as memory, can be expressed in words. We suppose, then, that this system is the semantic. The episodes which were the basis of the system are not accessible, but the negative attributes of self and other, her rage, together with the impulse to attack, can be verbalised.

Earlier or more severe traumata will be recorded in a way which is wordless, but probably involves images. At the earliest or most severe level, the traumatic memories will be wordless and perhaps imageless, recorded in a largely bodily way, as affects and impulses to act.

If the word 'affect' replaces that of 'instinct', my conception of the trauma zone is not dissimilar to Klein's infantile phantasy.

A difficulty in accepting Klein's notion of infantile phantasy is that it does not seem possible for the child to have the imaginative capacities which are required for this construction at the age at which Klein supposed it to be formed. Susan Isaacs approached this difficulty.

> It has sometimes been suggested that unconscious phantasies such as that of 'tearing [the breast] to bits' would not arise in the child's mind before he had gained the conscious knowledge that tearing a person to bits would mean killing him or her. Such a view does not meet the case. It overlooks the fact that such knowledge is *inherent* in bodily impulses as a vehicle of instinct, in the *aim* of instinct, in the excitation of the organ, i.e. in this case, the mouth.
>
> The phantasy that his passionate impulses will destroy the breast does not require the infant to have actually seen objects eaten up and destroyed, and then to have come to the conclusion that he could do it. This aim, this relation to the object, is inherent in the character and direction of the impulse itself and in its related affects.[12]

If we take the Jamesian view that 'every instinct is an impulse'[13] and that pugnacity, anger, and resentment are instincts[14] a certain concordance between the conception of 'unconscious phantasy' and the trauma zone becomes apparent. The affect of anger includes the impulse to attack. Perhaps Lavinia T.'s rage with her therapist included the wish to harm.

The trauma zone, unlike 'unconscious and phantasy', is conceived as unconscious not by means of repression but as the consequence of its representation in a module of the memory system which is not accessible to consciousness. However, although repression is not necessary to the unconsciousness of this system it may be a secondary and compounding factor. This may arise where the impulses at the core of the trauma system, of which the individual may or may not be directly aware, create sufficient anxiety to generate this defence. The idea that anxiety relating to destructive impulses is the cause of repression is evident in some of Klein's examples.[15]

A basic difference between the notion of the trauma system and 'unconscious phantasy' concerns the effect of the environment, that is, the caregiver. Klein considered that the origin of 'unconscious phantasy' was largely intrinsic. Her failure to recognise the effect of 'real-life experiences and situations', as Bowlby put it, has been criticised by many authorities.[16]

RESOLUTION OF A TRAUMATIC PSYCHOSIS

A graphic illustration of the monstrous attributions of the traumatising other, fused within a constellation of negative self attributes, is depicted in a series of paintings produced by a young woman called 'Jennifer', who was treated by my father, Ainslie Meares.[17]

The patient was a 19-year-old woman who was diagnosed as suffering schizophrenia. She had periods of hallucinations, formal thought disorder, and strong suicidal ideation. It became apparent, as the therapy progressed, that she had a history of trauma. It is now known that severely traumatised individuals may suffer prolonged auditory hallucinosis and other schizophreniform phenomena.[18] For example, some of these people hear voices in their head which they experience as foreign and which give commands and make derogatory remarks. There are no other manifestations of schizophrenia. In particular there is no formal thought disorder. Antipsychotic medication produces little change in the mental state. It is likely, then, that Jennifer suffered a condition which involved the mingling of disorders, one of which might be called a traumatic psychosis.

Jennifer had been given all the treatments available in the era before anti-psychotic medication. She had had extended ECT treatments, insulin coma, narco-analysis, the therapeutic armamentarium of the fifties. Nothing worked. One day she brought him a weird painting of monstrous and partly disintegrated figures. It conveyed a feeling of horror and constriction. He asked her about the painting. She identified one of the figures as herself, the 'bad one'. She also said that the red bits in the painting were sexual. In subsequent paintings, red zones continued to represent the sexual. This painting was the first of a series of about 200, painted over about seven years.

Her demeanour during the presentation of her paintings was different to that of the extraordinarily fearful silence which was her usual state. She was as if in a trance as she spoke about the paintings. She seemed so absorbed in them that she was oblivious of the therapist. She spoke in isolated sentences or phrases with pauses between them so that he could easily record what she was saying.

The first indication of the fusion between the traumatiser and herself is shown in a painting in which she represents herself as a hollow cage which is partly blue and black. This blue and black part is connected by a fragile neck to a precariously balanced head. Another part of the cage is made up of a red figure, apparently male, and also connected by another neck to the same head. One leg of this figure projects, phallic-like, from the cage. She seems not to completely understand what she has painted. She calls the figure in the cage 'he', although it is presumably herself. She said:

'Person in a container of some sort making a big effort to get out.
'One foot is big because he is trying.
'The other foot shrivels because it does not know what it is making the
    effort for.
'Does not know what it is trying to do.'

The image is of two people fused into a single system, a cage. 'A person turned into two persons,' she said. On considering the painting she became aware of the sexual imagery. She remarked: 'When I finished it, it looked rather rude.'

A later painting is split between two sides. The left is red and black, a sexual and evil chaos. This is her world. On the right is the world of normal people, where there is a sun shining, green appears and there is order. Of the left side, she says:

'That's me I suppose because I called it Harold.
'Harold is me.
'When I get stuck I talk to myself.
'I just use that name, it's a name I hate.'

Once again, there is a fusion of a male image, now clearly hated, with herself.

Soon after this painting, the traumatic imagery became overt in a picture of a frightening face of an old man with huge eyes and an image of vaginal penetration. This painting was followed by an increasing richness in the symbolic content of her paintings. A bird, which had been a minor motif in earlier paintings, became a dominant theme. There was something wrong with the bird. It had a third wing.

As the bird theme developed, a series of recurring images, including a monster and a blind fish chained to the bottom of the sea, which represented aspects of herself, began to appear. The culmination of this remarkable series of paintings, which was associated with Jennifer's recovery, was a painting in which the bird flew free of the phallic third wing.[19]

CONCLUSION

The imagery of this series of paintings conveys essential features of what I am calling malignant internalisation. The frightening, hated image of the traumatising other now seen in monstrous form, is fused with the helpless victim, whose body-self is misshapen and fragmented.

In summary, malignant internalisation differs from normal internalisation in the following ways. It arises in a state of anxiety compared with one of well-being. It involves a sense of enthralment rather than the freedom which is found in the playful origins of the normal process. Moreover, the state of self is diminished or almost lost. The other is experienced as alien, not integrated into the personal system. Paradoxically, this image is fused with, as if intruded into, the residual self. This largely adualistic experience contrasts with the normal process in which a state of self is established in relation to another who is typically idealised. Although linked to the other, he or she is distinct, so that the experience is dualistic. Also in the traumatic condition, the other is an illusion, no longer a person-illusion. Finally, normal internalisation is associated with, and determines, stable forms of relatedness, whereas the traumatic process underlies shifting, oscillating and discontinuous forms of relatedness.

Chapter 11

The evocative context

Distant memories arise unexpectedly, stirred by some element of our immediate experience. A certain smell of mist, for example, might bring back a street in another town, its quietness, the small stone houses, and cobbles shining after rain. Marcel Proust vividly tells of this flooding back of a scene from the past, which could not be rediscovered by voluntary means.[1]

He describes a day when he is overcome with boredom and lassitude. He tries a description of the scene before him, but fails. The following day is just as bad.

> I began now to draw on my memory for 'snapshots', notably snapshots it had taken at Venice, but the mere mention of the word made Venice to me as boring as a photographic exhibition and I was conscious of no more taste or talent in visualising what I had formerly seen than yesterday in describing what I had observed with a meticulous and mournful eye.[2]

Later in the day, as he is about to enter a house, he trips, and on recovering his balance, puts his foot on a paving stone which is lower than its neighbour. Suddenly 'a deep azure intoxicated my eyes, a feeling of freshness, of dazzling light, enveloped me'.[3]

> And then, all at once, I recognised that Venice which my descriptive efforts and pretended snapshots had failed to recall; the sensation I had once felt on two uneven slabs in the Baptistry of St Mark had been given back to me and was linked with all the other sensations of that and other days which had lingered expectant in their place among the series of forgotten years from which a sudden chance had imperiously called them forth.[4]

Such memories are evoked not only by particular stimuli but also by moods and feeling states. Freud gave an example. A man told him the following story:

Some years ago there were misunderstandings between me and my wife. I thought her too cold, and although I willingly recognized her excellent qualities we lived together without any tender feelings. One day, returning from a walk, she gave me a book which she had bought because she thought it would interest me. I thanked her for this mark of 'attention', promised to read the book and put it on one side. After that I could never find it again. Months passed by, in which I occasionally remembered the lost book and made vain attempts to find it. About six months later my dear mother, who was not living with us, fell ill. My wife left home to nurse her mother-in-law. The patient's condition became serious and gave my wife an opportunity of showing the best side of herself. One evening I returned home full of enthusiasm and gratitude for what my wife had accomplished. I walked up to my desk and without any definite intention but with a kind of somnambulistic certainty opened one of the drawers. On the very top I found the long-lost book I had mislaid.[5]

With the rekindled positive feelings for his wife, a renewed 'enthusiasm and gratitude', the young man regained access to the lost piece of information via the portal of the returning emotion.

Memories of traumata are reactivated in similar ways.[6] The activation of traumatic memories, however, differs from those of the Proustian kind. In typical circumstances, neither the triggering stimulus nor the return of the memory itself is identified by the subject. The following story provides an illustration.

The triggers are contextual cues which resemble, in some way, an aspect of the original traumatising environment. The most important of these cues are social. A second set of triggering events comes from the internal environment. These are most typically of an emotional kind.

MARY W.

Mary W. was 38 years old. She had endured physical abuse during childhood and during a long and loveless marriage which persisted, so she said, for the sake of her children. She had been badly depressed for some years. Various antidepressant medications failed to help her. She was treated for over a year by a talented nurse therapist working under supervision, who had met her during a period of hospitalisation. The therapy was very successful. The therapist had a style which depended upon 'conversational linking'. Her responses appeared natural, fluent, and rather simple. In fact, they were sophisticated. Each 'link' which she provided derived directly from a core element of the patient's last remark. She did not tamper with it, but added something, a small elaboration. The patterning had the form of the proto-conversation.

Mary was able to use her therapy in a way which seemed to have developmental significance. She took the form of the therapeutic conversation
away with her when she left her sessions, and would, from time to time,
have an internal conversation with her therapist. It was an experience which
may have resembled that of the aboriginal *Rai*.[7]

The *Rai* is a conception of great depth and complexity. They are, in a
sense, guardian spirits. Although they are spirits-of-the-dead with male and
female characteristics, they are more than this. They are always present.
Communication with them is necessary to the inward Dream Journey,
through which one becomes a person of high degree. The *Rai* are always
present but outsiders are regarded as ignorant of their presence. They are
necessary to well-being. As one aboriginal informant put it, 'The *Rai* never
let us become separated from them. We don't have pleasure (without them).
We might not be people in this world unless they had stuck with us right
through'.[8] This conception resembles the experience of the other, the 'life
of union', which is observed first in symbolic play, and later internalised.

Mary W.'s depression lifted during her therapy. She left her husband and
began a stable relationship with a woman with whom she set up house.
They had begun a small business together. The therapy was terminated as
the patient felt that she had gained what she needed. Put in her own way,
she expressed the sense that her conversations with her therapist had been
internalised.

Some months after treatment ended, the therapist was telephoned by
Mary from the scene of a car crash. It was as if she immediately needed to
recommence the therapeutic conversation. It was not a bad accident and
she was not badly hurt. She suffered severe bruising of her rib cage. The
main consequence was the return of her depression. She came back to her
therapist.

Mary W. could not understand the return of her depression. It seemed
to come in surges so that, as she said, she was 'going up and down'.
'Everything was going right until I had that accident,' she said. A further
difficulty was a changed feeling, which she had intermittently, towards her
partner, who it seemed, was being constructed in terms of a traumatic
memory system.

'I don't know what I want. I want to be by myself . . . Keep testing her
to see if she's going to hurt me.' To this the therapist replied with the
speculative statement: 'You're expecting to be hurt?' It seemed that this
was so. Mary had become wary of her partner, wanting to get away from
her. She said she was 'quite confused'. She couldn't work it out. It made
no sense. The relationship was a good one and supportive. Mary said of it:
'This is the first relationship that I haven't had my guts kicked in'.

On hearing this statement, the therapist remembered the report of the
chest X-ray taken after Mary's accident. It showed no recent rib fracture but
near the area where she had been struck was a callus on a rib indicating an

old fracture. This must have been caused by a blow when she was, quite literally, 'kicked in the guts'.

Mary seemed unaware of the link between her present injury and the past abuse. Although not clearly accessible to consciousness, memories of it entered conscious life, influencing the form of her language, in a condensed way. Terr gives several examples of the patient's language betraying the nature of the trauma.[9] The mother of one of these patients had tried to drown him as a child. He told Terr that as a young person he was 'scared to death of the water'. These incidents show that a therapist must always listen to the *precise* words of a conversation, since embedded within them may be a story, not properly told, and of which the subject is not entirely aware.

Her therapist did not press her for it nor did Mary spontaneously recover any memory associated with the rib callus. Neither did she directly connect her history of abuse to the recurrence of her depression. Nevertheless, she recovered her equilibrium in a relatively short time.

The contextual cues which trigger the traumatic system and which come from the outer world are not usually such discrete and concrete stimuli as that inflicted upon Mary. They are usually produced by the social environment and are often very slight. In clinical situations they may be produced by what Kohut called the therapeutic 'error'. This is not usually an error in a technical sense since the same behaviour with a different patient will not necessarily produce the same response. A well known example comes from Kohut himself. In his treatment of Miss F. he found that his silences provoked violent anger and presumably replicated the non-responsiveness of the original caregivers.[10]

Kohut's use of the term 'error', although not having quite its usual meaning, is felicitous. It makes clear that the therapist is involved in the patient's response. He or she had something to do with bringing it about. The word 'error' acknowledges that what is happening in the present is not merely a matter of individual pathology, the patient's 'fault'. Kohut believed that recognition of and working with these moments of error is the most important part of the therapeutic process. They are recognised by attending to 'the minute particulars'[11] of the conversation. The anecdote concerning Robin C., in Chapter 8, provides an example of the effect of the 'error'.

INTERNAL TRIGGERS

The reactivation and repetition of the traumata may come about in a manner which is apparently independent of external circumstances. It may be internally triggered. Hughlings Jackson gave a number of accounts which suggested that particular experiences and their related behaviours are triggered by a recurrence of the brain states associated with them.[12] The brain state characteristically associated with trauma is that related to high anxiety, the disorganising effects of which have been repeatedly demonstrated. However, this state is not the only affective means of reprecipitating the traumatic state. Brandchaft has described the malignant effect of the trigger which is the positive feeling at the heart of self.

Self has a core of positive feeling. This feeling tone gives value to that which is sensed as peculiarly personal. An accumulation of those feelings, which are generated in conversation, gives to the individual his or her sense of worth. These positive feelings are often no more than a vague well-being. Those that are the most vulnerable to trauma are the tender emotions.

An example of positive feeling as an internal trigger of the traumatic system was provided by Jane. Whenever she described an event or activity in which she felt pride or well-being, sooner or later the description would change to one of self-deprecation and devaluation. For example, she planned to set up a room in which she was going to make tapestries. There was pleasure in her voice. Then her face fell, her eyes looked down, and she said it was a stupid thing to do, she would be no good at it. When what had occurred was pointed out to her, she commented that she had never been any good at things like that.

In this case, both contextual and affective cues triggered her self-disparagement. Her facial expression and posture, when this system took over, suggested that the original impingements were shaming. Contextual circumstances that were in some way reminiscent of the shame situation triggered the negating system, in the same way that pride or well-being did. A more purely affective triggering, at least as it appeared clinically, is described by a man, David, in his forties. He said:

> The feelings of feeling good – I get to a point where I feel good, then suddenly I hit a brick wall. The other night I was doing something really interesting (a technical task) and I got a kick out of it and I was thinking this is great then suddenly I went 'whammo' . . . something stops me, like deflation, boom, deflated. I think, why it is? My father fears . . . stronger than me. Am I frightened? Why am I frightened? Am I frightened to show myself? Am I fearful of his anger? Was he such an ego that I would be a threat to him if I excelled and did better than he was.

Brandchaft outlined the main features of this phenomenon as it affected his patient Patrick. 'Whatever transient feeling of well-being, confidence, enthusiasm, or hope, arising from some still-active spring inside himself, Patrick experienced in the sessions would regularly disappear, relentlessly vitiated by some self-disparaging thought'.[13] Brandchaft remarked that 'that point at which the shift in feeling state from enthusiasm to malaise occurs continues to mark exactly the great divide of development derailment'.[14] An important aspect of the activity of this malignant system is that it is automatic. It is 'an internal and automatic replication of crucial developmental events of the child caretaker experience'.[15] Moreover, the system is sequestered from ordinary consciousness: 'Developmental traumata derive their lasting significance from the establishment of invariant and relentless principles of organisation that remain beyond the accommodative influence of reflective self-awareness or of subsequent experience'.[16]

'Invariant organising principles' is an expression which encapsulates the notion that the contents of the traumatic system are not organised in narrative form. Sequencing is often lost so that some traumatised people describe a series of critical or abusive phrases which automatically came into their minds when the trauma memories are triggered. There is no ordering of these sentences. They are disconnected. The principles underpinning the traumatic system cannot strictly be termed 'narrative', since the product does not have the sequencing, progressing, and evolving characteristics of a true personal narrative that depends on episodic and autobiographical memory. It is repetitive and invariant. The narrative is a thwarted one. It does not consist of episodes of personal history but, rather, of 'facts' the individual has to learn about himself or herself. The language is linear, offering few associational linkages. The individual is as if entrapped within the confines of the system.

I am calling this kind of a narrative a 'script' and using the word according to its literal meaning. This implies very limited voluntary control. The reality is imposed.

REPETITION-COMPULSION

Since the 'traumatic script' prescribes the part the individual is to play in his or her world and in relationship to other, it is manifest in the same patterning, on a number of scales. It will be evident on a microscopic scale during periods of disconnectedness from the other, since this state is a characteristic of the traumatic system. It is particularly likely to appear at the opening of a therapeutic session. At the other extreme, this system has the malignant effect of structuring the totality of the individual's experience. He or she tends, 'unconsciously', to build a life around the repetitive script. The individual is in the grip of what Freud called the 'repetition-compulsion'. David describes an incident in which this seems to be occurring.

> The other night my daughter had a baby . . . Coming back, I had this warm feeling, nice warmth, and I thought, gee this is nice, and then between (two towns) in the middle of the night I ran out of petrol . . . The feeling came over me, this car breaking down like this, breaking down was a failure. This feeling of failure then led me to scan (my life) 'Who loves me?'

Running out of petrol is obviously an event over which David had some control. 'Unconsciously', he constructs an event that breaks up his state of well-being. Whereas other people might be annoyed or frustrated by the breakdown, it confirms for him that he is 'a failure'.

The construction of one's personal world about what I have called in the past 'the impingeing narrative'[17] has a reverberating effect, tending to perpetuate the system. The individual may choose a partner whose responses resemble its 'facts'. For example, Carol, whose main presentation was that she was a hopeless person, unable to cope with ordinary living, had a husband who repeatedly reinforced this view. He was, to use her words, ceaselessly 'hounding her', or like an 'acid eating into' her. Yet, to use her own expression again, she could not but think that his view of her was 'reasonable'. She lived much of the time in a state of chronic dysphoria.

After a time, as Carol became increasingly aware of the operation of this system, the therapist posed a question. 'What if,' he asked, 'you told him to stop?' As it happens, she had, in fact, made such a request, for the first time, a few days previously. The effect was dramatic. She felt good. 'Living and breathing was easier'. Very soon, however, she felt she was living a 'delusion'. This state did not conform to what she knew as 'reality'. She relapsed into her usual state of dysphoria and hopelessness.

Carol's traumatic system was not merely repeated in microscopic form in the therapeutic conversation. Its pattern was replicated in larger shapes throughout her life. In fact, her whole life was built about it. This is more than an intermittent re-emergence of the traumatic system. How could this construction come about? There is no generally accepted answer to the question. It is often said that the individual re-enters the trauma zone in order to gain 'mastery' over it. Yet in the case of Carol the opposite of mastery is achieved. She feels helpless. At times, however, the 'mastery' explanation is plausible. For example, a woman who was sexually abused as a child becomes a prostitute in her mid-thirties not only for economic reasons but also to face and overcome 'the demons'.

Another explanation of repetition concerns attachment. The 'repetition-compulsion' sees the individual repeatedly enter the same form of unsatisfactory relationship. Attachment must play an important part when the original traumatiser was also the only source of care and affection. A traumatising caregiver may engender a 'pathological attachment' (see Chapter 13) in which the repetition of trauma creates growing insecurity, causing the traumatised child to cling more closely to the caregiver in order to reduce this insecurity.

Attachment alone, however, seems insufficient to explain fully the complexities of repetition compulsion. Perhaps Carol's own words give the best explanation. The trauma zone, however diminishing to her, is 'reality'.

The conviction that the trauma zone provides a reality which is embodied, based on feelings in the guts and muscles, is likely to arise particularly when the individual's sense of self is attenuated, flimsy, and when this person feels disconnected from others. Such relationships seem slight. The body feels insubstantial. The personal world is uneasy and without meaning. Its forms, as Carol put it, are mere delusion.

In order to discover some meaning, however unsatisfactory, one returns to the trauma zone, seeking out those people who resemble the cast of characters who inhabit it and who tell the subject who he or she is. This, in the case of Carol, is someone 'hopeless'.

Chapter 12

Priming and projective identification: on being constructed

Two weeks after meeting Ludwig Wittgenstein, who had come to Cambridge to study the philosophy of mathematics under him, Bertrand Russell wrote to Ottoline Morrell: 'My German engineer, I think, is a fool. He thinks nothing empirical is knowable – I asked him to admit there was not a rhinoceros in the room, but he wouldn't.'[1]

A year later Russell described Wittgenstein pacing 'up and down my room like a wild beast for three hours in agitated silence'.[2] Russell saw something comic in him,[3] also something uncivilised[4] and 'a little too simple'.[5] His storms and rages[6] were consistent with his style of argument which tolerated no other viewpoint[7] and which was delivered with such 'force that nearly knocks one down'.[8]

Russell's later descriptions of his student suggest that his question at one of their first meetings was not a chance one. He could have chosen any number of questions. 'Are we standing on water?' 'Is there wind blowing through the walls?' 'Is there a fire in the grate?' Instead he picked out an image of something rampaging, an unhappy animal, single-minded, angry, forbidding, and, in a way, stupid. In Russell's subliminal experience there *was* a rhinoceros in the room.

The image which came to Russell's mind would probably have seemed to him to be randomly chosen. Yet his subsequent descriptions of Wittgenstein suggested that the image was thrown up by the form of their relationship. This incident illustrates the main point of this chapter.

During a conversation, images and feelings come to one's mind which seem to have arisen fortuitously, as if from one's own personal system. They are the origins of behaviours or impulses to behave which, equally, seem to be freely selected. Yet if these images, feelings, and impulses to behave are thought about in a particular way, involving the associative function and removed from immediate stimuli, an awareness might arrive that these experiences did not appear randomly but were created by the experience of the relationship.

This phenomenon is often considered one of the forms of projective identification. A contribution to its understanding is provided by modern memory research, particularly as it concerns 'priming'.

PRIMING

The concept of priming depends upon a particular view of the unconscious which is implicit in a categorisation of memory functions put forward by Endel Tulving[9] which have been reviewed in previous chapters. The episodic form of memory is, in Tulving's terminology, 'autonoetic' which, since 'noesis' refers to mental activity, means an awareness of this activity.[10] Semantic memory, on the other hand is adualistic, lacking the reflective capacity. It is merely 'noetic'. It concerns knowledge of the world. One knows something to be a fact, but does not link a personal episode to this knowledge. One remembers, for example, the names of trees and birds, the value of coins, and the way to the airport without, at the same time, remembering the particular occasions when these things were learnt.

Other forms of memory are 'non-conscious' or 'anoetic'. They include the perceptual representation system (PRS)[11] which is operative at birth or even earlier. This contrasts with the developmental history of the episodic and semantic memory systems which emerge later in childhood.

The various modules of the memory must be presumed to function together in usual circumstances so that a single event is recorded in several different ways. This resonates with Freud's remark that 'what is essentially new in my theory is the thesis that memory is present not once but several times over'.[12] I have suggested, in earlier chapters, that the recording in memory of psychological traumata lacks the involvement of the later developing modules, in particular the episodic. When the memory is evoked by contextual cues, it is experienced in the present, without awareness of its origins in the past. In this sense, the memory is, at least in part, unconscious. In another language it is 'implicit'.

The perceptual representation system (PRS) is an aspect of 'implicit memory'[13] which causes an individual to be influenced by a past experience without awareness that he or she is remembering.[14] In the sense that it does not depend upon later maturing aspects of brain function, perceptual representation can be regarded as 'primitive'. However, this word should not imply relative inefficiency. Perceptual representation is extraordinarily accurate. By the end of the first week of life the baby recognises not only his or her mother's voice,[15] but also the shape of her eyes,[16] and the smell of her breast pad.[17]

This form of remembering does not involve 'meaning', but merely featural recognition. This is highly specific, and inflexible.[18] For example, babies learn to move a mobile by kicking when one of their legs is attached to the mobile by a string. When the mobile appears again a few days later they begin to kick. However, if the features of the mobile are changed, the babies kick only infrequently.[19]

This featural specificity suggests that the PRS consists of 'a multitude of distributed representations'.[20] The fact that these representations are not linked to systems of meaning is demonstrated in certain amnesic patients who are able correctly to read words aloud without understanding what they mean.[21] Thinking about meaning involves activation of the temporal and frontal lobes,[22] the latter of which is not necessary to the PRS.

Frontal lobe maturation,[23] and hippocampal function[24] are necessary to episodic memory, while the PRS appears to work independently of these structures.[25]

This kind of evidence suggests the PRS has a neurophysiological basis which differs from that of episodic and semantic memory. The PRS is a primitive system which operates not only before the brain is fully mature but also may remain active when the brain is impaired through damage, disease or toxin. Priming is an 'expression of' the operation of the PRS.[26]

Studies of priming often involve target stimuli, such as words, being shown to an individual, who may or may not remember them. When subsequent responses of the individual show an influence of the target, priming is indicated.

The influence is tested in a variety of ways. For example, a subsequent cue, say a fragment of the target word, produces the response of the complete word more readily than a control fragment derived from a word which was not a target. The priming effect is unrelated to whether or not the subject is able to recall the original presentation of the target. This suggests that priming is independent of the conscious memory systems.

The featural specificity of priming can be demonstrated in word studies of priming. Priming is stronger when the details of the type in the target are replicated in the subsequent testing for the possible influence of the target word.[27]

In another approach to the study of priming, negative target words, presented too quickly to be perceived, later produced hostile feelings towards a fictional person.[28] This effect has been studied recently using neuroimaging techniques.[29] For example, an angry face, which is associated with an unpleasant experience by means of a previously conditioned link to white noise, is presented for only 30 milliseconds followed immediately by a neutral face, which is shown for 45 milliseconds. The second face has a masking effect so that subjects report seeing only the neutral face, yet their bodily responses, in terms of skin conductance and activity in the right amygdala, show that the angry face has been subliminally perceived. An extraordinary aspect of this study was the finding that the response in the right amygdala was *absent* when the angry face was shown so that it could be consciously perceived.[30]

However, under these circumstances, the *left* amygdala was activated. The authors of this study remark that the absence of activity of the right amygdala when the subjects were able to report upon the perception 'indicates that processes related to conscious awareness, such as the engagement of language systems, may inhibit this neural response'. Their findings resonate with evidence from 'split-brain' patients showing that emotionally-laden visual stimuli produce greater autonomic responses when the subjects are not able to report upon them, than when they can.[31] The Morris et al. findings are also consistent with a single neuron study showing greater activation in the amygdala to stimuli which could not be recalled than to those that could.[32]

These and other findings[33] are consistent with Tulving and Schacter's suggestion that priming reflects the operation of an unconscious system of perceiving and remembering which is distinct from that of consciousness.

The proposal that priming is relatively independent of conscious memory is given further support by remarkable findings showing the effect of priming even during anaesthesia. Schacter and his colleagues[34] demonstrated that a list of words spoken during surgery showed a priming effect for those words when tested during recovery.

Tulving and Schacter[35] remark that 'we still know little about priming at this early stage of research. Nevertheless, it seems clear that it plays a more important role in human affairs than its late discovery would suggest'. It seems not improbable that a system resembling that studied in priming experiments had a part to play in Russell's choice of the rhinoceros image. It also seems likely that such a system has a part to play in the therapeutic conversation during which, at times, the therapist may act, or tend to act, as if he or she has been 'constructed' to play a particular part. My supposition is that this effect is magnified when the patient is in the grip of a traumatic memory system which he or she does not recognise as memory. In this case, the therapist begins to take on, in miniature form, the role of the original traumatiser.

A FIRST MEETING

The effect of cues and signals emitted by the other, but of which one is barely aware, is apparent not only in a well developed therapeutic relationship but also at its beginning. The following is an example. It concerns the first meeting between a young resident and his future patient.

The resident, Dr A., has had no experience of psychotherapy but he is sensible and sensitive. His responses are unmodified by the sophistication of a trained therapist's viewpoint. The patient has been allocated to him as part of his training programme.

The patient, Mrs C., is a married woman in her forties, who has lived for much of her life in an outback country town. The therapist knows little of her, apart from the fact that she has been unsuccessfully treated with antidepressants and that her admission was surrounded by an atmosphere of crisis and confusion.

Dr A. begins by trying to gain some understanding of Mrs C.'s current situation and problems. He receives no clear answers. Her voice is soft, sometimes barely audible. She conveys a sense of helplessness and power-lessness. Her responses are equable, indefinite, and confusing. However, it emerges that she and her husband have recently separated. Ambiguities surround the separation. Although they are separated, they may be getting back together. The therapist is unable to clarify whether the husband is actually at home or not. A faint tension underlies the conversation.

Despite the sense of obfuscation, Dr A. begins to understand an essen-tial feature of her experience of her husband. He 'covers everything up', does not want to hear accounts of emotional distress, of difficulties. Dr A. also realises that she herself does not recognise her emotional states. When talking of 'the' depression which brought her to hospital Mrs C. speaks of it as a force outside her own agency, something which chose to occupy her. She says: 'I never recognised it before I came here.'

Dr A. now attempts to understand the content of the depression. It seemed to begin two weeks before her admission to hospital, at about the time of her marital separation. She makes no connection between the two events.

As she begins to talk of her emotional states, it becomes apparent that the therapist makes responses which, in a minor but significant way, move away from what she had been saying. It is as if he is beginning to get caught up in a system which avoids emotional issues. Once again, Mrs C. complains about her husband who places a covert embargo on 'bringing anything up'.

Dr A. pursues this difficulty, asking about the things she wants to discuss with him. Her responses show that it is not only he who avoids the central issues of their life together. She says: 'It's very hard for me to talk about anything that goes too deep. Surface things are fine. When I'm feeling depressed, yeah possibly I can talk then. Now I've started to get better as far as the depression goes, I just want to close up again.' Dr A. tries to find out what things she would like to talk about.

She says: 'Anything that's ever happened irrespective of whether it's between him and I, or whether it's other things, he never discusses it.' And then, softly, so that it is barely audible, 'When my stepfather and grandson died he didn't talk about it. I tried to talk about it but he didn't want to know. Those sorts of things. Just backs off.' The therapist seems not to hear this news of a family tragedy. He replies: 'Since you've been in hospital, have you been able to talk about those things?'

His move away from the emotion laden topic parallels her own system of avoidance. Mrs C. replies 'Not really. They know about my grandson and stepfather dying.' Her voice sinks away. Dr A. asks a question designed to clarify the nature of these deaths. 'He killed my grandson and then he shot himself.' Dr A. asks 'Ah. How long ago did you leave Deniliquin?'

The therapist makes a remark which avoids the shock of the patient's revelation, as if the catastrophe must not be spoken about. The patient, so the therapist said, on being asked about it afterwards, seemed frozen and emotionless. It is as if, at her first meeting with him, she has constructed the other who is not allowed to enter the zone of emotional life but who is blamed for it. He has become, in one session, like the husband who does not talk about difficult and emotional issues.

In this case the 'construction' of the therapist comes about not only as a result of the patient's psychopathology but also because of the therapist's freshness. He has no preconceptions, no strong theoretical principles which guide his conversation, no 'technique'. He is open to the experience of the encounter in a way which causes him to be led into the nebulous and difficult conversation. He senses, and is taken over by, a covert pressure to play out the part of the other in a traumatic 'script'. It also seems likely that his sensitivity to particular priming signals is potentiated by his own developmental experiences.

PROJECTIVE IDENTIFICATION

The sense of being constructed, which is an almost inevitable part of the therapeutic process, is frequently conceived as a manifestation of projective identification. This term originates from Melanie Klein.[36] Her original description has stimulated a wide range of inquiry.[37] However, this chapter cannot encompass the complexities of projective identification nor engage with the controversies which surround the term. Rather, I focus upon a central feature of the concept, highlighted by Segal in her summary of Klein's description. 'Parts of the self and internal objects are split off and projected into the external object, which then becomes possessed by, controlled and identified with the projected parts'.[38] This paper considers the nature of this control.

In his explorations of this subject, Ogden points out that projective identification involves a sense of interpersonal pressure on the analyst to engage in an identification which comes from the patient's personal system. There is a feeling of coercion, as if one is being constructed to play out a particular part.[39]

One of the first to remark upon the feeling of coercion was Wilfren Bion. In his pioneering work on group therapy, he found the group developed a 'fantasy', or set up expectations about how he, as the therapist or director, should behave. There was a sense of being impelled towards acting out a particular role based on these expectations.[40] The power of this construction is conveyed by Ogden in his essay on 'the subjugating third'.[41]

The sense of coercion might be understood in terms of 'priming'. The data concerning priming suggest that its effects are likely to be particularly evident when the subject is in the grip of unconscious memories, that is those recorded in a memory system of an earlier or more primitive kind than the episodic. Traumatic memories, as we have seen, are likely to be stored in such early memory systems.[42] These memory systems provide a catalogue, or 'script',[43] of the attributes of self and other which are a consequence of the past traumata and which involve expectations regarding the form of the current relationship. When this memory system is triggered by contextual cues, we might suppose that the other is drawn into it by means of a subliminal awareness of signals related to these expectations. He or she begins to be 'constructed' by these signals.

The individual who finds himself or herself caught in the field of the other's traumatic memory system is likely to feel a constriction, a diminished sense of freedom, and a tendency to behave according to the expectations the subject has of the originally traumatising other. Dr A. found himself in such a situation and began, inexorably, to be taken into an intersubjective field in which various signals, of which he was barely aware, led him to evade the emotionally laden topic. In this way, he resembled Mrs C.'s husband and, presumably, replicated the behaviour of the original caregiver. The embargo upon discussion of distressing subjects in her childhood, and a consequent failure of the child to find any suitable responses to a certain range of her affective states, presumably led to her failure to recognise emotions such as depression.

THERAPEUTIC IMPLICATIONS

Feelings, impulses to impact, and images, such as the rhinoceros which came into Bertrand Russell's mind, are potential starting points in the exploration of the form of relatedness which underpins the therapeutic conversation. Taking the Russell–Wittgenstein anecdote as an example, it is necessary not only to realise that the one with whom we speak may experience himself or herself as an angry and unhappy animal but also that they are talking to a person who, in some covert way, 'makes' them feel and act like this, someone who is important to them but who sees them as a 'fool'.

An image, such as the rhinoceros, should not be taken as a direct transfer from one mind to another, nor should it be acted upon in its literal or concrete state. The idea that it is a product of priming leads to a necessary processing – a careful, imaginative, and unspoken mulling around – in order to arrive at some speculative understanding of the kind of implied relationship, including the attributes of its partners, which underpins the therapeutic conversation and which determines its form. The following incident provides an example of this process.

The patient is the middle-aged woman, Jane, who is depressed and has severe marital difficulties. The session is an early one. It begins almost incoherently.

'Today is the day of rationality . . .' She says, her eyes cast down. There is
    a long pause.

'It's not a feeling that . . .' Another pause, accompanied by a similar downcast look.
'When I spoke to you last time I said to you that I get this feeling that
I've got to be away in silence . . .'. Again the falling gaze and a pause
followed by another remark of a similar kind.

Following this passage of broken up and disconnected speech, during
which the therapist, Dr. B., makes no response, Jane's conversation becomes
more organised. She soon gives an account of her oscillating moods which
vary between calmness and 'throwing things'. She then touches upon her
feelings regarding therapy. 'I said I wasn't coming, I wasn't coming back
here any more, and when I finally realised why I didn't want to come back,
one, I'm embarrassed that I have to come, that I need to come, and two,
I'm ashamed.'

At this point, the words 'Don't be silly' come into the therapist's mind.
However, he does not say them but silently reflects upon his impulse. This
reflection leads him to the awareness of having been drawn into experiencing himself as the original other in his patient's personal system. To
have actually spoken the words that came into his mind would have been
belittling and devaluing. In a minor way, he would have shamed her. This
realisation enabled him to understand what had been happening in the
previous few minutes. In the halting, jumbled opening of the session, the
patient presumably felt herself exposed, in a situation of revelation in which
the response of the other was potentially humiliating. He now saw that his
silence, which was uncharacteristically total, devoid of murmurs or other
non-verbal vocalisations, provoked, in miniature form, the experience of
shame, seeming to show her the worthlessness of her observations. It was
as if he had been 'constructed' to play out a particular role.

Further reflection gave support for his formulation. The downcast expression which followed each incomplete and barely comprehensible remark at
the start of the session, he now recognised as stereotypic of shame. He also
remembered a story Jane had told about feeling compelled to go to a friend's
birthday party although she was unwell. The reason for going was that her
friend would have been humiliated if nobody came to her party.

The opening of this session can be conceived in terms of traumatic memories which are recorded in memory systems which are developmentally earlier
than the episodic. As a consequence they are unconscious. They provide a
catalogue of attributes of self and other which determine the form of the
current relationship. The 'script'[44] of this memory system tells Jane that
she is hopeless and incompetent in relation to someone who is critical and
devaluing. This is a transference experience, located in the present, without
an awareness of its past. Using the model of priming, it can be supposed
that her expectations of the other are conveyed by emotional signals of
which he or she is not consciously aware.

Since becoming aware of such unconscious constructions of self and other is central to the therapeutic process,[45] it is important to consider the way in which this awareness is fostered and also how it is impeded. As a first step in gaining this awareness, we enter a particular 'form of relatedness'. This is necessarily so. 'Unless the analyst affectively enters the patient's relational matrix or, rather, discovers himself within it . . . the treatment is never fully engaged'.[46] We become part of the experience we are trying to understand. In doing so, the analyst uses a curious double processing.

The doubleness involves being taken into the patient's personal system while, at the same time, monitoring this experience. This dual process can be hindered at either of its poles. In the first case, the therapist may not sufficiently enter the experience. This may come about through excessive reliance on a technique.

The subtle sense of pressure to behave in a particular way can be over-ridden by a strongly habitual method of therapeutic responding. For example, in the case of Mrs. C., a certain kind of experienced therapist may have focused on the deaths in Deniliquin without, at the same time, being aware of compulsion to avoid the issue.

The necessary monitoring of responses and behaviours during the thera-peutic conversation may also be hindered by technique. In essence, this mon-itoring depends upon the therapist asking himself and herself: 'Why did I do or say that? I wonder why I feel, think, or imagine as I do now?' If the answer is 'What I am doing now is what I always do', the awareness that one has entered the other's personal system may not arise. For example, had Dr. B. been a therapist who was often silent, it might not have occurred to him that his behaviour had anything to do with his patient's behaviour. He may have considered her incoherence a manifestation of the deficiencies, or psychopathology, of a single person as an 'isolated mind'.[47]

A more widely remarked upon failure of monitoring of one's own psychic process comes about through a congruence between the response which is expected and towards the enactment of which the therapist feels impelled, and the therapist's own personal system. For example, a therapist whose early life was marked by lack of valuation may not realise that his or her failure to give value or validation is an aspect of his or her patient's personal system. The patient expects nothing; the therapist gives nothing. The fit between them obscures the subtle sense of coercion which is often the starting point of unravelling a traumatic memory system.

The monitoring of one's psychic process and the subsequent 'mulling around' may not be sufficient to detect this subtle coercion. Indeed, it is sometimes argued[48] that the 'construction' does not become apparent until it has been acted upon. How does one sense that such responses are a mani-festation of the slight pressure induced by priming signals? Perhaps it is a faint feeling of discomfiture which gives the alert, a subtle sense of disso-nance between the actual response and another, unacted upon response, which would have been more freely made. This discomfiture includes bodily feelings and is an example of what Schwaber[49] called 'state'. Monitoring of this wordless and rather nebulous background experience, which is with us all the time, is important as a reflection upon specific impressions, such as words or images.

In considering the effect of priming, it is necessary to conceive it as bi-directional. In describing the move towards the intersubjectivitist viewpoint, Levenson wrote: 'Rather than emphasis on the patient as a discrete histor-ical process, interest shifts to the immersion of therapist-patient in their common transformational field and, most important, to their unique creation of each other'.[50] Something of this effect may, perhaps, help to explain subsequent events in the relationship between Dr. B. and Jane.

On realising the system of devaluation in which he had been caught up, Dr. B. did not, at first, make any interpretation. Instead, he changed his behaviour. He began to respond in a way which gave value to what she told him.

Her conversation finally revealed the nature of the original traumata. Spontaneously bringing up her parents' responses to her, she first of all excused them, explaining that whatever they did, she always believed that they were doing it because they believed it was right. This was so 'even if they made you feel like an idiot'. This remark was consistent with the hypothesis that a partly unconscious system of memories of being repeat-edly shamed determined the form of relatedness underpinning the therapeutic conversation.

How the patient spontaneously arrived at the understanding is not clear. It is tempting, however, to suppose that the therapist's reflection upon his experience and his attempt to understand who he was in relation to his patient had a subliminal influence creating a priming effect operating in the reverse direction.

Finally, the notion of priming leads us back to Freud's famous remark about 'evenly suspended attention'.[51] The idea that a particular state of mind is required in order to allow one 'to catch the drift of the patient's unconscious with his own unconscious' is given support, and gains addi-tional import, from studies such as that of Morris et al.[52] Their findings seem to imply that ordinary language-based consciousness may inhibit subliminal responses to the priming signals relating to emotional states. The therapist concerned with translating the patient's productions into secondary process, the so-called 'orderly therapist',[53] may not, in his or her state of mind, have access to crucial information concerning the form of relatedness in which he or she is immersed.

The state of mind to which Freud alluded involves disengagement from immediate stimuli and from what might be called a linear form of mental function.[54] Such a disengagement is necessary not only for the patient[55] but also for the therapist. Freud recommended that the therapist 'surrender himself to his own unconscious mental activity, in a state of evenly-suspended attention, to avoid as far as possible, reflection and the construction of conscious expectations, not to try to fix anything that he hears particularly in the memory'. Evidence from the study of priming suggests that a release of left brain dominance in order to allow the activity of the right might be necessary 'to catch the drift of the patient's unconscious' emanating in the signals of priming. Freud was suggesting a certain kind of therapeutic discipline which might facilitate such a release.

SUMMARY

This chapter concerns the therapist's sense, which arises from time to time, of a subtle pressure to behave in a particular way. This phenomenon is an aspect of 'projective identification'. In this chapter it is understood in terms of the recently described phenomenon of 'priming'. Studies of priming show that a subject may record and be influenced by stimuli of which he or she is not conscious or which he or she may not afterwards recall. In the therapeutic session, the therapist is 'constructed' by such stimuli so that he or she begins to play out a part in the patient's personal system. This effect may be unusually strong when the patient is in the grip of traumatic memories of an unconscious kind.

Priming studies indicate that an awareness of the effect is likely to be obscured by a mental state which is that of the ordinary, language-based, consciousness characteristic of secondary process. Freud's recommendation concerning the therapist's 'evenly suspended attention' suggests adoption of a discipline which allows a release from the dominance of this kind of consciousness, so permitting a subliminal awareness of priming signals and 'the drift of the patient's unconscious'.

Chapter 13

Satellites of trauma

William James wrote that in certain patients, 'we have revealed to us whole systems of underground life, in the shape of memories of a painful sort which lead a parasitic existence, buried outside of the primary fields of consciousness and making irruptions there into' of various kinds.[1]

The individual with a traumatic past is constantly under threat from such 'parasitic' life forms, which might, at any moment, move in, obliterate the sense of self, taking up, as it were, all the space within, as if there were nothing else. In order ceaselessly to guard against this disaster, the traumatic system is hedged about with systems of protection which are designed to prevent their activation.[2] Two important forms of protection involve 'avoidance' and 'accommodation'. These defensive stratagems and the activity of the traumatic anxiety which lurks behind them are major impediments to development of traumatised individuals.

In addition to the 'avoidant' and 'accommodative' systems which metaphorically surround the trauma zone, there are related systems of behaving and experiencing in relating to others which have the purpose of making up for the traumatic failures of the caregiving environment. I am calling them 'autogenous'. Another category of the sub-systems related to trauma is found, as it were, within the trauma zone itself. It has a 'restorative' purpose. It is frequently unrecognised or labelled 'resistance' within the therapeutic relationship and 'maladaptive' outside it. It has the function, whenever the traumatic experience is reactivated, of re-establishing some semblance of a sense of self, however unsatisfactory this may be.

AVOIDANCE

Traumata are of many kinds, as we have seen. Consequently, there are multiple strategies for avoiding a repetition of the trauma. A child who has become terrified in learning to swim, later avoids the water; a woman traumatised by a bushfire can no longer live on the farm. However, the traumata with which psychotherapy is most concerned are those which have occurred in the interpersonal sphere. A most important category of protective behaviours arises from damage to an intensely personal zone of experiencing which is at the heart of self.

At the core of self is a group of feeling-laden thoughts, images and memories which are sensed as necessary to the integrity of the individual. They are given a value which arises from the positive feelings, the 'warmth and intimacy', with which they are imbued. Their devaluation leads to a sense of damage and devastation, as noted in Chapter 8.

Damage to this core of images, moments, and so on, which is linked to feelings of affection, can come about through repeated criticism, ridicule, or simple lack of responsiveness. Robin C., whose story was briefly told in Chapter 8, was a victim of such a damaging environment.

Robin C. adopted a social posture designed to prevent being known. He had a pleasant demeanour and was well liked, but avoided intimate relationships. Nobody could enter his most personal and private world for fear that, in some way, devastation would follow. What was deeply felt or valued could be spoken of to his therapist only in a form which was disguised, in a dull and monotonous voice. He lived a false-self form of existence which is analogous to a mask.[3] Kohut described this kind of situation. He wrote: 'A wall of defenses is subsequently built up which protects the psyche against the re-activation of the infantile wish . . . for parental approval'.[4]

ACCOMMODATION

The second principal system of protection is built around the other main source of personal damage – the threat of loss of the other upon whom existence seems to depend. Separation anxiety, as remarked previously, is a fundamental issue in considering damage to personality development.

People whose principal traumatic experience involves abandonment, or fear of abandonment, build for themselves a way of living with others which is designed to guard against the loss of the other, who is necessary to existence, and who, through his or her absence, can inflict catastrophic anxiety.

This system typically arises as a consequence of the failures of the mother, or other caregivers, to respond in a way which connects with the child's feeling-based reality. These failures are experienced as mini-separations and evoke anxiety. This anxiety drives the child towards re-establishing the bond with her. The child behaves in a way which it believes is required in order to regain contact with the mother. This involves a sacrifice. The child, in complying to what seems to be demanded, will jettison those emotional responses which threaten the link with the caregiver. He or she emits only those expressions which are acceptable even if these expressions are not congruent with the bodily states which accompany emotions. As a consequence, the developing individual senses a diminished aliveness which, in later life, he or she will describe as 'deadness' or even 'falseness'. In essence, the child gives up the later developing system of intimacy, which depends upon the revelation of inner states, in favour of attachment, the stronger, earlier imperative. The relationship is one of 'non-intimate attachment'.[5]

Non-intimate attachment implies alienation. This was noted by an early descriptor of this system, R. D. Laing.[6] Since the system of a person relating in this way 'arises in compliance with the intentions or expectations of the other, or with what are imagined to be the other's intentions of expectations'[7], it is alien. It is also foreign in another way. Since the system is outside of self, 'partially autonomous and out of control, it is felt as alien'.[8]

Bernard Brandchaft, who has described this system, calls it 'pathological accommodation'. It is based on 'pathological attachment'.[9]

Pathological attachment is qualitatively different from the ordinary affectionate attachment between parent and child, which is without anxiety. It is characterised by the child's feeling of well-being and sense of 'ownership' of his or her experience. The relationship is consistent with, and allows exploration. There is a certain freedom in it.

Pathological attachment, on the other hand, is based on anxiety and driven by the need to reduce anxiety. It grows as anxiety begins to obliterate a tenuous stream of consciousness.[10] The paramount aim is now to regain a sense of security.[11] This need prevails over that of self, the pursuit of which is jettisoned.

There is a sense of constriction and entrapment in this relationship, which involves disconnectedness between the individual and the attachment figure. Consequently it is triggered by a sense of disconnectedness from the therapist. It is often evident, in miniature form, at the beginning of a session or after a vacation break. For a few minutes before he or she goes into therapy mode, in apparent random and colloquial chit-chat, the patient seeks the re-connection. The therapist's face is scanned; the patient may be particularly charming, or concerned about the therapist's well-being.

The system gathers complexity when the other, typically a spouse, begins to realise how it works. He or she now uses emotional distancing as a form of sanction in the manner of the parents of Lavinia T. Through coldness or silence, he or she inflicts a fear in the subject, manipulating him or her into compliance.

The story of Mrs C. (Chapter 12) illustrates aspects of the accommodative system.

AUTOGENOUS SYSTEMS

Autogenous systems refer to constellations of behaviours which arise when the other has failed the developing individual in a particular way, causing the individual to perform this function for himself or herself. The child is forced to become self generating, that is, to function autogenously.

The 'caretaker self', described by Winnicott,[12] is a common 'autogenous' system. The caregiving function of the parent fails and the child is forced to provide this function for himself or herself, adopting a somewhat artificial stance of independence and often vicariously experiencing the feeling of being nurtured through his or her own provision of care for others. An extraordinary finding[13] in a series of traumatised individuals is that one third of them worked in the health professions.

An autogenous system is often displayed in subtle ways which may not be easily detected. For example, an interpretation may lead to a cheerful and matter-of-fact response. This 'sensible' demeanour belies the failure of the interpretation which leaves the patient with the feeling that he or she is alone and must look after things in his or her own way.

A common 'autogenous structure' involves grandiosity. The other is required to respond in a way which gives value to the developing individual's sense of personal being. When the other fails, the subject takes on for himself or herself the role of valuation, adopting a posture of pride and superiority which has a feeling of fakeness about it.

Kohut described the intermittent appearance of grandiosity in his exploration of narcissistic personality disturbances. He conceived the shifts in self state in terms of 'vertical' and 'horizontal splits'. In 'vertical' terms, the self state alternated between grandiosity, which denied 'the frustrated need for approval', on one hand, and a profound sense of emptiness and low self esteem on the other. In addition, a horizontal 'split' or 'repression barrier', created an avoidance system which is 'manifest by the patient's emotional coldness and by his insistence on keeping his distance from objects from whom he might want narcissistic sustenance'.[14]

The autogenous systems of behaviour are variants of the false self, but arise in different ways to those which seek to avoid retraumatisation. However, they are obstructions to the discovery of a personal existence which has vitality and is associated with well-being.

RESTORATION

Another category of sub-system related to the trauma system is found, as it were, embedded in it. Its function is to restore, albeit in an unsatisfactory and maladaptive way, something of the sense of self which is lost when the traumatic system is re-evoked.

The quasi-positive nature of the restorative system is disguised since it appears to be merely an aspect of the trauma and its enactment.

An illustration of the restorative system comes from the case of a man who often became absorbed in the maintenance of his motorcycle. During the session, from time to time, he would recount in boring details, his difficulties in finding bike parts, problems with his motorcycle, and so on. It was apparent that these monotonous accounts followed periods of disconnection from his therapist. These disconnections were often the result of some element of the therapist's behaviour activating a traumatic memory system relating to the patient's authoritarian father.

Although the linear language, the dull voice, and the outer orientation were all indications that a disjunction between patient and therapist had taken place, his conversation involved something more. It turned out that the only person the patient remembered as giving him care when he was a child was his grandfather. He felt content being with his grandfather while the old man tinkered with machines, such as his motorcycle. Repetitive tinkering with and a preoccupation with motorcycle parts was his way of holding himself together. His boring account of his motorcycles' problems was not resistance, but a means of restoring a threatened sense of personal existence.[15]

The forms of the restorative system are multiple. They are often, incorrectly, treated as if they were circumscribed symptoms or behaviours.[16] They appear with the evocation of the traumata memory system and take place within that experience. They include, for example, self-mutilation, bingeing, pathological wandering, and certain sexual behaviours. In many cases, the behaviour has the effect of re-establishing, in a quasi-symbolic way, the feeling of relatedness with the other who is necessary to existence. A man cross dressed, for example, when he felt he had, in an emotional sense, lost his wife. They were attached to each other but she was often remote and unreponsive. At times when he felt particularly shut off from her his dressing in female clothing was soothing. It was as if by becoming her he could reconnect with the feeling of being with her.

This man was first treated by behaviourists (this was 30 years ago). They removed the fantasy relating to his cross dressing by means of aversive deconditioning. With the solace of the restorative system gone, he became catastrophically depressed and made a serious suicide attempt.

A self-restorative basis for self-mutilation was described by a woman of 35, who had been both neglected and sexually abused. When she was about six or seven she found that the only time she would get a hug from her mother was when she hurt herself accidentally. She then started to cut herself to gain this solace. It soon began to fail as her mother realised what was happening and reverted to her system of neglect. Nevertheless, the child found that cutting herself was still soothing. There remained within the act of cutting something of the soothing effect of her mother's care. The patient described it: 'I remember I used to feel much better inside. I didn't feel so empty, so lonely somehow.' In this way, the self-mutilation was an integrating act.

CONCLUDING REMARKS

The behaviours described in this chapter have the purposes of protecting, maintaining, or restoring the sense of personal being. They are underpinned by anxiety. They must be approached with these bases in mind, using the same empathic method which is necessary to the more fundamental task of integrating the trauma system into self as the stream of consciousness. This matter is touched upon in the following two chapters.

Part III

Integration

Chapter 14

Transforming the chronicle

The therapeutic conversation begins in the language of alienation. A principal therapeutic task is to transform this kind of conversation into another, the form of which shows the emergence of self in patternings which resemble the stream of consciousness.

Certain theorists[1] consider that human beings are condemned by their nature to an existence of inevitable alienation. An important aspect of the argument involves words.

When the child first begins to use words, they are provided by others. One expresses oneself not by means of gestures and body movements, which are one's own, but by means of signs and symbols which come from outside oneself, by means of an extra-personal system. Since one represents oneself, and communicates this representation, in codes which are created by others and which do not arise from a personal reality, one lives in a system of alienation. Although this argument makes sense in theoretical terms, it does not make experiential sense. As Helen Keller[2] movingly intimated, words provide an immense enlargement of life. They allow us to link with the experiences of others. Rather than alienation, language provides the possibility of intimacy. How can these opposing views of conversation be reconciled? An answer involves the form of language used.

In Chapter 4 it was argued that during symbolic play, the peculiar language and the form of the child's playing are manifestations of a particular kind of mental activity which transforms both the things and the words of the outer world into the thoughts and words of the inner and personal world. The transforming function which is evident in symbolic play is also, we suppose, a quality of the stream of consciousness. Those things of the world, including words, which are taken into it are given a certain feeling-tone, which gives them a sense of the personal. They are 'owned'. However, not all things and words are invested with this aura. Although our conversations are made of the words of others, to these words will be attached varying degrees of otherness and varying degrees of 'one's-own-ness'. Conversations in which there is no, or limited, evidence of the transmuting force of the stream of consciousness will be those of relative alienation.

Amongst the various forms of this kind of conversation, two major categories can be discerned. They might be called chronicles and scripts. This chapter concerns the chronicle, while the following approaches the script.

THE CHRONICLE

Despite the fact that in the clinical situation we are confronted with many different forms of conversation, a tripartite classification, made in terms of narratives, chronicles and scripts, has a heuristic value. It gives us a way of talking about the storying of which the therapeutic encounter is made up.

A chronicle is a primitive history. The Oxford English Dictionary defines it as a 'detailed and continuous register of events in order of time; a historical record, especially one in which the facts are narrated without philosophic treatment, or any attempt at literary style'. The clinical chronicle is, characteristically, a catalogue of problems with the family, with work, and of symptoms. Nothing comes from an interior world. The individual's experience is dominated by events, the language is linear, and there is a relative poverty of metaphoric usage. Furthermore, there is no pleasure in the conversation. The chronicling conveys a sense of deadness, without creative aliveness.

An explanation of this state of affairs can be derived from the developmental schema built around two fundamental forms of human conversation.

Since the development of symbolic play depends upon pre-intimate relatedness, a child who has been relatively deprived of this kind of care will also have a diminished access to that form of mental activity which is necessary to the establishment of self. He or she will be oriented towards the outer world, caught in the zone of adaption. Experience will come, overwhelmingly, from external sources, and be recounted, in linear form, as a series of reactions, with little evidence of the third term, which is a manifestation of self.

The form of the chronicle can be predicted from Jacksonian theory. The repeated failures of the caregivers will have the effect of repeated miniature traumata. Each one, in a small way, is a blow to the child's embryonic experiencing of self.[3] This passively traumatic environment will impede the usual developmental trajectory which Jackson postulated, that is, a progression towards states of greater complexity which involve increased voluntary control.

The less complex nature of chronicle relative to narrative is implied in the dictionary definition which highlights the fact that chronicle is without 'philosophical treatment'. Put another way, it is unprocessed. The things that have happened are recounted as if they have not entered that form of non-linear mental activity which is the basis of the stream of consciousness.

More limited voluntary control is exhibited in sequencing. Whereas the narrative form of conversation has a spontaneous quality, influenced by the movements of inner life, the freedom of the chronicle is diminished.

The sequence is imposed from without, by the environment, including the environment of the body.

There is little evidence of the individual's capacity to roam about in time. He or she is caught in the present. The conversation is dominated by episodic memory. The remote past which depends upon autobiographical memory, is barely mentioned.[4]

The chronicle, which reflects a state of disconnection from inner experience, is told in a relationship of disconnection. It emerges in an established therapeutic relationship when the atmosphere of intimate relatedness is broken up. It should not be understood as resistance nor, as Enid Balint implies in a discussion of a case of this kind,[5] should the memory failure be considered a consequence of repression. It is the manifestation of damage. The damage is likely to have been of the kind identified by Balint[6] herself in an earlier paper entitled 'On being empty of oneself'. She felt this state was the result of a mismatch between infantile experience and maternal perception. 'Misrecognition', to use her word, is another way of describing misattunement or failure of appropriate responsiveness to the child's core reality. It is precisely the condition which triggers the child's experience towards the outer world, leaving the inner zone stunted, depleted, and at times, painfully vacant. This state is shown in the form of the language of clearly maltreated chldren. These children, as toddlers, use fewer internal-state words than other children. Also, they are more context bound in their use of internal-state language than their peers.[7]

RESONANCE

People who tell their story as a chronicle seem to be trapped by the sensory environment. The catalogue is of events, descriptions of the world as it impacted upon them. They live almost entirely in the 'real'. Little evidence of the imaginary or the symbolic is to be found. They suffer from a painful state which might be called 'stimulus entrapment'.[8] The stimuli which preoccupy them, and which come to the forefront of consciousness are not only those coming from others in the environment, but from the body. The catalogue involves, characteristically, complaints of various discomforts, headaches, and other pains, which at times take up much of the conversation. In technical language, 'somatisation' is prominent.

Since the individual who recounts the chronicle is in the state of disconnection from others, there is boredom, lack of vitality, and unease, experienced by both partners in the conversation. A way out of this impasse is to create the atmosphere of connectedness with another person which allowed symbolic play to come into being, and which is necessary to the emergence of inner life, and a feeling of 'aliveness'. This then is the therapist's first objective.

The attempt to establish a connectedness differs from an approach which is based on the notion of resistance. In this case the therapist, finding that very little of what the patient says comes from an inner zone, concludes that the conversation is a kind of protective flack designed to keep the therapist out, or even, perhaps, an attempt to sabotage therapy. The therapist's interventions, based on this idea, lead to remarks about the uselessness of this form of conversation. This is the stance of 'foreignness'. It leads to further disconnection.

Rather than pointing out the deficiency evident in the chronicle form of conversation, the therapist must move against his or her own inclinations. He or she shares the alienation of the patient. In this state, responses come to mind which are induced by this state and so perpetuate it. Rather than acting in the way which seems natural in the face of a boring conversation, one tries to move within it, to become part of it in the manner of James' 'intimate' philosopher. Rather than withdrawing interest from the tedious conversation, one listens intently.

The process is slow and laborious. It must depend upon the use of a language which resembles Vygotsky's 'inner speech', which is qualitatively different from 'external speech'.[9] It is also often abbreviated so that, as Vygotsky observed, subjects are omitted and 'only predicates are left'.[10] The grammar has the form which is likely to potentiate the emergence of the third term. The language is directed towards an emergent state. It often has a speculative, wandering, or incomplete form.[11]

In a sense, the objective is akin to the establishment of a feedback loop, a resonance which not only enhances the state of reflection, but also creates the beginning of the reverberation which may be necessary to the creation of complexity. The therapist's apparently simple remarks can be seen as the triggers of complexity. Since the session typically starts in a state of disconnection and relative alienation, this kind of intervention is likely to be common as the conversation begins. One colleague spoke of 'kick-starting' the session.

The effective forms of resonance are 'within' the patient's experience, that is they are empathic, however simple or abbreviated they may be. Examination of the transcripts of work with patients whose conversation was of the chronicle kind showed that such remarks lead to a fall in preoccupation with the body and, at times, an increase in the complexity of the conversation.

Simple resonance involves a response to that which is most personal in the patient's most recent remark. It is a step towards a more complex form of responding which involves an attempt to understand the chronicle as a reflection of some more interior or imaginative state, something which is nearer to an individual reality than the surface chatter might suggest.

This more complex form of resonance depends upon the view that although the patient's account seems to be nothing more than a reading off of the events of the world as they impinge against him or her, these events are selected. In this way, they have some personal quality. An imaginative exploration of this selection may lead to the discovery of an implicit metaphor. Metaphor is a means of visualising the inner world.

THE DISCOVERY OF IMPLICIT METAPHOR

Words can be used as signs or symbols. They are used as signs in the linear language of adaption.

A sign refers to an aspect of a collective reality, to known features of the environment. A bus conductor's badge, the pedestrian crossing indicator, are signs. The chronicle is told in the language of signs.

A symbol, on the other hand, can refer to entities or ideas which are *not* part of the observable world. The word symbol refers 'especially to a material object representing, or taken to represent, something immaterial or abstract, as a being, idea, quality, or condition'.[12] Symbols serve to represent realities which cannot be seen or grasped.[13] Examples of such realities are the personal, the religious and the scientific. The Cross and $e = mc^2$ are both symbols. In an individual sense, symbols are needed to portray the inner world of feelings and imaginings, so that all words for affects are metaphors, dead or alive.[14]

With the establishment of an inner life at about four, a particular language is required which allows one to convey to others aspects of one's inner reality. This depends, in particular, upon the use of metaphor. Self is manifest in a particular form of the symbolic function.

The metaphoric process is the direct descendant of symbolic play. In both cases, things of the world are chosen and made to express what the player wishes in order to represent personal states. There is a reciprocal relation. The outer world is necessary to the bringing into being of an inner or personal world. In this process, particular aspects of the outer world become also part of the personal. They are now, in a sense, part of oneself.

The use of metaphor to describe inner states signifies the emergence of true symbolisation. The words are now free of representing things whereas in symbolic play the word was *part* of the thing. (It would be more accurate to call symbolic play proto-symbolic.) Predictably, those who have been denied the necessary caregiving environment of 'pre-intimate relatedness', engage in conversations which are hypo-symbolic.

In essence, the therapist's goal is to participate in the creation of a feeling of 'aliveness' in an individual whose sense of ordinary living is one of 'deadness'. The task will involve the bringing into being of an inner life in someone for whom such an experience is limited, interrupted, or fragmentary. The first moves towards this goal involve setting up a kind of resonance which is analogous to the proto-conversation. While in this form of relatedness, which involves early elements of a non-linear, non-directive, associative state, one attempts to discover the means of representing an emergent zone of self, which is felt as interior. In symbolic play, the things of the world are used. In later life it must be words, but words used in a way which resembles the toys, as symbolic. However, this is not simple. The therapist cannot use his or her own metaphors, however clever or apt. In this case, he or she is speaking a language which is foreign to someone the currency of whose conversation is words as signs.

Metaphors have to be 'found' in the intersubjective field. In this way, they are shared, to be 'played with' together. Robert Hobson gave an example of this process in his interview with Mrs Jones.

Mrs Jones had been ill for three years. She was investigated for nine months by neurologists for what they understood to be vertigo. It eventually emerged that this was not vertigo at all, but the dizziness which accompanies panic attacks. In addition to panic attacks, Mrs Jones had a series of phobias and a generalised anxiety disorder. Following her discharge from neurological care, she was treated extensively in a behavioural manner with no improvement. She was eventually admitted to hospital for intensive treatment. The symptoms did not abate. Moreover, those caring for her found it impossible to get any important personal story from her. Although the events of her life were told, nothing of an intimate nature was revealed. Her conversation tended to be dominated by accounts of her symptoms and her bodily complaints. Her case was puzzling and she herself seemed to be unreachable. She was pejoratively labelled 'a somatiser'. Hobson, who was visiting Sydney at the time of her hospitalisation, was asked to see her in order to make suggestions about her management. In a single interview he was able to give her a sense that she was understood and at the same time to understand her, discovering, with her, the fundamental psychodynamics underpinning her symptoms.

Instead of merely tolerating her account of her symptomatology, as her previous medical advisors and her behaviour therapists had done, he listened intently.

In telling him of her panic attacks, which she did not label as such, she focused on her dizziness. This was a personal selection. She did not tell him of the beating heart, the constriction in the gut, the sweating palms, the shakes. Since it was chosen, it had a personal significance. It was an implicit metaphor.

Rather than merely noting the 'dizziness' and inquiring about the other symptoms in the manner of a check list which someone relating in the manner of 'foreignness' might have done, he attempted to understand the dizziness as much as possible. He found that it was associated with the fear of falling. This was usually towards the left. In order to overcome this fear Mrs Jones would lie down. He asked about her position on the bed, which side she lay on. Was she right handed? It seemed that the left side was the one which had something wrong with it. After exploring the symptom he offered the speculation that the left side felt like an unknown part of her. The videotape showed a clear relaxation and increase in vitality on the patient's part after this remark. After attempting to discover an underlying metaphor in this state of stimulus entrapment, Hobson then began to elaborate it. He told her the story of the origin of sinister, of the evil omen of the birds flying to the left. This brief story which might be called an 'offered narrative' appealed to the imaginary and symbolic. It elaborated the metaphor in narrative terms.

The metaphor does not remain static but changes and develops with the conversation, in a thematic manner. Hobson[15] calls it the 'moving metaphor'. It evolves in the to and fro of a resonance which is larger than that of conversational linking. It is a movement towards triggering the kind of mental activity which underpins the stream of consciousness. This non-linear state, arising out of a previous linearity, can be seen as the result of a reverberation between two poles of representation.

RESONANCE AND COMPLEXITY

Edgar Levenson, whose concept of resonance I borrow, has for many years been describing a change in conceiving the therapeutic relationship from the traditional to the intersubjective. The former relationship was conducted in the manner of James' 'foreignness' while the latter resembles his description of the 'intimate' philosopher. Levenson contrasts the kind of therapist's remark which is a 'transmission of information across interpersonal space' with another form of communication which has more to do with 'interpersonal resonance'. 'Out of the resonance, a patterning emerges. It is as though all the harmonic variations of the same melody light up'.[16] Put another way, resonance has the effect of triggering a previously linear system into one of complexity.

Levenson's metaphors, which he uses to describe the nature of the intersubjective field, anticipated those of non-linear mathematics. The field involves 'connections, patterns, harmonies'.[17] Its temporal dimension 'is neither an arrow nor a boomerang but a kaleidoscopic shifting of the patterns of consequence'.[18] This approach is contrasted with the traditional orientation: 'The *hubris* of the stimulus–response precept, where every cause had its effect and every phenomenon its explanation, no longer applies. Interpretation, explanation, understanding, belief in the one-to-one relationship of the event and the word, were the mainstays of psychoanalytic theory and practice in the mechanical model.'[19]

A metaphor which illustrates the remarkable effect of a relatively simple resonance is provided by Mandelbrot's[20] fractal geometry. He demonstrated how out of a simple reverberation between representations, complex and beautiful patterns could emerge.

Mandelbrot's equation starts with a representation (Z) which is then squared (Z^2) and a constant c added to it. $Z^2 + c$ becomes the new Z which is squared and the constant c added to it and so on. Mandelbrot suggested that his iterative mathematics predicts the meandering form of a river. Hans-Henrick Stolum[21] made a formal study of this hypothesis. 'Meandering,' he stated, 'is caused by the operation of the opposing processes which are linked by a complex feedback that is partly under local geometrical control: lateral migration acts to increase sinuosity, whereas cutoffs (the formation of oxbow lakes) act to decrease it'. Using simulations and empirical data, he was able to show that the meandering stream could be seen as a self-organising process which can be understood in terms of Mandelbrot's theorem. It is tempting to suppose that the doubling, or resonance, provided by the emergence of the reflective process in human life participates in the creation of the stream of consciousness.

A non-linear system, as Prigogine and Stengers point out, can be triggered into large changes of state, by small alterations within it. 'A small fluctuation may start an entirely new evolution that will drastically change the whole behaviour of the macroscopic system'.[22]

Although the metaphors of non-linear mathematics can be taken too far in attempting to understand the emergence of self, the concept of resonance offers an image which is helpful in guiding the therapeutic approach to the problem of the chronicle. The chronicle cannot be altered by so-called interpretations or by instructions to enter a more personal and associative form of conversation. Nor is a waiting strategy particularly useful. The Mandelbrot image of reverberations between initially very small representations which are slowly enhanced and amplified, offers a way of conceiving what must be done. The aim is to foster maturation of a personal system which, in terms of the Jacksonian hierarchy, is ill-developed. A state of greater maturity will be manifest in a conversational form of greater complexity.

Chapter 15

Flights and perchings

An ideal conversation is associative, dependent upon a non-linear psychic state, shared by both partners, which allows spontaneity and free movement of the mind. This kind of conversation is not usually possible until near the end of therapy. It is a goal towards which the treatment is directed.

The form of this conversation has the 'shape' of the stream of consciousness as James described it. He wrote:

> Like a bird's life, it seems to be made of an alternation of flights and perchings. The rhythm of language expresses this, where every thought is expressed in a sentence, and every sentence closed by a period. The resting-places are usually occupied by sensorial imaginations of some sort, whose peculiarity is that they can be held before the mind for an indefinite time, and contemplated without changing; the places of flight are filled with thoughts of relations, static or dynamic, that for the most part obtain between the matters contemplated in the periods of comparative rest.[1]

The 'perchings' can be seen as small moments of 'insight', that is, they are seen with the eyes of the mind. A scene is created and contemplated. The visualisation of inner life implied in the Jamesian description is crucial. A 'sensorial imagination' is at work.

The moments of contemplation, the perchings, come out of a previous flux, the flight. The 'perchings' are part of the total movement, with its sense of flow. They are not discontinuous or sequestered from the rest of inner life. These miniature forms of insight, when this term is used in its original sense, provide a way of considering how insight might be approached in the clinical situation. This 'inner view' must be integrated with the sense of self as the stream of consciousness. The experience of 'insight' is analogous to those moments of contemplation which James called 'perchings'.[2]

The difficulty with the achievement of insight in the clinical situation is that those experiences which must be made 'conscious' are discontinuous from self as the stream of consciousness.

Activation of a traumatic memory system breaks up a previous psychic state. Consciousness is taken over by another kind of mental activity which is linear, so operating according to laws which differ from those governing the non-linearity of the stream of consciousness. The separation of this system is further marked by a change in affect. The positive feeling, however muted, which is at the heart of the stream of consciousness is replaced by a negative state, which is unpleasant.

Repeated incursions into consciousness of the traumatic system, which is 'unconscious' in that it is not experienced as memory, are disruptive of ordinary living and impede development. Overcoming the effect of psychic imprints left by traumata is a major therapeutic task.

In the past, the therapeutic approach to the traumatic memory system has focused on direct attempts to change the 'script' which organises the experience. This 'script', as previously remarked, is more primitive than the chronicle, showing less complexity, and very little voluntary control. It is triggered almost automatically. It tells the individual that he or she is bad, worthless, stupid, weak, and in the presence of a critical, devaluing, intrusive, other. In other words, the script is composed of transference phenomena.

Since the individual is unaware that this 'reality' which he or she now inhabits comes from memory and is not 'real', some therapists address this distortion directly in transference interpretations which seek to give the patient 'insight' in the form of self knowledge, and to correct the distortion. Although this approach seems to make sense, recent evidence suggests that this manner of insight interpretation is likely to be ineffective.[3]

The difficulty of this kind of 'transference interpretation' becomes clear when we consider it from the point of view of integration. Since the therapist's remarks are directed towards knowledge and facts, they are addressed to the wrong system, the semantic. The conversation stays in the 'trauma zone'. Indeed, the therapist himself or herself is now likely to be caught up in it. Observations which are of benevolent intent are experienced as confirmation of the 'script', that is, of one's badness, uselessness, in the face of someone who is devaluing, distancing, and so on.[4] Unwittingly, what was meant to be helpful is sensed as derogation.[5]

The notion that the traumatic memory system must be integrated into the stream of consciousness changes the whole emphasis of therapeutic behaviour. There must be a stream of consciousness before integration can occur. Priority is therefore given to the establishment of this experience. The therapist's first task is to develop a relationship with the patient in which it is possible for a mental activity, which is non-linear and feeling based, to emerge.

Second, the traumatic system can only enter the stream if it is made of the same kind of experience. Whereas inner life is visualised, the traumatic system is not. In order to facilitate its integration, it must slowly be converted, in the context of a relationship in which the associative form of mental activity is operative, into an experience which can be 'looked at'. Visualisation is fundamental to the process of integration.

The narrative form of the stream of consciousness is made up of scenes.[6] In order that the traumatic systems and their satellites can be viewed, they must slowly be 'brought before the eyes', and built up, bit by bit, through imaginative immersion in the patient's experience.[7] It is never enough to point out, say, someone's 'guardedness'. It is necessary to work towards the reconstruction of an episode which shows the cause of such guardedness. It might involve, for example, an attack upon value. This piecing together of this scene often involves an awareness of how one is being 'constructed' so as to become the other in this stereotypic drama. The eventual visualisation of the experience places it in a different mode of mental processing to that which depends upon semantic or more primitive forms of memory.[8]

Development of insight seen in this way does not depend upon what is 'true' or 'untrue', 'real' or 'unreal', but upon the creation of a mental picture by discovery of implicit metaphors and through imaginative use of the data of the therapeutic conversation. The achievement of an insight in this circumstance indicates a widening of 'internal sight' or 'mental vision',[9] an enhancement of the reflective capacity.

OLIVIA

Something of the complexity of the operation of the trauma system, and its pervasive and subtle influence upon the therapeutic encounter is illustrated by the case of Olivia. Olivia had a very difficult upbringing. As far as we are aware, she was not physically or sexually abused, but she was emotionally abused. She was a troubled adolescent who, at one stage, ran away to live on the streets and to survive by prostitution. Police, however, rescued her within a few days and she was returned home. Despite her difficulties, she managed to complete a university course, gaining a degree in psychology. For a time she worked in an adolescent inpatient psychiatry unit. However, she could not maintain recovery and in her twenties she was treated for a number of disorders including depression and a range of phobias. She also had multiple somatic complaints. She was unable to work except intermittently as a part-time cleaner. Relative to her abilities, her life is now restricted. She still lives with her parents. Since she is panphobic, she has great difficulty in travelling, attending cinemas, and so on.

For the first two years of therapy she was stuck in the chronicle mode of conversation. She has now changed a great deal. She is functioning better, and there is a sense, at least at times, of vitality and the imaginative in her conversation. However, these unfoldings of the zone of the personal are usually brief. The following extracts show the continuing operation of a traumatic system, the basis of which is an attack upon the value at the core of self. This system 'constructs' the other, and is hedged about by systems of avoidance and accommodation.

The session to be discussed begins, if the therapist were to describe it, with her telling him that during the weekend she was able to go out to afternoon tea. This is good news, since it indicates that she is overcoming some of her phobic difficulties, which include generally avoiding social occasions. She then goes on to describe how one of her friends at the afternoon tea upset her by contradicting her. She appears to deal well with this since she seems able to reflect upon her experience of this encounter. This bald summary of the opening of the sessions is accurate as far as it goes. However, a consideration of the actual conversation, the words as they were used, including the life or otherwise that was in them, shows a far more detailed and complicated story, which involves the relationship with the therapist. As she told him her story, the difficulties at the party with her friend were being played out with him, although this microscopic re-enactment of her trauma was so subtle that it was barely discernible.

The session begins with the words, spoken in a dead voice, in the manner of the chronicle 'It was drizzling on Saturday'. She then remarks that it cleared up, after which her voice lifts and she says, 'I had a busy weekend', the word 'busy' is stressed. In a bright and lively voice, as if she is pleased, she says 'I went out to afternoon tea', and gives a little laugh. There is a pause, very brief, after which the therapist says 'yup'. She then says 'yup' in a voice that is now matter-of-fact. She then begins to talk about how she managed to get to the afternoon tea.

In this tiny fragment, at the opening of the session, the whole system of the trauma is laid out.

Olivia says 'I had a busy weekend'. Her voice, however, says she had a _good_ weekend. Why does she not use the word good? Is she afraid? Does she fear that anything that is good that is her own doing, her own creation, will be devalued? Yet she is clearly pleased as the little laugh shows. The pause following her announcement, we might suppose, is to allow the therapist to make some remark which acknowledges her achievement, which recognises that she has taken a step forward in overcoming her phobic symptomatology. What she is recounting is a triumph. Yet the therapist, who is a warm and empathic individual says 'yup'. What has happened? If he were asked, the therapist would probably say that he did not feel that anything was expected of him. Put another way, he has been constructed. He has become part of her traumatic system. This small fragment of conversation suggests that Olivia expects that anything that comes from within her, anything that is personal, will be devalued by not being acknowledged. Perhaps it will even be attacked. However, she, to some extent, protects herself from this event.

She protects herself, first of all, by her use of words. The good feeling which is at the heart of self, and which came from her feeling of achievement, is obscured in her description of the weekend as 'busy' rather than 'good'. A second means of protection involves the gap in the conversation which she provides for him to resonate with her feeling of pleasure, which is shown in the little laugh. This gap is so small that he barely has time to realise what has happened. In this way, also, she is protected. If he fails, she can feel that she had not revealed herself, he did not really know how she felt.

The next question to ask is why should the word 'busy' be used instead of 'good'. In the traumatic state, the individual is disconnected in terms from the other. Separation anxiety arises. The traumatised individual now needs to establish attachment to the other in some way or another. This will involve, in most cases, the child or the traumatised individual, behaving in a way which he or she considers will gain the approval of, and so enhance the attachment to, the other. Perhaps Olivia felt that if she were a busy girl her mother would be pleased with her. If she bustled about doing household chores this would gain some positive regard from her mother who, it seemed, was excessively self-centred. Put another way, the word 'busy' is a reflection of a system of accommodation. Consistent with this speculation is the fact that Olivia now has a part-time cleaning position.

Although what happens in the opening moments of this session goes too fast to be properly processed, the therapist now engages with Olivia in a way in which allows the whole story, which was implicit in the first few sentences, to become quite clear.

Olivia describes the afternoon tea party and as she does so the matter-of-fact tone of voice once again brightens. She says that when she entered the party, the other guests 'couldn't believe it'. On this occasion, although there was pleasure in her voice, she does not allow the therapist the chance to fail. She gives him no pause in which, once again, he can become the traumatising other who gives no value to what she does.

The conversation then goes on to describe the incident in which her friend puts her down. This involves a discussion about adolescent sexuality. Olivia, of course, is an expert in the difficulties of young people not only through her own history, but through her professional work. Her friend, however, dismisses her viewpoint as if it were of no consequence.

The therapist knows he must explore this incident since it seems not unlikely that it will show the lineaments of a trauma system. In particular, the feelings at the core of this story must be laid out.

He approaches this task by asking no questions, and making no assumptions about how she felt. His words, in such circumstances, would seem to come from outside, from the zone of 'foreignness'. Instead of conversing in this way he tries to enter into her experience. He stays with her in her description of the incident, helping her to build it up, in the manner of 'resonance', a kind of 'doubling'. The patient's voice rises and she says spontaneously 'I just felt this flare of anger'. This revelation, since it is her own, is far more important than the therapist having said to her, 'That must have made you angry', although, of course, he would have known that was the case. The patient now *owns* the discovery of her feelings.

At this point it must be said that, though the therapist might be developing a picture of the traumatic memory system as it is shown in Olivia's relationship with her girlfriend, this endeavour does not conform to the usual manner of transference interpretation since it is not linked to the immediate experience between patient and therapist. A traditional understanding of Olivia's story regarding her friend might be that she is *really* talking about her relationship with her therapist. This is not exactly so.

When the therapist fails to give an acknowledgement of Olivia's pleasure at her overcoming her phobic symptoms by turning up to a party, she begins to talk about the form of a traumatic relationship. A plausible explanation for this behaviour is as follows. The therapist's failure, although minuscule, triggers the traumatic memory system. Within this memory system the patient now begins to tell a story which shows its outlines. Since the story has been triggered by the disjunction it does reflect something of the form of the relationship between patient and therapist at that moment. Put another way, the story that is being told by Olivia, and which comes from the past, is being played out in the present in a minor, subtle, and barely discernible way between patient and therapist. However, an intervention which suggests that the patient's experience with her friend is a replication, in a minor way, of that with the therapist is likely to be greeted with puzzlement and rejection, since the immediate experience is, in a way, unconscious. In fact Olivia's therapist has, on a number of occasions, attempted to make such an intervention. She merely replies by saying that her relationship with her therapist is quite different from those of the rest of her life.

The traditional transference interpretation involves another linking. It relates a current incident to the patient's developmental history. The story about Olivia's girlfriend has not only a trigger in the present but also a model which comes from the past. It would be quite appropriate for her therapist to suggest that perhaps that flare of anger she felt with her girlfriend would also have been experienced by Olivia in relation to one or other of her parents. The danger of this behaviour, however, is that Olivia's compliance and willingness to accommodate will cause her to agree to this suggestion. This passive acceptance of the therapist's superior knowledge of her, leaves her with a diminished sense of her ownership.

What the therapist actually does is to make remarks which stay in a conversational mode, but which in an empathic way, amplify what Olivia has said. He sees his behaviour as enhancing the power or effectiveness of a feedback loop. 'Like you were dismissed,' he says. Soon, Olivia spontaneously says 'There are visions of my mother here'. Her own realisation of the origins of her flare of anger are far more powerful and useful than the therapist having given her this piece of 'insight'. Her capacity to reflect upon her experience and to connect it with her past is a remarkable achievement in a person who had seemed, a year or so ago, almost devoid of the capacity for reflection. This capacity, together with the associational linking which led to her recovery of something from the past, shows, in words, the emergence of self.

Some minutes later, the therapist is continuing in his amplifying mode, making attempts to understand her experience.

'Did you feel almost like a nothing?'
'No not a nothing. Just someone who didn't count. You couldn't give much
    weight to anything I said,' she replies.
'You would almost be a ghost, wouldn't you, hovering round without any
    substance to you.'
'I guess that is what it is. With people who really know me, I'm worthless.'

This passage, which is typical of the conversation, reflects another remarkable change in the way Olivia talks with her therapist. She is able to use the metaphors he offers, arriving at an understanding of the core of her traumatic system. She realises that those closest to her diminish her sense of personal value. She is not led to this conclusion by any clever intervention which in effect shows her that the therapist knows something she does not. His remarks are speculative, giving her the opportunity to have the insight as her own and to respond in a way which is not compliant. She rejects the idea of being 'a nothing', reformulating the proposal in her own way.

His language is sophisticated, in a way of which he is probably not aware. He says 'You would almost be a ghost', not 'You must have felt like a ghost'. This form of expression pictures another Olivia, whom she can contemplate. In helping her to reflect upon her experience, he enhances the coming into being of the 'doubling' which is necessary to the experience of self.

His choice of metaphor is a resonance with her word 'weight'. She implies that she is made 'weightless' by the devaluing response of her friend. Although he is not quite accurate in that he interprets 'weight' in terms of substance rather than value, his image is 'good-enough'.

The conversation continues in the manner of the above passage, as if they are playing around with her experiences at the party. It emerges that not only was she angry, she also felt humiliated. He says that to be shamed or humiliated is like being physically hit:

'It's like you've been beaten up, in a way.'
'Yes, that's how it feels. You think you're getting on to a safe topic, then
    bang. It's like being king hit from behind. You're not expecting it . . .'
'Which is what your mother did, isn't it?'

She blocks his attempt to link the humiliating incident to her developmental history. Although she has previously told him of this earlier in her therapy, she makes a doubtful acquiescence which has the effect of negation. Why should this be so? Is it an effect of the structuring of his language? Alternatively, does his remark appropriate her own realisation of this connection? If this were the case, it might be like a theft or intrusion.

Despite this minor break up in the flow of their conversation, she is able to return to her feelings of being humiliated. She says she was in 'total shock. How can I answer this?' She goes on to say her decision is to 'shut up and join the conversation on books or something'. Then after a pause, which is filled by his 'm'mm', her voice lifts and she says:

'The other thing was, I didn't feel frightened, and to feel like I need to get out of there. But I was very aware of what was happening to me. And I thought . . .'
'Sounds good'. His voice is warm and affirming.
'Yeah.'
'That sounds good.'

These apparently simple interventions by the therapist are important. With his responses he gives value to her new-found ability to reflect upon her inner states. He seems no longer to be in the grip of the construction of him made by her trauma system which presumably prevented such responses at the beginning of the session. As connectedness has grown during their conversation, the salience of the trauma system has diminished. It has not entirely melted away, but now its hold is weak. The fact that it persists is shown by his having to interrupt her, almost speak over the top of her, in order to utter his first 'Sounds good'. However, after her 'Yeah', she gives him space to say it again.

His remark encourages her further to reflect upon the scene, in the manner of a 'perching'. 'I thought I'm not sure my problem here is with Shirley, or if it's, like, the dynamics of what was happening.'

They jointly attempt to understand these dynamics. After some digressions, she says:

'They're probably feelings I've had for a long time, but I just became really aware of them and some of the causes of them. But I'm still not sure. I'm thinking "Who's got the problem here, is it them or is it me?"'

An effective intervention of the therapist, which must be based not in theory but in the empathic capacity, results, in a typical case, with a response from the patient which shows increased complexity. This is evident in Olivia's apparently simple and colloquial reply. The temporal domain now includes a past which is operating in the present; her perspective is multiple, shifting from her past to her present, to her inner life, and to a view of others.

'So you're clearer about something.' His remark, once again, is sophisticated. He resonates with her achievement of some form of insight in order to give it a 'reality'. However, he uses no technical terms like 'insight' or 'consciousness'. Rather, he simply acknowledges that she is 'clearer about something', as if a picture is coming into focus. His remark might be seen as an invitation to a 'perching'.

'Yeah. But unless I decide whose problem it is, I'll continue to feel belittled.' She begins to explore, by implication, the notion that there must be something wrong with people who try to make others feel small. However, she cannot avoid feeling that the problem is hers.

'I'm not strong enough or together enough to cope with it.'
'It's almost as if you've lost your voice,' he says.
'Yeah, yeah. I guess that's how I felt.'
'Yeah, then talk about trivial things,' by which he means the books.
'Yeah.'
'Sort of superficial things.'
'Yeah, because anything personal to me feels like it just leads to attack.'

The whole traumatic system is now revealed but not as a result of insight interpretations. By means of a continuing process, fostered by the therapist's quiet and patient empathy, Olivia herself arrives at the appropriate conclusion. 'Insight' has emerged through the provision of a scaffolding of understanding.

MINUTE PARTICULARS

The above account is taken from an audiotape. Both 'Olivia' and her therapist were glad to allow its presentation here. It shows, unidealised, the actual process of therapy which had a successful outcome. It is important that it is not perfect. A therapist who knows everything that is passing through his or her patient's mind, who misses nothing, and whose interpretations are always 'accurate' would be disaster. It is necessary not only for those in therapy, but for everybody, to feel that the private world of imaginings, ideas, and emotions is intact, and one's own, not to be breached.[10] What is required of the therapist is a responsiveness that, in the Winnicottian phrase, is 'good-enough'.

It does not matter particularly that the therapist missed what happened in the opening sentences. It will happen again. The trauma system will be evoked repeatedly in the therapeutic encounter and make its impact on the conversation in subtle ways. It would be inappropriate for the therapist to pounce on every shift of feeling-tone. Such behaviour would hinder their mutual movement towards a form of conversation which has the 'shape' of play and the stream of consciousness. This is the principal priority, as previously remarked. However, once this has begun, to some degree, the second aim must be pursued.

The traumatic memory system must be integrated into self as the stream of consciousness. In the context of a non-linear form of mental activity[11] these half-known experiences must be brought into 'view'. However, 'insight' must be gained not once but many times. A 'working through' is required.

As the conversation between Olivia and her therapist evolves and progresses, the work will continue to involve extensive examination of particular episodes of the patient's life. Increasingly, however, attention will shift towards those much smaller episodes which take place in the moment-to-moment movements of the conversation between patient and therapist. The conversation will become as much concerned with the intricacies of what is going on in the present, in the room, as with stories from the world beyond. As the conversation with Olivia has shown, this exploration cannot be done by taking a stance 'outside' the conversation, as an observer might do who views a scene, a play, or a piece of machinery, which is the work of somebody else.

Conversation is the result of an interplay between two minds whose words begin to create a third zone which was not previously existent and which would not have arisen but through the activity of the single minds alone. The therapist, as participant, cannot, without breaking up this shared creation, suddenly take a role in which he or she is the objective observer of the patient as subject. This new subject—object form of relationship is discontinuous with the conversational flow, like the emergence of traumatic memory. What the 'objective observer' says by way of interpretation does not work, since it is in a zone of experience split off from that of the stream of consciousness.

Yet, at the same time, the therapist must be an observer. He or she has to play out a paradox. He or she must stay within the intersubjective experience and at the same time become aware of the shifts in the patient's, as well as his or her own, states and behaviours. This is just one of the 'doublings' in which the therapist is required to engage.

The double stance of the therapist, who is both participant and observer of the conversational experience, leads, in ideal circumstances, to an exploration and representation of the 'minute particulars' which show the unconscious determination of certain aspects of the therapeutic conversation. In the session just described they would include the news of the 'busy weekend' and the rejection of his transference connections between her mother and her friend, although she can make the connection herself. The perchings in the flight of conversation must involve not only Olivia and her friends and her past but also the present in which she and her therapist find themselves.

Epilogue

Chapter 16

The death of Narcissus

The myth of the double is a kind of sub-text to the basic story of this book, which is woven about William James' concept of self. This is double, made up of two poles which, for the sake of brevity, are called the 'I' and the 'me'. I have conceived the developmental process in terms of this doubleness.

We are not born with an 'I' and a 'me'. Rather, we begin life as 'I' and the 'other', a doubling which is slowly taken inside. In order for this internalisation to occur, the other takes on a representing function which is a re-knowing, or re-cognition, of a feeling kind, showing the infant a nascent 'me'. This representing takes place in the context of play, which is underpinned by a non-linear form of mental activity. A 'matching' representation creates a sense of vitality and well-being.

The representing function is slowly taken on by the infant, once again in the context of play. At first, the representing of emergent aspects of the 'me' is performed by the body, by means of imitation. With the advent of symbolic play, the representation of the personal moves beyond the limitations of the body, to include language and material objects. What is important about this activity is that it displays a transformation of words and things that are taken from others and from the external environment, into the words and the scenes of the personal. We are able to observe, in the external world, the coming into being of a cardinal feature of the stream of consciousness, the feeling that this experience is 'mine'.

The appearance of an internal doubling, and a 'me' that is made up of an experiential stream of feeling-laden images, memories, imaginings, and ideas, is a major advance in maturation. It is accompanied by a sense, not often expressed, of an internal dyad who, as it were, can converse. The realisation of this fundamental change in the nature of his psychic life, which occurred when he was five, was vividly described, in later life, by Edmund Gosse.

> It is difficult to define impressions so rudimentary, but it is certain that it was in this dual form that the sense of my individuality now descended upon me, and it is equally certain that it was a great solace to me to find a sympathizer in my own breast.[1]

In essence, this momentous event involves what was two becoming one. The sense of the other, whose resonance with one's personal world is such that he or she is felt as like oneself, is transformed into an inner experience. The two becoming one is a principal feature of the myth of the double identified by Otto Rank (1884–1939), a pioneer of the psychoanalytic study of myth.[2] The myth of Narcissus can be seen as portraying the arrest of this transformational process.

Myths organise and represent aspects of human existence in a particular and peculiar way. These representations, like those of symbolic play, are underpinned by a non-linear, associational kind of mental activity which is the vehicle of symbolisation.[3] The resultant organisation cannot be understood in terms of the linear and logical mode of mental function, nor can it be directly translated into this function. The 'meaning', if one can use such a term, of a myth is neither single nor simple. A myth from the Australian Dreamtime, for example, may have purposes and value which are at once explanatory, informative, and moral. It might tell of aspects of the origin of the world; of the life cycle of a particular plant; and of certain relationships between human beings. No one element replaces others. Skeins of meaning are interwoven. The myth of Narcissus is not to be understood at face value as, for example, a parable on the perils of vanity.

A form of doubleness which James and Jackson saw as essential to self is understood in this book in a 'materialistic' way, that is, it is explained in terms of brain function. Until quite recently, a different explanation was dominant. The movements of psychic life were conceived as having a substance which differed from that which seemed to contain them. The psyche was spiritual and so immortal, whereas the body was made of earthly components, and mortal. The myth of the double, in Rank's view, represents the combining 'in one person the mortal and the immortal self'.[4] This is a stage in a larger collection of myths, the myth of the hero, which is a representation of the pathway towards individuation. Rank briefly reviewed stories of twins, such as Romulus and Remus, in which it was necessary for one to die in order that the other attained the status of hero. The necessary progression was from the dyad to the individual.

Since myth is not to be understood as a simple story, it must be approached in a different way. The method of Lévi-Strauss is intriguing. It depends upon the idea that 'there is no single "true" version of (the myth) of which all the others are but copies or distortions. Every version belongs to the myth'.[5] From these various versions the 'gross constituent units'[6] are extracted. These units consist of 'relations'.[7]

However, it is not the isolated units of relations which provide the key to the myth but bundles of such relations.

> The true constituent units of a myth are not the isolated relations but *bundles* of *such relations*, and it is only as bundles that these relations can be put to use and combined so as to produce meaning.[8]

This method resembles, in its fundamentals, the process of averaging which is used to extract a hidden wave-form from a mass of electrical activity recorded from the brain. A stimulus evokes an electric potential change at the cerebral cortex which is obscured by informational 'noise'. The evoked potential is not apparent in the raw electroencephalogram (EEG). However, if the stimulus is repeated, and the EEG segments which follow it are averaged, a new wave-form emerges which has a shape quite unlike the raw EEG. It is as if the raw EEG segments were recorded on celluloid and placed on top of each other so that one could peer down through the various 'versions' and discern a pattern which could not be seen before.

There are two main versions of the Narcissus myth.[9] The first comes from Ovid. The beautiful youth Narcissus was loved by the nymph Echo, who was a chatterer. She upset the goddess Hera because her conversation distracted Hera from surveillance of her husband's dalliance with the other nymphs. As a punishment, Hera deprived Echo of the capacity for speech, except for the ability to repeat what others had just said. Echo tried to make Narcissus love her but failed because, it seems, she could not converse but only echo. After he rejected her, she pined away in lonely glens until only her voice remained.

Narcissus, following this, came across a pool, clear as silver, in which he saw the form of a beautiful youth with whom he fell in love. After a while he recognised the youth as himself. He lay by the pool grieving that he was unable to possess the beautiful image. In thrall to the image, unable to leave it, he, like Echo, withered away, or alternatively, killed himself in despair.

A second version comes from Pausanias. In this story, Narcissus was grieving after the death of his twin sister, who was like him in every way, except for her sex. In attempting to find a replacement for her he used his reflected image as a means of solace. This led to the same result as that described by Ovid.

Another aspect of the myth concerns the flower which sprang from the site of Narcissus' death. It has associations with deadness. Narcissus oil is a *nar*cotic, that is, it is a sedative, or deadening potion.[10] Havelock Ellis, who Freud[11] acknowledged as the originator of the term 'narcissism', notes that Wieseler, writing in 1856, believed that the myth of Narcissus was

> nothing else than the history of the flower. Narcissus has a water-god as father because the flower grows by the water, and his mother was Liriope because the flower is a lily. The name of the personification is the name of the being's symbol, and the name indicates the effects of frost, terror, syncope, death, these effects being attributed to the action of the plant.[12]

The prominent constituent elements of the myth are the youth of Narcissus; the twin–double motif; forms of conversing–responding; deadness–

aliveness; and the reflected image. Frazer believed that this last element is
the key to the Narcissus myth.

Frazer found that the reflected image motif appears in many cultures.[13]
Almost invariably it is conceived as the 'psyche' or soul, what James called
the spiritual self.

At this point, a 'meaning' of the Narcissus myth begins to appear which
is quite different to the straightforward and literalistic explanation of Ovid,
who saw the fate of Narcissus as a punishment for his treatment of Echo.
The meaning hinges on several binary oppositions. (Such oppositions, Lévi-
Strauss considered, are characteristic of the structure of the myth.)

The most important binary opposition concerns responding–not
responding. The other who is sensed as like himself can respond effectively
either because like Echo, before the spell is cast upon her, she has a gift
of engaging others in conversation or because, like a twin, she 'knows' him.
She can respond in a way which is a re-knowing or a re-representation of
that which is most personal of his experience. When Echo loses her gift
and the twin sister dies, Narcissus is bereft. His search now is for a replacement, but his need is not fulfilled. The image which is like himself cannot
respond in the manner of resonance but only with duplications. Between
Echo and the reflecting pool, he is caught in a cage of mirrors, between an
awareness of need and a failure of its fulfilment. He is deprived of that
kind of responsiveness which is the essence of intimacy, which engenders
vitality and well-being, and which confers value. As a consequence he is as
if deadened, and withers away. He suffers a 'developmental arrest'. The
maturational movement towards the creation of the duplex self cannot go
on. The progress towards internalisation of the other as a kind of double,
who first appeared in the proto-conversation, is halted.

The story of Narcissus, in this way, is a symbolic representation, as if in
a dream, of the main thrust of the second part of the book which concerns
an interruption in the development of self either as a consequence of trauma,
which has the effect of uncoupling or dedoubling consciousness, or through
a failure of the caregiving environment to provide the emotional resonance
needed by the developing individual.[14]

The final section touches upon the therapeutic task. The goal of the therapeutic work, in essence, is redoubling. It is to revive and to foster the
developmental impetus towards the establishment of the 'duplex' self.

The development of self is related to a form of memory in which the
past can be metaphorically 'seen'. States in which the sense of self is deficient are dominated by forms of memory in which the component of
'visualisation' is lacking. The individual is unaware that he or she is remembering. In such states, the therapist has the task of taking part in the mutual
struggle to represent that which cannot be seen. His or her empathic stance
implies a position akin to an auxiliary 'I' attempting to potentiate a shared
'view' and creation of an emergent 'me'.

The heart of the matter, as in the story of Narcissus, is deadness and aliveness. Above all, the therapeutic aim is to develop a form of conversation in which 'aliveness' emerges out of deadness.[15] What is required is a form of language, resembling the artistic process as Susanne Langer defined it, which strives towards the finding of 'expressive forms to present ideas of feeling'.[16]

Notes

I The self in conversation

1 Meares (1990); Meares (1993a); Meares and Coombes (1994); Meares and Lichtenberg (1995).
2 Meares (1998).
3 Meares (1999a).
4 Paul Brown and Onno van der Hart (1998) distinguish between 'dissociation/integration' and 'repression/abreaction' models in the field of trauma. In this book the former model is elaborated so as to apply to personality disorder.
5 Stevenson and Meares (1992, 1999); Meares (1993a); Meares et al. (1999a).

2 I, me, myself

1 Jung (1953, #1165).
2 Kohut (1977, pp.310–11).
3 Harter (1983, p.226).
4 Ryle (1949, p.17).
5 Ryle (1949, p.10).
6 Ryle (1949, p.36).
7 Ryle (1949, p.40).
8 Oxford English Dictionary.
9 Ryle (1949, p.10).
10 Ayer (1936).
11 Meares (1985).
12 Russell (1921, p.18). Russell seemed to live as if split between two personal worlds. In one he was driven by a relentless quest to reduce all knowledge to logical forms. The other world, in which he was alone, was one of profound and passionate feeling. The consequence of this split between aspects of his nature was that he became, as he said, like a ghost. He wrote:

> Underlying all occupations and all pleasures I have felt since early youth the pain of solitude. I have escaped it most nearly in moments of love, yet even there, on reflection, I have found that the escape depended partly upon illusion. I have known no woman to whom the claims of intellect were as absolute as they are to me, and wherever intellect intervened, I have found that the sympathy I sought in love was apt to fail. What Spinoza calls 'the intellectual love of God' has seemed to me the best thing to live by, but I have not had even the somewhat abstract God that Spinoza allowed himself to whom to attach my intellectual love. I have loved a ghost, and in loving

a ghost my inmost self has itself become spectral. I have therefore buried it deeper and deeper beneath layers of cheerfulness, affection, and joy of life. But my most profound feelings have remained always solitary and have found in human things no companionship. The sea, the stars, the night wind in waste places, mean more to me than even the human beings I love best, and I am conscious that human affection is to me at bottom an attempt to escape from the vain search for God.

(Russell, 1967–9, II, p.38)

Russell's autobiography is a remarkable document, revealing a man who was, in his own way, heroic, but also tragic.

13 Meares (1985).
14 Damasio (1994).
15 Myers (1986, p.1).
16 E.g. Gregory (1961).
17 Ellenberger (1970).
18 Van der Kolk and van der Hart (1989).
19 Daniel Dennett (1991, 1995), however, revived his name by reference to the Baldwin effect. Noam et al. (1983) have been advocates of his significance.
20 He wrote: 'Unable to integrate traumatic memories, they seem to have lost their capacity to assimilate new experiences as well. It is . . . as if their personality has definitively stopped at certain point, and cannot enlarge anymore by the addition, or assimilation of new elements' (Janet, 1911, p.532. Cited by van der Kolk et al. 1996; my translation).
21 Bringuier (1980, p.3).
22 Van der Veer and Valsiner (1994, p.345).
23 James (1909, p.17).
24 Cited by Myers (1986, p.589).
25 James (1892, p.176).
26 Ogden (1994a, 1994b, 1995).
27 Ellenberger points out that the distinction between I, Me and Self has also been made by George Herbert Mead, who had once lived in William James' house. Ellenberger also notes that Mead's tripartite distinction resembles Janet's 'individu, personage, and moi'. Ellenberger finds it difficult to understand how Janet could have influenced Mead, and speculates that both may have come to this formulation after reading Josiah Royce and James Mark Baldwin (Ellenberger, 1970, p.406). Baldwin was a close friend of Janet (Ellenberger, 1970, p.349).
28 Lévi-Strauss (1979, pp.3–4).
29 James (1892, pp.153–4) This sentence does not appear in the 1890 volume.
30 Meares (1990, 1993a); Meares and Lichtenberg (1995).
31 James (1890, I, p.238).
32 Meares (1980, 1984).
33 The other major 'process' philosophers were Henri Bergson (1859–1941) and Alfred North Whitehead (1861–1947). Both maintained that actuality has a fluent, stream-like quality, and that ultimate reality is moving and dynamic. Whitehead, after collaborating with Bertrand Russell on their 'Principia Mathematica' (1910–13) broke away to pursue a quite different path. He moved to Harvard where he influenced such philosophers as Susanne Langer.
34 See Wittgenstein (1953).
35 Myers (1986, p.377).
36 Myers (1986, p.351).
37 'I' is not a camera. It is active. The centrality of attention in the function of 'I' is crucial. It is a cardinal feature of Freudian 'ego' (Freud, 1939, pp.145–6).

38 James (1892, p.177).
39 Baldwin (1906, pp.93–4).
40 Baldwin (1906, pp.93–4).
41 James (1890, I, p.226).
42 James (1890, I, p.297).
43 James (1890, I, p.297).
44 Galton (1883, p.45).
45 Galton (1883, p.85).
46 Galton (1883, p.86).
47 Flavell et al. (1993).

3 Conversational play

1 Wittgenstein (1953, #7).
2 Monk (1990, p.330).
3 Meares et al. (1982).
4 De Casper and Fifer (1980), Trevarthen (1987, p.364).
5 Trevarthen (1987, p.364).
6 Kaye (1982).
7 Trevarthen (1974).
8 Quoted by Wittgenstein (1953, #1).
9 Trevarthen (1987, p.365).
10 Trevarthen (1983) called it 'primary intersubjectivity'.
11 Milgrom-Friedman et al. (1980).
12 Ogden (1998).
13 Darwin (1934, p.64).
14 Langer (1941).
15 De Villiers and de Villiers (1979).
16 She based her viewpoint on the Kelloggs' (1933) data.
17 De Laguna (1927, p.307).
18 Pettito and Marentette (1991).
19 Locke and Pearson (1990).
20 Pettito and Marentette (1991).
21 Penman et al. (1981).
22 Bruner (1983, p.47).
23 Bruner (1983, p.49).
24 Bruner (1983, p.52).
25 Bruner (1983, p.60).
26 Stern (1985).
27 Kaye and Charney (1980).
28 Bruner (1983, p.62).
29 Bruner (1983, p.62).
30 Hobson (1993, p.145).
31 Uzgiris (1991, p.226).
32 Uzgiris et al. (1989) studied matching of each other's acts in face-to-face engagement between mothers and their babies at different times during the first year of life. They found that imitation was rare in the younger babies. The replication of certain of the mother's facial expressions (e.g. tongue protrusion) demonstrated by Meltzoff and Moore (1977) may not indicate true imitation, which involves two models, but a form of echopraxia.
33 Winnicott (1960).
34 Baldwin (1895, p.1).

35 See Meares and Lichtenberg (1995) for an outline of the argument of the German writer Friedrich Schiller (1759–1805).
36 Huizinga (1938).
37 Baldwin (1906, p.128).
38 Baldwin (1906, p.128).
39 Brandchaft (1993).
40 Sroufe and Wunsch (1972).

4 Two forms of human conversation

1 Bruner (1983).
2 Piaget (1951).
3 Piaget (1926, p.243).
4 In that the other in this situation is an extension of the child's embryonic self, he or she is a 'selfobject' as Kohut conceived it (eg. 1971, p.xiv). Baldwin anticipated this idea in remarking of the child that 'to be separated from his mother is to lose part of himself, as much so as to be separated from a hand or foot' (1895, pp.338–9). However, Kohut went beyond Baldwin in pointing out that the caregiver has a *responsibility* to behave, at least for significant periods, in the manner implied by this metaphoric limb.

   However, the selfobject concept is, to some extent, controversial, understood by different authorities in different ways (Meares, 1993a, pp.40–2). Kohut himself, in later definitions of the term, described behaviour which is essentially different from the caregiver in Piaget's 'life of union'. Kohut wrote that: 'The patient feels the analyst is substituting for his or her psychic structure' . . . 'as the supplier of his self-esteem, as the integrator of his ambitions, as the concretely present idealised power that dispenses approval and other forms of narcissistic sustenance' (Kohut, 1977, p.16).

   Kohut's final and succinct definition of selfobject is 'that dimension of our experience of another person that relates to this person's functions in shoring up our self' (Kohut, 1984, p.49).

   This definition describes a potential pathology. It might simply refer to an audience. The difference between this concept and that of the 'life of union' is extremely important but its elaboration is beyond the scope of this discussion. Although I consider Kohut's selfobject is the most important contribution to psychoanalytic theory in the last thirty years (see Meares, 1996a, 1996b) the ambiguities of the term have caused me generally to prefer expressions such as 'pre-intimate relatedness' in order to make clear my own meaning and in order to fit with the main theme of the book.
5 A particular aspect of this illusory personage is given value and materialised as a teddy bear, doll, or similar object which is a focus of affectional feeling – Winnicott's transitional object. In his seminal description (1953) of this special possession, Winnicott conceived the teddy bear, or whatever it is, as symbolising the breast (or the mother). In the conception put forward here, the 'symbolisation' is dual, involving both the caregiver, experienced in a special way, and a projection of self. Although the transitional object is 'not-me' it is also 'me'.
6 Kohlberg et al. (1968, p.695).
7 Watkins (1986, p.50) citing Shields (1979).
8 James (1890, I, p.226).
9 Baldwin (1906, p.124).
10 Baldwin (1906, p.112).
11 Baldwin (1906, p.112).

12 Baldwin (1906, p.113).
13 Baldwin (1906, p.116).
14 James (1890, I, p.223).
15 Wood Jones (1924, p.118).
16 A study of the monologues uttered before sleep by a two-year-old in her crib showed more of the social or linear form of speech than would be predicted from Vygotsky's description of 'private speech' (Nelson, 1989). It may be that crib speech differs from the speech which accompanies symbolic play. In the former case the child is often reviewing events of the day; in the latter setting, the child is telling an *imaginary* story with the aid of objects which help to portray it.
17 Piaget (1926, p.43). Jung used the same term in his essay distinguishing between two types of thinking (Jung, 1912). In this essay Jung refers to Baldwin, James and Janet. One wonders if the term originally comes from Janet, who had influenced Piaget.
    Freud (1911) also distinguished between two kinds of thinking. However, his primary process is not equivalent to the non-linear form of mental activity described here. First, he conceived primary process as relatively immature and thus, implicitly, inferior to secondary process. Second, since primary process is directed towards a goal, albeit one disguised by the processes of condensation and displacement, it is essentially linear (Meares, 1977c).
18 Vygotsky (1962, p.149).
19 Piaget(1926, p.40).
20 Watkins (1986, pp.53–4) is critical of Vygotsky's view that the principal purpose of this form of language is self-regulatory. She is also critical of his notion that the dialogue is between the child and a projected aspect of his or her self. She considers that it is with an imaginary other. My view, as previously stated, is that the conversation is with a dual imaginary person deriving from *both* self and other.
    The notion of the dialogic self, implicit in Watkins' thesis, is echoed in the work of Hermans (e.g. Hermans et al., 1992; Hermans and Hermans-Jansen, 1995).
21 Meares (1990, 1993a).
22 Meares and Orlay (1988). A disruption of the sense of privacy is a cardinal feature of disorders of self (e.g. Meares, 1994).
23 Put in different words, the child discerns a 'theory of mind' (Perner et al., 1987; Gopnik and Astington, 1988; Wellman, 1990; Whiten, 1991; Hobson, 1993). Fonagy and Target call this process 'mentalisation'. They point out that it depends upon the establishment of secure attachment (Fonagy and Target, 1997; Fonagy 1998). The feeling of safety is necessary to the creation of the embryonic self.
24 Mitchell (1988).
25 Van der Veer and Valsiner (1994, p.354).
26 This developmental background is necessary to the understanding of Hobson's highly condensed statement: 'I can only find myself in and between me and my fellows in human conversation' (Hobson, 1985, p.135).
27 Oxford English Dictionary.
28 Recent brain imaging studies demonstrate an extraordinary fragmentation of brain function. This has been most clearly displayed in the visual system. Whereas we suppose that the vision of a particular object enters us all in one piece, like taking a photograph, the actual situation is quite different. Rather, multiple aspects of the image are processed independently (Kosslyn, 1988). The processing of the various pieces of information relating to an image takes place

at a number of levels and scales. At a relatively microscopic level, in the prefrontal cortex, the identity of the object is processed separately from the space in which it is located (Wilson et al., 1993). Moreover, the colour, the depth, and the movement of the object are all treated separately (Livingstone and Hubel, 1988) in multiple processing streams (de Yoe et al., 1994). At a finer level, one set of neurons is dedicated to orange-red colours, another to objects with high-contrast diagonal left to right (Horgan, 1993). The bits of the image are then brought together to create the perception of a single object. The brain function which 'binds' together the disconnected bits of the image to be brought together is unknown.

A well-known hypothesis, developed by Wolf Singer (see references in Roelfsema et al., 1997) and made well known by Crick and Koch (1990) concerns the potentially integrating effect of electric patterning in the brain which oscillates at a 40Hz frequency.

Integration is also likely to involve a synchrony of activation in widely dispersed brain sites contributing to their co-ordination (e.g. Roelfsema et al., 1997).

Our group has shown that the pattern of activity, which reaches a maximum at about 300 milliseconds following the presentation of a stimulus, is deficient in people suffering from borderline personality disorder. These people characteristically exhibit a disconnectedness between the elements of psychic life (Meares et al., 1999c).

'Binding' is likely to occur at several levels and scales, as previously remarked. What is suggested here is that the mental activity underpinning play may have a role in the integration necessary at higher levels than that occurring at the 300 millisecond level. Such higher scale integration is necessary for the drawing together of large and complex organisations of experience.

29 Meares (1977, pp.93–102); Meares and Lichtenberg (1995).
30 Bower (1974).
31 The fragmentation of the child's existence is briefly reviewed in Meares (1993a, pp.47–58).
32 Piaget (1926, p.74).
33 Cited by Piaget (1929, p.149).
34 Bruner (1990). There is a growing interest in the relationships between narrative, self and psychotherapy. White and Epston (1990) see psychotherapy as the 'restorying' of unassimilated experience. McLeod (1997) has recently reviewed this field of interest. The best known psychoanalytic contributors to it are Spence (1982) and Schafer (1992).
35 Janet described a total of 591 patients and reported a traumatic origin of their psychopathology in 257 (Croq and le Verbizier, 1989).
36 Janet (1901, p.34).
37 Janet (1901, p.222).
38 Janet (1901, p.77).
39 Janet (1901, p.211).
40 Bruner (1986).
41 Amsterdam (1972); Lewis and Brooks-Gunn (1979).
42 Baldwin (1906, p.244).
43 James (1909, pp.35–6).
44 Holmes (1996).
45 James (1909, p.31).
46 Murray (1938, p.31) cited by Bowlby (1971, p.280).
47 Meares and Anderson (1993).
48 Bergson (1911, pp.13–14).
49 Wittgenstein (1922).

50 Wittgenstein (1953, p.viii).
51 Using Wittgenstein's work as a background, Hobson develops this idea from the therapeutic point of view, seeing language games as 'forms of life' 'akin to some existentialist notions such as modes of 'being-in-the-world' or 'being-with-others' (Hobson, 1985, p.20). The term language-game, he notes, refers 'to the whole act, consisting of language and the actions into which it is woven' (p.47).
52 An experimental study of group function, conducted on Hobson's Unit in London, suggested that a linear interpretive style of therapeutic intervention was unlikely to be effective. Rather, a movement towards the construction of a group 'story' seemed to offer the hope of benefit (Meares, 1973).

   Hobson and I (Meares and Hobson, 1977) suggested that therapeutic language of a logical, linear kind is likely to be alienating, causing a sense of disconnectedness from the patient, who needs to move into a more associative mode of mental function. A different kind of therapeutic language is required.

   In recent years Thomas Ogden has been exploring the nature of this requisite language. His focus is upon the different languages of 'deadness' and 'aliveness'. Dead therapeutic language has the staleness of the stereotypic intervention of a particular theoretical ideology. Put another way, it is a language of alienation, since it uses the words of someone else. A language of aliveness, although apparently 'ordinary', will have something of the effect of poetic expression. Ogden uses Robert Frost as a model (Ogden, 1997a, 1997b, 1997c, 1998, 1999).
53 Keats (1821); Meares (1981).

5 Memory

1 See conversation reported in Meares (1993a, pp.56–7).
2 Hering has an interesting connection with the origins of psychoanalysis. His name is still remembered as the original descriptor of the Hering–Breuer reflex, the nervous control of respiration. His partner in this discovery was a medical student, Josef Breuer, who was to become more famous as the collaborator with Freud in producing 'Studies in Hysteria' in 1895. It seems likely that Breuer had something to do with Hering inviting the young Freud, in 1884, to join him as his assistant in Prague (Jones, 1953, I, p.244). It also seems likely that Freud was influenced by Hering's ideas. They must have been made familiar to him by Joseph Breuer, who became his intimate friend, when they both worked in the laboratories of Ernst Brücke, the Professor of Physiology in Vienna from 1849 to 1891 (Jones, 1953, I, p.183).

   Freud remarked that Brücke was 'the greatest authority who affected me more than any other in my whole life' (Jones, 1953, I, p.31). He was presumably the inspiration behind Freud's pioneering attempt to create a neural basis of mind (Freud, 1895).
3 Freud (1926, p.205).
4 Butler (1880, pp.115–16).
5 Galton (1883, p.187).
6 Galton (1883, p.187).
7 Galton (1883, pp.192–3).
8 Galton (1883, p.187).
9 Galton (1883, p.202).
10 Galton (1883, pp.203–4).

11 Galton (1883, pp.203–4). Galton's ideas had some influence on early psycho-analytic thought. Stimulated by Galton (Jung, 1905–41, #730), Wilhelm Wundt introduced the word association test into German psychology in 1883 (Jung, 1905–41, #868). Jung, for a time, used this means of investigating psychic life. Wundt's influence was enormous. He was initially assistant to Helmholz, whose school made a profound impression upon Freud (Jones, 1953, I, p.45). Like Freud, Wundt attempted to develop a 'physiological psychology'. Freud's method of free-association resembles Galton's associative explorations of which Freud may have been aware (Zilboorg, 1952, p.492).

12 This organisation approximates to 'self-representation' (Hartmann, 1950). Since memories are dependent upon protein changes in cells (Hyden, 1973; Davis and Squire, 1984), 'self-representation' might be conceived as a structure in contrast to the process nature of self. However, the substantiality of the intra-neuronal protein is by no means fixed, but a part of a dynamic metabolism (Rose, 1993, pp.182–9).

13 James (1890, I, pp.648–9).

14 Jackson (1931–2, II, p.361).

15 James (1890, II, p.650).

16 Tulving (1972, 1983).

17 Baddeley et al. (1984).

18 Crovitz (1970). Like Galton, Crovitz uses cue words to elicit episodic memo-ries (e.g. Crovitz and Schiffman, 1974; Crovitz and Harvey, 1979), so that now the method is often called the Galton–Crovitz test. Robinson (1976) is another to have employed the Galton approach.

19 Tulving (1993a).

20 Cohen and Squire (1980).

21 Schacter (1992).

22 Gazzaniga (1989).

23 Talland (1965).

24 Baddeley (1990, p.208).

25 Personal communication. This story might be seen as illustrating the opera-tion of 'implicit' memory (see next section of chapter).

26 Kail (1984); Nelson (1984).

27 Carpenter (1974).

28 MacFarlane (1975).

29 De Casper and Fifer (1980).

30 Tulving and Schacter (1990); Schacter (1992).

31 Mandler (1984); Ashmead and Perlmutter (1980).

32 Reviewed by Fivush and Hudson (1990).

33 Nelson (1989).

34 Dudycha and Dudycha (1941); Pillemer and White (1989).

35 Nelson (1992). Perner and Ruffmann (1995) point out that episodic memory, as defined by Tulving, requires 'the autonoetic consciousness of having *experienced remembered* events'. They produce evidence suggesting that children cannot encode events as experienced before the age of about four to five years. At this point the child discovers the concept of 'innerness' (Meares and Orlay, 1988).

36 Hudson and Nelson (1986).

37 Nelson (1978); Nelson and Gruendel (1981).

38 Bartlett (1932, p.295); Bartlett cites Halbwachs (1925) 'Les Cadres Sociaux de la Mémoire'.

39 Edelman (1992). This stage of the development of the capacity for reflection is crucial but it is not an end point. The 'decentration' which it represents is presumably, at least for some people, a process which goes on throughout life.

Important progressions occur during the period between 7 and 11 years and at adolescence (Inhelder and Piaget, 1958).

40 Humphrey (1992), arguing in a different way, has also suggested that the emergence of 'mind' depends upon the emergence of such a feedback loop.

41 This maturation is likely to involve the pre-frontal cortex, particularly the orbito-frontal cortex (Schore, 1994). Pre-frontal function is essential to episodic memory (Shallice et al., 1994; Tulving et al., 1994).

Wheeler et al. (1997) argue that frontal function is not only necessary to this memory but also to autonoetic consciousness, i.e. the stream of consciousness.

42 Vygotsky and Luria (1994).

6 Uncoupled consciousness

1 Janet called this sequestered form of psychic life a 'subconscious fixed idea'. Jung, who worked with Janet during the winter of 1902–3, elaborated Janet's concept in his formulation of the 'complex'.

2 In a personal communication Paul Brown points out that Janet 'used the term désagrégation psychologique in "L'Automatisme Psychologique" (1889) but by 1898 in "Les Névroses et idées fixes" (and thereafter), used the term dissociation almost exclusively'.

3 The term 'splitting' seems to have been first used by Otto Rank in 1909 in *The Myth of the Birth of the Hero* (see Rank, 1914, p.86).

4 Janet (1907, p.172).

5 See Ellenberger (1970).

6 An example of the misunderstanding and neglect is the view that dissociation is merely an alternate term for repression (e.g. Rycroft, 1987, pp.197–8). The distinction between dissociation and repression is often conceived as the difference between 'vertical' and 'horizontal splitting', respectively.

7 Waller et al. (1994).

8 Janet (1907, pp.114–16).

9 Holen (1993); Cardeña and Spiegel (1993); Koopman et al., (1994); Shalev et al. (1996).

10 E.g. Chu and Dill (1990).

11 Janet (1907, pp.51–2).

12 Jackson (1931–2, II, p.96).

13 Myers (1986).

14 Janet (1907, p.3).

15 Ellenberger (1970, p.403).

16 Jackson (1931–2, II, p.4).

17 Jackson (1931–2, II, p.9).

18 Jackson (1931–2, II, p.42). This conception approximates to a view of the brain–mind relationship which is currently influential in the field of neuroscience. Nancy Andreasen summarised the position: 'The mind is the expression of the brain and these two are separable for purposes of analysis and discussion but inseparable in actuality. That is, mental phenomena arise from the brain, but mental experience also affects the brain' (Andreasen, 1997).

19 Freud (1891, pp.206–8).

20 Jackson (1931–2, II, p.85).

21 Jackson (1931–2, II, p.93).

22 Jackson (1931–2, II, p.96).

23 Jackson (1931–2, II, p.42).

24 Jackson (1931–2, II, p.82).

25 Jackson (1931–2, II, p.41).
26 Freud (1891, p.208).
27 Jackson (1931–2, II, p.82).
28 Jackson (1931–2, II, p.98).
29 Jackson (1931–2, II, p.82). This is something of a joke since Ribot was greatly influenced by Jacksonian ideas. Jackson is using Ribot's summary of his own ideas as support for his system. Ribot was, in Ellenberger's view, Janet's main mentor.
30 Jackson (1931–2, II, p.399).
31 Jackson (1931–2, II, p.84).
32 Damasio (1994, p.243).
33 Damasio (1994, p.225).
34 Damasio (1994, p.240).
35 Jackson (1931–2, II, pp.395–6).
36 Jackson (1931–2, II, p.4).
37 Jackson (1931–2, II, p.11).
38 Jackson (1931–2, II, p.13).
39 Jackson (1931–2, I, pp.379, 390).
40 Janet (1907, p.58). Schenk and Bear (1981) reported that 33 per cent of 40 patients with temporal lobe epilepsy showed some dissociative phenomena. The dissociative phenomena occurred in the post-ictal period.
41 Terr (1993, pp.29, 201).
42 Sullivan (1953, p.314).
43 Sullivan (1953, p.152).
44 Jackson (1931–2, I, pp.404–5).
45 Van der Hart and Nijenhuis (1995); Scheflen and Brown (1996); Elliott (1997); van der Hart et al. (1999).
46 Schacter et al. (1982); Schacter (1996).
47 Berrington et al. (1956).
48 E.g. Chu and Dill (1990).
49 Terr (1988, p.103).
50 Van der Kolk (1996, p.287).
51 Janet (1901, p.488).
52 Lewis (1992).
53 Freud (1914, p.150).
54 Cited by van der Kolk et al. (1996, p.53). My translation.

7 Disrupted maturation: the dissolution hypothesis

1 Herman et al. (1989); Zanarini et al. (1989); Ludolph et al. (1990).
2 Golomb et al. (1994).
3 Waller et al. (1994) identified four cardinal features of dissociation (i) disturbances in memory; (ii) depersonalisation/derealisation; (iii) discontinuity of personal existence; (iv) hallucinatory phenomena.
4 Claparède (1911, p.67).
5 Meares (1980).
6 Jackson (1931–2, II, p.129).
7 Meares and Grose (1978).
8 Meares (1984).
9 Hadamard (1945).
10 West (1996, p.52).
11 West (1996, pp.52–3).

12 Jackson wrote 'The view I take is that the sudden and excessive discharge in an epileptic paroxysm produces an exhaustion of nerve-tracts which have been travelled by excessive current in that paroxysm' (1931–2, II, p.55). After a slight attack, 'the patient declares himself to be "knocked up"' (1931–2, II, p.60), i.e. very fatigued. Exhaustion is central not only to Jackson's understanding of automatisms but also to that of Pierre Janet, who remains the outstanding authority on the subject of automatisms which are the consequence of psychological trauma (Janet, 1907, p.333).

13 Again this was anticipated by James. Quoting Mill, he wrote that: 'if the constitution of consciousness were that of a string of bead-like associations, "we could never have any knowledge except that of the present instant" . . . "each of these momentary states would be our whole being" (James, 1890, I, pp.605–6). We live in the illusion of what James called the 'specious present'. The notion of a personal time which differed from scientific time was also proposed by Bergson, whose conception of 'durée' was widely influential before the positivist era.

14 Garbutt (1997).

15 Janet (1907).

16 Goldman-Rakic (1995, p.57).

17 Baddeley (1984).

18 Dias et al. (1996).

19 Ellenberger (1970, p.376).

20 Cited by Ellenberger (1970, p.376).

21 Cited by Ellenberger (1970, p.376). It is of interest that Ellenberger considers that the dissolution theory of Jackson resembles 'Janet's general theory of the désagrégations psychologiques' (Ellenberger, 1970, p.360).

22 Those who have been traumatised in childhood show an impairment of autobiographical memory (Parks and Balon, 1995). Williams and his colleagues studied people who have attempted suicide. This group of individuals typically include those with personality disorders. However, Williams and his colleagues do not investigate this aspect of diagnosis. Their diagnostic procedure included only measures of depression. Nevertheless, this study produced interesting and suggestive data. Their patients tended to produce generic rather than specific autobiographical memories (Evans et al., 1992). The former, as outlined in Chapter 5, tend to develop earlier than the latter. Kuyken and Brewin (1995) also showed that depressed women who had been abused in childhood had autobiographical memories of a more generic kind than depressed women who had not been abused. These findings, taken together, tend to support the dissolution hypothesis.

23 The syndrome of hysteria was officially discarded as a diagnostic entity in 1980. It was broken up into its constituent parts. They included a severe disruption of personality development (borderline personality); a pronounced tendency to complain of, and seek medical attention for, bodily complaints for which, in many cases, no cause could be found (somatisation disorder); and various dissociative and conversion disorders. The diagnostic catalogue of 1980 (DSM-III) implied these were distinct diagnostic entities. Although this is sometimes the case, the distinctions are often artificial. There is considerable overlapping (Herman, 1994, pp.123–7). This is now implicitly acknowledged in a more recent diagnostic manual (DSM-IV) in which dissociative states are among the diagnostic criteria for borderline personality and conversion disorders are necessary to the diagnosis of somatisation disorder. There is a relationship between dissociative states and somatisation (Saxe et al., 1994; Walker et al., 1992) and also a relationship between somatisation, dissociative states, and abuse (Pribor et al., 1993; Maynes and Feinauer, 1994). There is an association between

somatisation disorder and Cluster B personality disorder (Lillienfield et al., 1986), the various categories of which overlap with borderline personality disorder (Stone, 1994). Like borderline personality disorder those with somatisation disorder (Morrison, 1989) and severe dissociative states (Putnam et al., 1986; Coons et al., 1988; Ross et al., 1989; Ross et al., 1991; Chu and Dill, 1990) have a childhood history typically scarred by sexual and/or physical abuse.

24 Janet (1901, p.22).

25 Meares and Horvath (1972). Horvath et al. (1980). Habituation failure could not be explained in terms of arousal since these patients were significantly less aroused than those with anxiety disorders who did not show habituation failure, merely slowing.

26 Meares et al. (1999).

27 This group of patients also shows an impairment of the fine tuning of attention. People with somatisation disorder respond more than controls to irrelevant stimuli, but less than the undamaged group when confronted with meaningful stimuli (James et al., 1989a; James et al., 1989b). An animal model for these deficits is given by Zhang et al. (1997).

Cortico-fugal tracts having a modifying effect on attention are found, as higher order mechanisms, in other species whose sensory capabilities are superior to humans. Bats, for example, hunt insects by means of radar. They emit a particular frequency (61KHz) and then detect its reflection by means of nerve cells which are tuned to this frequency for fine frequency analysis. The corticofugal system mediates a positive feedback which sharpens and adjusts the tuning of neurons at earlier stages in the auditory processing pathway. When the cortico-fugal system is lost the animal still hears, but the fine tuning is lost (Zhang et al., 1997). Analogous effects are found in attentional processes of humans who have been subjected to trauma (McFarlane et al., 1993).

28 James et al. (1990).

29 Meares (1997).

30 Basing his conclusion on an extensive review, Schore (1994) considers that affect regulation depends upon the right orbito-frontal cortex. This is consistent with the recent findings of Goyer et al. (1994) who used positron-emission tomography to examine rates of cerebral glucose metabolism in 17 patients with various personality disorders. They showed a significant inverse correlation between a life history of impulsive aggressiveness and activity in the frontal region.

31 Jackson (1931–2, II, p.25).

32 McGuire et al. (1996) conducted brain imaging studies in which subjects first read aloud and then, in a second test, read aloud but heard the words spoken by someone else, transmitted through earphones. In the second situation, when the words heard were not in their own voice, there was bilateral activation of parts of the temporal cortex. In another study with schizophrenic subjects who suffered hallucinosis, the experimental situation was repeated. When the words they heard were not spoken in their own voice, there was *no* activation in the temporal cortex. Frith and his colleagues concluded that the temporal cortex formed part of a system of self monitoring, tracking, and evaluating, which was lost in those who suffered hallucinosis.

33 Luria (1973, p.24).

34 Kolb and Wishaw (1990, p.338).

35 Janet argued against such a distinction. He wrote:

Psychology is not independent of physiology, but it demands a more delicate and more profound physiology than that of digestion or of respiration.

The study of nervous and mental diseases, far from being able to do without physiological and medical information, will more and more demand a much more thorough physiology and medicine. The treatment of these diseases, far from being possible after brief medical study, will fall to the most accomplished clinician and will require the use of all forms of examination and all the most delicate methods.

(Janet, 1924, p.302)

36 Herman (1992) considers that borderline personality disorder can be seen as a variant of 'complex post-traumatic stress disorder' (p.126). The authors in a volume edited by Zanarini (1997) warn that there is not a simple relationship between a history of sexual abuse and the borderline condition. Other possible aetiological factors, such as family environment and neurological abnormality, must be taken into account in addition to the effect of abuse.
37 The notion of a 'cascade' implies that the emergence of self as the stream of consciousness involves more than the capacity for introspection. See also Fonagy and Target (1997, pp.680–1) who distinguish between reflective function and self-reflection.
38 The hypothesis is outlined in somewhat greater detail in Meares et al. (1999b).
39 Schore (1996).

8   A theory of value

1 James (1892, pp.153–4).
2 James (1890, I, pp.297).
3 Meares (1976).
4 James (1902, p.478).
5 Jung (1948, #61).
6 Jung (1936, #23).
7 Meares (1977a, pp.52–6; 1993a, pp.59–73).
8 Passmore (1968, p.606).
9 Ayer (1936).
10 Urban (1909, p.53).
11 Urban (1909, p.53).
12 Urban (1909, p.23).
13 Urban (1909, p.38).
14 Urban (1909, p.39).
15 Urban (1909, p.39).
16 Urban (1909, pp.36–7).
17 Urban (1909, p.40).
18 Perry (1926).
19 Dewey (1939).
20 Urban (1909, p.426).
21 Russell (1918, p.109).
22 Wittgenstein (1953, #527).
23 Wittgenstein (1953, #544).
24 Heidegger (1962, p.178).
25 Damasio (1999) gives this idea a neurophysiological basis.
26 Urban (1909, p.2).
27 Meares (1977a, pp.52–6; 1993a, pp.59–73).
28 Sroufe and Wunsch (1972).
29 Russell (1967–9, I, p.209).
30 Lewis et al. (1990); Allessandri et al. (1990).

31 Kagan (1981, p.57).
32 Lewis (1992, p.94).
33 Partridge (1983).
34 Oxford English Dictionary.
35 Durkheim (1915).
36 Balint (1963).
37 Balint (1987).
38 Winnicott (1965, 1971).
39 Balint (1968).
40 Kohut (1971, 1977, 1984).
41 Kohut (e.g. 1977, p.5).
42 Sullivan (1953, p.214).
43 Sullivan (1953, pp.203–16).
44 Lee et al. (1995).
45 Suttie (1935, p.19).
46 Suttie (1935, pp.86–100).
47 Meares (1976).
48 Meares (1993a, pp.17–18).
49 Brandchaft (1993).
50 Meares and Hobson (1977).
51 Hobson (1985).

9 Feeling creates reality

1 Her wandering might be understood as a minor fugue state in which auto-biographical and episodic memory may be lost while semantic memory remains (see Schacter, 1996, for a very useful and authoritative summary of memory disturbance in this and other conditions).
2 Anthony (1973).
3 Terr (1981; 1983).
4 Terr (1993, p.28).
5 Isaacs (1952, p.78).
6 James (1902, p.479n).
7 Moscovitch (1995, p.229).
8 Moscovitch (1995, p.233).
9 Moscovitch (1995, p.230).
10 Moscovitch (1995, pp.230–5).
11 Moscovitch (1995, p.247).
12 Spiegel (1995).
13 Terr (1993, p.226).
14 Tulving (1993b).
15 Tulving (1993b).
16 The Cognitive Analytic Therapy of Ryle (1990) as I understand it, approaches these attributions and their consequences in action.
17 Klein (1975).
18 Partridge (1983).
19 Mauss (1970, p.1).
20 Mauss (1970, p.58).
21 Mauss (1970, p.41).
22 Nin (1966, p.243).
23 Nin (1966, p.317).
24 Nin (1969, p.249).
25 Nin (1969, p.11).

26 Meares (1995).

10 Malignant internalisation

1 The authoritative definitions of Laplanche and Pontalis (1973) make clear the technical difference between these terms.

Identification is 'the psychological process whereby the subject assimilates an aspect, property, or attribute of the other and is transformed, wholly or partially, after the model the other provides. It is by means of a series of identifications that the personality is constituted and specified' (p.205). However, identification refers to a person whereas internalisation refers to intersubjective relations (p.208). Since this larger compass must also include the people in this relationship, I prefer the term 'internalisation'.

2 The mother's imitative behaviour is mentioned by Papousek and Papousek (1977) and Trevarthen (1977). It has been specifically examined by Uzgiris et al. (1989).

3 Winnicott (1967) wrote of the mother's face as a mirror.

4 Meltzoff and Moore (1977).

5 Piaget (1951).

6 Uzgiris (1991).

7 Baldwin (1906, p.87).

8 Baldwin (1895, p.338).

9 Genet (1967, p.150).

10 The word 'reversal' is an attempt to capture a main feature of the phenomenon, in which the subject's state reverberates between the two poles of the traumatic experience (Meares, 1993a, pp.87–100; Meares, 1993b). The term is derived from Freud's notion of 'reversal into the opposite' (Freud, 1915a, pp.126, 127). His idea is elaborated by Laplanche and Pontalis (1973, p.399). The reverberations of role are often between activity and passivity, between 'sadism' and 'masochism'. The 'sado-masochistic' oscillation described by Kernberg (1968), and others, makes clear the states of hatred, revenge, fear and sense of cruelty which are found within the traumatic complex.

11 See Chapter 7.

12 Isaacs (1952, pp.93–4).

13 James (1890, II, p.285).

14 James (1890, II, p.409).

15 Klein (1975, p.393).

16 Grosskurth (1986, p.402).

17 Meares (1958).

18 See e.g. Middleton and Butler (1998).

19 This case illustrates some of the principles underlying a therapeutic approach to the traumatic system. The therapist avoided making any interpretations derived from prior theory. Although, as he said, many interpretations of the classical kind were obvious to him, he did not make them. Instead, his remarks were directed towards gaining or conveying an understanding of his patient's immediate experience. The treatment was conducted in a way which encouraged symbolic activity. In papers published in the *Lancet* (Meares, 1961, 1962), he discussed the basis of his patient's recovery, which could not be explained in terms of orthodox theory. The patient had not recovered by means of gaining 'insight' into unconscious mental states. He speculated that the most important therapeutic factor was the physician's understanding of his or her patient.

11 The evocative context

1 I am grateful to Professor Pierre Beumont for pointing out this passage to me.
2 Proust (1951, pp.208–9).
3 Proust (1951, p.210).
4 Proust (1951, p.211).
5 Freud (1915b, p.55).
6 Daniel Schacter (1996, pp.62–4) in a short essay on 'cue- dependent memory' considers that Endel Tulving has contributed most to the understanding of retrieval of memories. He introduced what he called the 'encoding specificity principle' (Tulving and Thompson, 1973; Tulving, 1983).

    Retrieval of memories depends not only on cues, but also on one's particular 'state' or mood when experiencing the event to be remembered. For a review of 'state-dependent learning' which focuses on the effect of intoxication, see Eich (1989). The event, if experienced during intoxication, tends to be better remembered in a similar state. Mood-congruent and mood-dependent memory is reviewed by Bower (1992).
7 Cowan (1992, pp.65–9).
8 Cowan (1992, p.66).
9 Terr (1993, pp.97–8, 137–8).
10 Kohut (1971, pp.286–7).
11 Hobson (1985, p.161) refers to Blake: 'Art and Science cannot exist but in minutely organised particulars' (Jerusalem, III, 55: 60–8).
12 Jackson (1931–2, II, p.384).
13 Brandchaft (1993, p.216).
14 Brandchaft (1993, p.215).
15 Brandchaft (1993, p.215).
16 Brandchaft and Stolorow (1990, p.108).
17 Meares (1995).

12 Priming and projective identification: on being constructed

1 Monk (1991, p.39).
2 Monk (1991, p.64).
3 Monk (1991, p.53).
4 Monk (1991, p.73).
5 Monk (1991, p.65).
6 Monk (1991, p.73).
7 Monk (1991, p.53).
8 Monk (1991, p.65).
9 Tulving (1972, 1983).
10 Tulving (1985).
11 Tulving and Schacter (1990).
12 Freud (1896, p.173).
13 Graf and Schacter (1985).
14 Schacter (1996, p.161).
15 De Casper and Fifer (1980).
16 Carpenter (1974).
17 MacFarlane (1975).
18 Tulving and Schacter (1990).
19 Rovée-Collier (1993).
20 Tulving and Schacter (1990).
21 Swartz et al. (1980).

22 Démonet et al. (1992); Peterson et al. (1990).
23 Shallice et al. (1994); Tulving et al. (1994).
24 Bechara et al. (1995).
25 Schacter et al. (1996).
26 Tulving and Schacter (1990).
27 Schacter (1991).
28 Bargh and Pietromonaco (1982).
29 Morris et al. (1998).
30 Study of the role of the amygdala in emotional learning has gained impetus from the work of Le Doux (1996).
31 Ladavas et al. (1993).
32 Fried et al. (1997).
33 E.g. Rugg et al. (1998).
34 Kihlstrom et al. (1990).
35 Tulving and Schacter (1990).
36 Klein (1946).
37 See Ogden (1994b, p.97). Ogden notes that the term projective identification refers to a 'wide range of psychological–interpersonal events. They include the earliest form of mother–infant communication (Bion, 1962), fantasied coercive incursions into and occupation of the personality of another person, schizophrenic confusional states (Rosenfeld, 1952), and healthy "empathic sharing" (Pick, 1985, p.45)' (Ogden, 1994b, p.98). Laplanche and Pontalis define it as both an attack and a defence (Laplanche and Pontalis, 1973, p.356).
    Investigations of the phenomenon, other than those already mentioned, include those of Malin and Grotstein (1966), Ogden (1979, 1982, 1990, 1997a), Meissner (1980), Grotstein (1981), Kernberg (1987), Joseph (1987), and Sandler (1987, 1993).
38 Segal (1973, p.27).
39 Ogden (1990, p.151).
40 Bion (1955).
41 Ogden (1994b, pp.97–106).
42 Meares (1995).
43 Meares (1998).
44 Meares (1998).
45 Gabbard (1995).
46 Mitchell (1988, p.293).
47 The 'isolated mind' is an expression used by Stolorow (1997) and Stolorow and Atwood (1992, pp.7–28; 1997) to illustrate the essence of the older one-person psychology. It arises out of their exploration and elaboration of the intersubjective approach (Atwood and Stolorow, 1984; Stolorow et al. 1987).
48 E.g. Renik (1993).
49 Schwaber (1998).
50 Levenson (1972, p.221).
51 Freud (1920–2, p.239).
52 Morris et al. (1988).
53 Meares and Hobson (1977).
54 Meares (1977, 1986, 1990, 1993a).
55 Meares (1973, 1986, 1993a, 1997).

13 Satellites of trauma

1 James (1902, p.235).
2 These systems are driven by what Anna Ornstein (1974) has called 'a dread to repeat'.
3 Meares (1993a, pp.119–24).
4 Kohut (1971, p. 198).
5 Meares and Anderson (1993).
6 Laing (1959, pp.94–105).
7 Laing (1959, p.98).
8 Laing (1959, p.96).
9 Brandchaft (2000).
10 Meares and Hobson (1977); Meares (1986).
11 Neither Laing (1959) nor Winnicott (1960), in their pioneering descriptions of system of the compliant false self, show that this motivation is primary and the basis of the system. Neither account mentions anxiety. Both suggest that the purpose of the false self system is to hide the 'true self' (Winnicott, 1960, p.152). I argue that this is not the case (Meares, 1993a, pp.119–24). The latter motivation is related to the system of avoidance which is made up of a quite different series of behaviours, such as stubbornness, which have the characteristic of non-compliance. It is analogous to a mask. Nevertheless both 'mask-like' and 'compliant' systems often co-exist.
12 Winnicott (1960).
13 Middleton and Butler (1998).
14 Kohut (1971, p.198).
15 Meares (1992).
16 Perverse sexual activity is a prominent example, as Arnold Goldberg has recently argued (1995). Goldberg points out the therapist must imaginatively 'enter into' this system in order to re-establish the sense of connectedness which is necessary to beneficial change. In many cases, in his experience, the creation of such a form of relatedness will cause the salience of the perverse sexual activity to diminish markedly without any direct focus on the behaviour itself (personal communication).

14 Transforming the chronicle

1 Most notably Lacan (Lemaire, 1977, p.176).
2 Keller (1936).
3 Janet wrote of the aetiological significance of repeated apparently small or innocuous events, of 'a host of slight repeated fatigues or, even little emotions, each one insignificant in itself' (Janet, 1924, p.275). I am indebted to Dr Jeff Yates, who has been investigating Janet's concept of exhaustion, for this reference.
4 Garbutt (1997). These findings are cited in Meares (1998).
5 Balint (1963).
6 Balint (1987).
7 Beeghley and Cichetti (1994). This study appears to show evidence of the early emergence of the accommodative system. Maltreated children produced fewer utterances about negative affect (hate, disgust, anger, bad feelings) than non-maltreated children. The investigators explained their findings in terms of parental disapproval of the expression of this class of affects. 'Thus, maltreated children, in an attempt to control their anxiety, may modify their language (and perhaps even their thinking) to prevent the anxiety engendered by certain

aspects of language and discourse in general' (Cichetti and Toth, 1995). Cichetti and his colleagues have carried out a series of interesting and important studies of maltreated children which are reviewed in Cichetti and Toth (1995).

8 Meares (1997).
9 Vygotsky (1962, p.149).
10 Vygotsky (1962, p.145).
11 Meares and Hobson (1977).
12 Oxford English Dictionary.
13 Meares and Coombes (1994).
14 Meares (1985).
15 Hobson (1985).
16 Levenson (1991, pp.7–8).
17 Levenson (1972, p.220).
18 Levenson (1972, p.91).
19 Levenson (1972, p.220).
20 Mandelbrot (1983).
21 Stolum (1996).
22 Prigogine and Stengers (1984, p.14).

15 Flights and perchings

1 James (1890, I, p.243).
2 Empathic language might be seen as having a 'picturing' function. The conversational partners try to depict, as if on an imaginary cinematic screen, a 'view' of inner life (Meares, 1983).
3 It is a widely held view that insight through interpretation is 'the supreme agent in the hierarchy of therapeutic principles' (Bibring, 1954, p.763).

An influential study conducted by David Malan (1976) seemed to confirm a conviction that transference interpretation is of major curative significance. However, his method, which depended upon therapists' accounts of their sessions, is not satisfactory. More recent studies which involve taped recordings produce, in the main, opposite results. These studies, comprehensively reviewed by Henry et al. (1994), tend to show that transference interpretation correlates negatively with outcome.

One of the better known of the studies cited came from Piper et al. (1991). These and other findings cannot be ignored. Yet the management of transference phenomena as implied in previous chapters, is central to the therapeutic process. A puzzle is presented. A partial answer to it will be evident in the main argument of this chapter.
4 Thomä and Kächele, in their authoritative text, write 'The transference neurosis is said to be resolved by the patient's realisation that his perceptions in the analytic situation are, to a greater or lesser degree, gross distortions' (Thomä and Kächele, 1987, p.54). This idea determines a kind of therapeutic practice which may help to explain findings such as those of Piper et al. (1991).
5 Meares and Hobson (1977).
6 Narrative is made up of scenes. Readers of stories construct mental models of the situation and characters described (Bower and Morrow, 1990).
7 Joseph Lichtenberg (1989a; 1989b) has highlighted the essential element of this process with his concept of 'model scenes'. (See also Lichtenberg et al., 1992.)
8 The fundamental role of visualisation in the development of a narrative of self might be questioned on the grounds that blind people could not, if this were so, develop a self, a proposal which is absurd. However, an intriguing study,

recently reported, suggests that visualisation of experience, of a kind, also occurs in blind people. Using brain imaging methods, Sadato et al. (1996) found that during a tactile discrimination task, Braille readers showed activation of those areas of the cortex which are to do with vision. Congenitally blind subjects showed the same activation of the primary visual cortex as those people blinded later in life.

9 Oxford English Dictionary
10 Meares and Hobson (1977).
11 Anna Ornstein (1994) suggests that a mental activity resembling the creative or poetic process is necessary to the piecing together and integration of the traumatic story.

16 The death of Narcissus

1 Gosse (1907, p.58).
2 Rank (1958, pp.62–101).
3 See Cassirer's (1946) distinction between discursive (logical) and mythical thought. Kirk (1970) reviews some of the controversies concerning the definition of myth.
4 Rank (1958, p.93).
5 Lévi-Strauss (1968, p.218).
6 Lévi-Strauss (1968, p.211).
7 Lévi-Strauss (1968, p.211).
8 Lévi-Strauss (1968, p.211).
9 Hammond and Scullard (1970); Graves (1960); Rank (1958).
10 See Partridge (1983) who links the etymology of 'narcotic' to the Greek, *narke*, meaning torpor.
11 Freud (1905, p.145, n.1).
12 Ellis (1928, p.347).
13 Frazer (1922, p.193).
14 In my view, it also conveys the essence of Kohut's approach to narcissistic personality disorder, which can be seen as implicitly dependent upon a theory of value and attacks upon value.
15 Thomas Ogden (1997a, 1997b, 1997c, 1998, 1999) has recently been exploring the nature of this kind of language.
16 Langer (1957, p.112). This idea is resonant with the main theme of Hobson's work entitled 'Forms of Feeling' (Hobson, 1985).

References

Alessandri S, Sullivan M, and Lewis M (1990) 'Violation of expectancy and frustration in early infancy', *Developmental Psychology* 26: 738–44.

Amsterdam B (1972) 'Mirror self image reactions before age two', *Developmental Psychology* 5: 297–305.

Andreasen N (1997) 'Linking mind and brain in the study of mental illnesses: a project for a scientific psychopathology', *Science* 275: 1586–93.

Anthony S (1973) *The Discovery of Death in Childhood and After*, Harmondsworth: Penguin.

Ashmead DH and Perlmutter M (1980) 'Infant memory in everyday life'. In: M. Perlmutter (ed.), *Children's Memory: New Directions for Child Development*, no.10, San Francisco: Jossey-Bass.

Atwood G and Stolorow R (1984) *Structures of Subjectivity: Explorations in Psychoanalytic Phenomenology*, Hillsdale, NJ: The Analytic Press.

Ayer AJ (1936) *Language, Truth and Logic*, London: Gollancz.

Baddeley A (1984) 'Memory theory and memory therapy'. In: B Wilson and N Moffat (eds), *The Clinical Management of Memory Problems*, London: Croom Helm.

Baddeley A (1990) *Human Memory: Theory and Practice*, Hillsdale, NJ: Lawrence Erlbaum.

Baddeley A, et al. (1984) 'Commentary on Tulving's elements of episodic memory', *The Behavioural and Brain Sciences* 7: 238–57.

Baldwin JM (1895) *Mental Development in the Child and the Race*, New York: Macmillan.

Baldwin JM (1906) *Thoughts and Things*, Vol.I, London: Swan Sonnenschein; New York: Macmillan.

Balint E (1963) 'On being empty of oneself', *International Journal of Psychoanalysis* 44: 470–80.

Balint E (1987) 'Memory and consciousness', *International Journal of Psychoanalysis* 68: 475–83.

Balint M (1968) *The Basic Fault: Therapeutic Aspects of Regression*, London: Tavistock.

Bargh JA and Pietromonaco P (1982) 'Automatic information processing and social perception: the influence of trait information presented outside of conscious awareness on impression formation', *Journal of Personalilty and Social Psychology* 43: 437–49.

Bartlett F (1932) *Remembering*, Cambridge: Cambridge University Press.

Bechara A, Tranel D, Damasio H, Adolphs R, Rockland C, and Damasio AR (1995) 'Double dissociation of conditioning and declarative knowledge relative to the amygdala and hippocampus in humans', *Science* 269: 1115–18.

Beeghley M and Cichetti D (1994) 'Child maltreatment, attachment and the self system: emergence of an internal state lexicon in toddlers at high social risk', *Development and Psychopathology* 6: 5–30.

Bergson H (1911) *Matter and Memory*, London: Allen & Unwin.

Berrington W, Liddell D, and Faulds G (1956) 'A re-evaluation of the fugue', *Journal of Mental Science* 102: 281–6.

Bibring E (1954) 'Psychoanalysis and the dynamic psychotherapies', *Journal of the American Psychoanalytic Association* 2: 745–70.

Bion WR (1955) 'Group dynamics: a review'. In: M Klein, P Heimann, and R Money-Kryle (eds) *New Directions in Psychoanalysis*, London: Tavistock.

Bion WR (1962) *Learning from Experience*, New York: Basic Books.

Bower G (1992) How might emotions affect learning? In: S-A Christianson (ed.), *The Handbook of Emotion and Memory: Research and Theory*, Hillsdale, NJ: Erlbaum.

Bower G and Morrow D (1990) 'Mental models in narrative comprehension', *Science* 247: 44–8.

Bower T (1974) *Development in Infancy*, San Francisco: Freeman.

Bowlby J (1971) *Attachment*, Harmondsworth: Penguin.

Brandchaft B (1993) 'To free the spirit from its cell'. In: A Goldberg (ed.), *Progress in Self Psychology*, Vol.9, Hillsdale, NJ: Analytic Press.

Brandchaft B (2000) *Accommodative Structures of Pathological Attachment*, Hillsdale, NJ: Analytic Press. (In press.)

Brandchaft B and Stolorow R (1990) 'Varieties of therapeutic alliance', *The Annual of Psychoanalysis* 18: 89–114.

Bringuier J-C (1980) *Conversations with Jean Piaget*, trans. B Gulati. Chicago: University of Chicago Press.

Brown P and van der Hart O (1998) 'Memories of sexual abuse: Janet's critique of Freud, a balanced approach', *Psychological Reports* 82: 1028–43.

Bruner J (1983) *Child's Talk: Learning to Use Language*, London: WW Norton.

Bruner J (1986) *Actual Minds, Possible Worlds*, Cambridge, MA: Harvard University Press.

Bruner J (1990) *Acts of Meaning*, Cambridge, MA: Harvard University Press.

Butler S (1880) *Unconscious Memory*, London: David Bogue.

Cardeña E and Spiegel D (1993) 'Dissociative reactions to the Bay Area earthquake of 1989', *American Journal of Psychiatry*, 474–8.

Carpenter G (1974) 'Mother's face and the newborn', *New Scientist* 61: 742.

Cassirer E (1946) *Language and Myth*, trans. S Langer. New York: Harper.

Chu J and Dill D (1990) 'Dissociative symptoms in relation to childhood physical and sexual abuse', *American Journal of Psychiatry* 147: 887–92.

Cichetti D and Toth S (1995) 'A developmental psychopathology perspective on child abuse and neglect', *Journal of the American Academy of Adolescent Psychiatry* 34(5): 541–65.

Claparède E (1911) 'Recognition and "me-ness"'. In: D Rapaport (ed.), *Organization and Pathology of Thought: Selected Sources*, New York: Columbia University Press, 1951.

Cohen N and Squire L (1980) 'Preserved learning and retention of pattern analysing skills in amnesia: dissociation or knowing how from knowing that', *Science* 210: 207–10.

Coons PM, Bowman ES, and Milstein V (1988) 'Multiple personality disorder: a clinical investigation of 58 cases', *Journal of Nervous Mental Disorders* 176: 519–27.

Cowan J (1992) *Mysteries of the Dreaming*, Bridport: Prism Press.

Crick F and Koch C (1990) 'Towards a neurobiological theory of consciousness', *Seminars in the Neurosciences* 2: 263–75.

Croq L and le Verbizier J (1989) 'Le traumatisme psychologique dans l'oeuvre de Pierre Janet', *Annales Medico-Psychologiques* 147: 983–87.

Crovitz HF (1970) *Galton's Walk: Methods for the Analysis of Thinking, Intelligence and Creativity*, New York: Harper and Row.

Crovitz H and Harvey M (1979) 'Early childhood amnesia: a quantitative study with implications for the study of retrograde amnesia after brain injury', *Cortex* 15: 331–5.

Crovitz H and Schiffman H (1974) 'Frequency of episodic memories as a function of their age', *Bulletin of the Psychonomic Society* 4: 517–18.

Damasio A (1994) *Descartes' Error*, New York: Grosset Putnam. London: Papermac, 1996 (latter edition cited here).

Damasio, A (1999) *The Feeling of What Happens*, New York: Harcourt Brace.

Darwin CR (1934) *The Expression of Emotions in Man and Animals*. Revised and abridged, C Beadwell, London: Watts & Co.

Davis H and Squire L (1984) 'Protein synthesis and memory: a review', *Psychological Bulletin* 96: 518–57.

De Casper AJ, Fifer WP (1980) 'Of human bonding: newborns prefer their mother's voices', *Science* 208: 1174–6.

De Laguna G (1927) *Speech: Its Function and Development*, New Haven, CT: Yale University Press.

Démonet JF, Chollet F, Ramsey S, Cardebat D, Nespoulous JL, Wise R, Rascol A, and Frackowiak R (1992) 'The anatomy of phonological and semantic processing in normal subjects', *Brain* 115: 1753–68.

Dennett D (1991) *Consciousness Explained*, Harmondsworth: Penguin.

Dennett D (1995) *Darwin's Dangerous Idea*, Harmondsworth: Penguin.

De Villiers P and de Villiers J (1979) *Early Language*, Cambridge, MA: Harvard University Press.

Dewey J (1939) *Theory of Valuation*, Chicago: University of Chicago Press.

De Yoe E, Felleman D, van Essen D, and McClendon E (1994) 'Multiple processing streams in occipitotemporal visual cortex', *Nature* 371: 151–4.

Dias R, Robbins T, and Roberts A (1996) 'Dissociation in prefrontal cortex of affective and attentional shifts', *Nature* 280: 69–72.

Dudycha GJ and Dudycha MM (1941) 'Childhood memories: a review of the literature', *Psychological Bulletin* 38: 668–82.

Durkheim E (1915) *The Elementary Forms of Religious Life*, trans. J Swain, New York: Free Press, 1965.

Edelman G (1992) *Bright Air, Brilliant Fire: On the Matter of Mind*, New York: Basic Books.

Eich E (1989) 'Theoretical issues in state dependent memory'. In: H Roedinger III and F Craik (eds), *Varieties of Memory and Consciousness: Essays in honour of Endel Tulving*, Hillsdale, NJ: Erlbaum.

Ellenberger HF (1970) *The Discovery of the Unconscious*, London: Allen Lane Press.

Elliott D (1997) 'Traumatic events: Prevalence and delayed recall in the general population', *Journal of Consulting and Clinical Psychology*, 65: 811–20.

Ellis H (1928) *Studies in the Psychology of Sex*, vol. VII, Philadelphia: Davis.

Evans J, Williams JMG, O'Loughlin S and Howells K (1992) 'Autobiographical memory and problem-solving strategies of parasuicide patients', *Psychological Medicine* 22: 399–405.

Fivush R and Hudson JA (eds.) (1990) *Knowing and Remembering in Young Children*, New York: Cambridge University Press.

Flavell J, Green F, and Flavell E (1993) 'Children's understanding of the stream of consciousness', *Child Development* 64: 387–96.

Fonagy P (1998) 'An attachment approach to treatment of the difficult patient', *Bulletin of the Menninger Clinic* 62: 147–69.

Fonagy P and Target M (1997) 'Attachment and reflective function: their role in self-organization', *Development and Psychopathology* 9: 679–700.

Frazer J (1922) *The Golden Bough*, abridged edition. London: Macmillan.

Freud S (1891) *Appendix B: Psycho-physical Parallelism*, S.E. 14: 206–8. London: Hogarth.

Freud S (1895) *Project for a Scientific Psychology*, S.E. 1: 283–388. London: Hogarth.

Freud S (1896) 'Letter to Wilhelm Fliess'. 06.12.1896. In: *The Origins of Psycho-Analysis: Letters to Wilhelm Fliess, Drafts and Notes: 1887–1902*, London: Imago, 1954.

Freud S (1905) *Three Essays on the Theory of Sexuality*, S.E. 7, London: Hogarth.

Freud S (1911) *Formulations in the Two Principles of Mental Functioning*, S.E. 12: 215–26, London: Hogarth.

Freud S (1914) *Further Recommendations in the Technique of Psychoanalysis: Recollection, Repetition and Working Through*. S.E. 12: 145–56, London: Hogarth.

Freud S (1915a) *Instincts and Their Vicissitudes*, S.E. 14: 117–40, London: Hogarth.

Freud S (1915b) *Introductory Lectures in Psychoanalysis. Parts I and II*, S.E. 15, London: Hogarth.

Freud S (1920–2) *Two Encyclopaedia Articles (A) Psychoanalysis*, S.E. 18, London: Hogarth.

Freud S (1926) *Freud and Ewald Hering*, S.E. 14: 205, London: Hogarth.

Freud S (1939) *An Outline of Psychoanalysis*, S.E. 23, London: Hogarth.

Fried I, MacDonald KA, and Wilson CL (1997) 'Single neuron activity in hippocampus and amygdala during recognition of faces and objects', *Neuron* 18: 875–87.

Gabbard G (1995) 'Countertransference: the emerging common ground', *International Journal of Psycho-Analysis*, 76: 475–85.

Galton F (1883) *Inquiries into Human Faculty and its Development*, New York: Macmillan.

Garbutt M (1997) *Figure Talk: Reported Speech and Thought in the Discourse of Psychotherapy*, unpublished Ph.D. thesis, Macquarie University, Sydney.

Gazzaniga M (1989) 'Organisation of the human brain', *Science*, 245: 947–52.

Genet J (1967) *The Thief's Journal*, Harmondsworth: Penguin.

Goldberg A (1995) *The Problem of Perversion*, New Haven and London: Yale University Press.

Goldman-Rakic P (1995) 'Anatomical and functional circuits in prefrontal cortex of non-human primates: relevance to epilepsy'. In: H Jasper, S Riggio, and P Goldman-Rakic (eds), *Epilepsy and the Functional Anatomy of the Frontal Lobe*, Raven Press: New York.

Golomb A, Ludolph P, Westen D, et al. (1994) 'Maternal empathy, family chaos and the etiology of borderline personality disorder', *Journal of the American Psychoanalytic Association* 42: 525–48.

Gopnik A and Astington J (1988) 'Children's understanding of representational change and its relation to the understanding of false belief and the appearance–reality distinction', *Child Development* 59: 26–37.

Gosse E (1907) *Father and Son*, Harmondsworth: Penguin, 1983.

Goyer P, Andreason P, Semple W, Clayton A, King A, Compton-Toth B, Schulz S, and Cohen R (1994) 'Positron-emission tomography and personality disorders', *Neuropsychopharmacology* 10: 21–8.

Graf P and Schacter DL (1985) 'Implicit and explicit memory for new associations in normal subjects and amnesic patients', *Journal of Experimental Psychology: Learning, Memory and Cognition* 11: 501–18.

Graves R (1960) *The Greek Myths*, vol.I., Harmondsworth: Penguin.

Gregory I (1961) *Psychiatry*, Philadelphia: Saunders.

Grosskurth P (1986) *Melanie Klein: Her World and Her Work*, London: Maresfield.

Grotstein J (1981) *Splitting and Projective Identification*, Northvale, NJ: Jason Aronson.

Hadamard J (1945) *An Essay on the Psychology of Invention in the Mathematical Field.* Princeton, NJ: Princeton University Press.

Hammond N and Scullard H (1970) *The Oxford Classical Dictionary*, Oxford: The Clarendon Press.

Harter S (1983) 'Developmental perspectives on the self system'. In: P Mussen (ed.), *Handbook of Child Psychology*, vol.4, New York: Wiley.

Hartmann H (1950) 'Comments on the psychoanalytic theory of ego'. In: *Essays on Ego Psychology*, New York: International Universities Press, 1964.

Heidegger M (1962) *Being and Time*, trans. J Macquarie and E Robinson, London: SCM Press.

Henry W, Strupp H, Schact T, and Gaston L (1994) 'Psychodynamic approaches'. In: A Bergin and S Garfield (eds) *Handbook of Psychotherapy and Behaviour Change*, New York: Wiley.

Herman J (1992) *Trauma and Recovery*, New York: Basic Books. Paperback, London: Pandora, 1994. The latter edition cited here.

Herman J, Perry J, and van der Kolk B (1989) 'Childhood trauma in borderline personality disorder', *American Journal of Psychiatry* 146: 490–5.

Hermans H and Hermans-Jansen E (1995) *Self-narratives: The Construction of Meaning in Psychotherapy*, New York and London: Guilford Press.

Hermans H, Kempen H, and van Zoon R (1992) 'The dialogical self: beyond individualism and rationalism', *American Psychologist* 47: 23–33.

Hobson RF (1985) *Forms of Feeling: The Heart of Psychotherapy*, London: Tavistock.

Hobson RP (1993) *Autism and the Development of Mind*, Hillsdale, NJ: Laurence Erlbaum.

Holen A (1993) 'The North Sea oil rig disaster'. In: JP Wilson and B Raphael, *International Handbook of Traumatic Stress Syndromes*, New York: Plenum Press.

Holmes J (1996) *Attachment, Intimacy and Autonomy*, Northvale, NJ: Jason Aronson.

Horgan J (1993) 'Fractured functions. Does the brain have a supreme integrator?' *Scientific American* 269: 16–17.

Horvath T, Friedman J, and Meares R (1980) 'Attention in hysteria: a study of Janet's hypothesis by means of habituation and arousal measures', *American Journal of Psychiatry* 137: 217–20.

Hudson JA and Nelson K (1986) 'Repeated encounters of a similar kind: effects of familiarity on children's autobiographical memory', *Cognitive Development* 1: 253–71.

Huizinga J (1938) *Homo Ludens: A Study of the Play Element in Culture*, London: Maurice Temple Smith, 1970.

Humphrey N (1992) *The History of Mind*, London: Chatto and Windus.

Hyden H (1973) 'Changes in brain protein during learning'. In: G Ansell and P Bradley (eds), *Macromolecules and Behaviour*, New York: Macmillan.

Inhelder B and Piaget J (1958) *The Growth of Logical Thinking from Childhood to Adolescence*, trans. A Parson and S Milgram, New York: Basic Books.

Isaacs S (1952) 'The nature and function of phantasy'. In: M Klein, P Heimann, S Isaacs and J. Rivière (ed.), *Developments in Psychoanalysis*, London: Hogarth Press.

Jackson JH (1931–2) *Selected Writings of John Hughlings Jackson, Vol. 1 and 2* (ed. J. Taylor), London: Hodder.

James L, Gordon E, Kraiuhin C, and Meares R (1989a) 'Selective Attention and auditory event related potentials in somatization disorder', *Comprehensive Psychiatry* 30: 84–9.

James L, Gordon E, Kraiuhin C, Howson A, and Meares R (1989b) 'A modified selective attention auditory-related potential paradigm suitable for the clinical setting', *International Journal of Psychophysiology* 8: 61–71.

James L, Gordon E, Kraiuhin C, Howson A, and Meares R (1990) 'Augmentation of auditory evoked potentials in somatization disorder', *Journal of Psychiatric Research* 24: 155–63.

James W (1890) *Principles of Psychology*, Vols. I and II, New York: Holt.

James W (1892) *Psychology: Briefer Course*, London: Macmillan.

James W (1902) *Varieties of Religious Experience*, New York: Longmans; London: Collins-Fontana, 1960. (The latter edition is cited here.)

James W (1909) *A Pluralistic Universe*, New York: Longmans, Green. Replicated 1996, Lincoln: University of Nebraska Press. This edition cited here.

Janet P (1901) *The Mental State of Hystericals*, trans. CR Corson, London and New York: Putman.

Janet P (1907) *The Major Symptoms of Hysteria*, New York, London: Macmillan.

Janet P (1911) *L'Etat Mental des Hysteriques*, 2nd edn, Paris: Alcan.

Janet P (1924) *Principles of Psychotherapy*, Freeport, NY: Books for Libraries.

Jones E (1953) *Sigmund Freud: Life and Work,* Vol.1., London: Hogarth.

Joseph B (1987) 'Projective identification: some clinical aspects'. In: E Spillius (ed.) *Melanie Klein Today, Vol. 1: Mainly Theory*, New York: Routledge, 1988.

Jung CG (1905–41) 'Experimental researches'. In CG Jung: *The Collected Works*, Vol.2, trans. L Stein, London: Routledge & Kegan Paul.

Jung CG (1912) 'Two kinds of thinking'. In: CG Jung *The Collected Works*, vol.5, trans. R Hull, London: Routledge & Kegan Paul.

Jung CG (1936) 'The Tavistock lectures'. In: CG Jung *The Collected Works*, vol.18, trans. R Hull, London: Routledge & Kegan Paul.

Jung CG (1948) 'The self'. In: CG Jung *The Collected Works*, vol. 9ii, trans. R Hull, London: Routledge & Kegan Paul.

Jung CG (1953) 'Foreword to Frieda Fordham: introduction to Jung's psychology'. In: CG Jung *The Collected Works*, Vol.18, trans. RFC Hull, London and New York: Routledge & Kegan Paul.

Kagan J (1981) *The Second Year: The Emergence of Self Awareness*, Cambridge, MA: Harvard University Press.

Kail R (1984) *The Development of Memory in Children*, New York: WH Freeman & Company.

Kaye K (1982) *The Mental and Social Life of Babies*, Chicago: Chicago University Press.

Kaye K and Charney R (1980) 'How mothers maintain dialogue with two-year-olds'. In: O Olson (ed.), *The Social Foundations of Language and Thought*, New York: Norton.

Keats, J (1821) *The Letters of John Keats, 1814–1821*, vols 1 & 2, ed. HE Rollins, Cambridge MA: Harvard University Press.

Keller H (1936) *The Story of My Life*, New York: Doubleday.

Kellog WN and Kellog LA (1933) *The Ape and the Child*, Toronto: McGraw-Hill.

Kernberg O (1968) 'The treatment of patients with borderline personality organisation', *International Journal of Psychoanalysis* 49: 600–19.

Kernberg O (1987) 'Projection and projective identification: developmental and clinical aspects'. *Journal of the American Psychoanalytic Association,* 35: 795–819.

Kihlstrom JF, Schacter DL, Cork RC, Hurt CA, and Behr SE (1990) 'Implicit and explicit memory following surgical anesthesia', *Psychological Science* 1: 303–6.

Kirk GS (1970) *Myth: Its Meaning and Functions in Ancient and Other Cultures,* London: Cambridge University Press.

Klein M (1946) 'Notes on some schizoid mechanisms'. In: M Khan (ed.) *Envy and Gratitude and Other Works 1946–1963,* London: Hogarth, 1975.

Klein M (1975) *Love, Guilt and Reparation and Other Works: 1921–1945*, London: Hogarth.

Kohlberg L, Yaeger J, and Hjertholm E (1968) 'Private speech: four studies and a review of theories', *Child Development* 39: 691–735.

Kohut H (1971) *The Analysis of the Self*, New York: International Universities Press.

Kohut H (1977) *The Restoration of the Self*, New York: International Universities Press.

Kohut H (1984) *How Does Analysis Cure?* ed. A Goldberg, Chicago: University of Chicago Press.

Kolb B and Wishaw I (1990) *Fundamentals of Human Neuropsychology*, 3rd edn, New York: Freeman.

Koopman C, Classen C, and Spiegel D (1994) 'Predictors of post traumatic stress symptoms among survivors of the Oakland/Berkeley, California, firestorm', *American Journal of Psychiatry* 151: 888–94.

Kosslyn S (1988) 'Aspects of a cognitive neuroscience of mental imagery', *Science* 240: 1621–6.

Kuyken W and Brewin C (1995) 'Autobiographical memory functioning in depression and reports of early abuse', *Journal of Abnormal Psychology* 104: 585–91.

Ladavas E, Cimatti D, Del Pesce M, and Tuozzi G (1993) 'Emotional evaluation with and without conscious stimulus identification: evidence from a split-brain patient', *Cognition and Emotion* 7: 95–114.

Laing RD (1959) *The Divided Self*, Harmondsworth: Penguin.

Langer S (1941) *Philosophy in a New Key*, Cambridge, MA: Harvard University Press.

Langer S (1957) *Problems of Art*, New York: Scribner.

Laplanche J and Pontalis J-B (1973) *The Language of Psychoanalysis*, New York: Norton.

Le Doux J (1996) *The Emotional Brain*, New York: Simon & Schuster.

Lee K, Vaillaint G, Torrey W, and Elder G (1995) 'A 50-year prospective study of psychological sequelae of World War II combat', *American Journal of Psychiatry* 152: 516–22.

Lemaire A (1977) *Jaques Lacan*, trans. D Macey, London: Routledge & Kegan Paul.

Levenson E (1972) *The Fallacy of Understanding*, New York: Basic Books. Reissued in: *The Master Work Series*, Northvale, NJ: Jason Aronson, 1995. This edition cited here.

Levenson E (1991) *The Purloined Self: Interpersonal Perspectives on Psychoanalysis*, New York: William Alanson White.

Lévi-Strauss L (1968) *Structural Anthropology*, London: Allen Lane.

Lévi-Strauss L (1979) *Myth and Meaning*, New York: Schocken Books.

Lewis M (1992) *Shame: The Exposed Self*, New York: The Free Press.

Lewis M and Brooks-Gunn J (1979) *Social Cognition and the Acquisition of Self*, New York: Plenum.

Lewis M, Alessandri S, and Sullivan M (1990) 'Expectancy, loss of control and anger in young infants', *Developmental Psychology* 26: 745–51.

Lichtenberg J (1989a) *Psychoanalysis and Motivation*, Hillsdale, NJ: The Analytic Press.

Lichtenberg J (1989b) 'Model scenes, motivation, and personality'. In: S Dowling and A Rothstein (eds), *The Significance of Infant Observational Research for Clinical Work with Children, Adolescents and Adults*, Madison, CT: IUP.

Lichtenberg J, Lachmann F, and Fosshage J (1992) *Self and Motivational Systems: Toward a Theory of Psychoanalytic Technique*, Hillsdale, NJ: The Analytic Press.

Lillienfeld SO, van Valkerberg C, Larntz K, and Akiskal HS (1986) 'The relationship of histrionic personality disorder to antisocial personality and somatization disorders', *American Journal of Psychiatry* 143: 718–22.

Livingstone M and Hubel D (1988) 'Segregation of form, color, movement, and depth: anatomy, physiology, and perception', *Science* 240: 740–9.

Locke JL and Pearson D (1990) 'The linguistic significance of babbling: evidence from a tracheotomized infant', *Journal of Child Language* 17: 1–16.

Ludolph P, Westen D, Misle B, Jackson A, et al. (1990) 'The borderline diagnosis in adolescents: symptoms and developmental history', *American Journal of Psychiatry* 147: 470–6.

Luria A (1973) *The Working Brain*, Harmondsworth: Penguin.

MacFarlane A, Weber D, Clark C (1993) 'Abnormal stimulus processing in PTSD', *Biological Psychiatry* 34: 311–20.

MacFarlane J (1975) 'Olfactory factors in human attachments'. In: M Hofer (ed.), *Parent–Infant Interaction*, Amsterdam: Elsevier.

McGuire P, Silbersweig D, and Frith C (1996) 'Functional neuro anatomy of verbal self monitoring', *Brain* 119: 907–17.

McLeod J (1997) *Narrative and Psychotherapy*, London, Thousand Oaks, New Delhi: Sage.

Malan D (1976) *The Validation of Dynamic Psychotherapy*, New York: Plenum.

Malin A and Grotstein J (1966) 'Projective identification in the therapeutic process', *International Journal of Psychoanalysis* 47: 26–31.

Mandelbrot B (1983) *The Fractal Geometry of Nature*, New York: Freeman.

Mandler JM (1984) 'Representation and recall in infancy'. In: M Moscovitch (ed.) *Infant Memory*, New York: Plenum.

Mauss M (1970) *The Gift*, paperback edition, London: Routledge.

Maynes L and Feinauer L (1994) 'Acute and chronic dissociation and somatized anxiety as related to childhood sexual abuse', *American Journal of Family Therapy* 22: 165–75.

Meares A (1958) *The Door of Serenity*, London: Faber.

Meares A (1961) 'What makes the patient better?' *Lancet* 1: 1280–81.

Meares A (1962) 'What makes the patient better?' *Lancet* 1: 151–3.

Meares R (1973) 'Two kinds of groups', *British Journal of Medical Psychology* 46: 373–9.

Meares R (1976) 'The Secret', *Psychiatry* 39: 258–65.

Meares R (1977a) *The Pursuit of Intimacy: An Approach to Psychotherapy*, Melbourne: Nelson.

Meares R (1977b) 'Structures'. In: R Meares, *The Pursuit of Intimacy: An Approach to Psychotherapy*, Melbourne: Nelson.

Meares R (1977c) 'Fantasy-thinking'. In: R Meares, *The Pursuit of Intimacy*, Melbourne: Nelson.

Meares R (1980) 'Body feeling in human relations: the possible examples of Brancusi and Giacometti', *Psychiatry* 43: 160–7.

Meares R (1981) 'On saying goodbye before death', *Journal of the American Medical Association* 246: 1227–9.

Meares R (1983) 'Keats and the "impersonal" therapist: a note on empathy and the therapeutic screen', *Psychiatry* 46: 73–82.

Meares R (1984) 'Inner space: its constriction in anxiety states and narcissistic personality', *Psychiatry* 47(2): 162–71.

Meares R (1985) 'Metaphor and reality', *Contemporary Psychoanalysis* 21: 425–45.

Meares R (1986) 'On the ownership of thought: an approach to the origins of separation anxiety', *Psychiatry* 21: 545–59.

Meares R (1990) 'The fragile spielraum: an approach to transmuting internalization'. In: A Goldberg (ed.), *The Realities of Transference: Progress in Self Psychology* 6, Hillsdale, NJ: Analytic Press.

Meares R (1992) 'Transference and the play space', *Contemporary Psychoanalysis* 28: 32–49.

Meares R (1993a) *The Metaphor of Play: Disruption and Restoration in the Borderline Experience*, Northvale, NJ: Jason Aronson.

Meares R (1993b) 'Reversals: on certain pathologies of identification'. In: A Goldberg (ed.), *Progress in Self Psychology*, Vol. 9, Hillsdale, NJ: Analytic Press.

Meares R (1994) 'A pathology of privacy: towards a new theoretical approach to obsessive-compulsive disorder', *Contemporary Psychoanalysis* 30(1): 83–100.

Meares R (1995) 'Episodic memory, trauma and the narrative of self', *Contemporary Psychoanalysis* 31(4): 541–55.

Meares R (1996a) 'The psychology of self: an update', *Australian and New Zealand Journal of Psychiatry* 30: 312–16.

Meares R (1996b) 'Reply to critique of "The Psychology of Self: an update"', *Australian and New Zealand Journal of Psychiatry* 30(6): 838–41.

Meares R (1997) 'Stimulus entrapment: on a common basis of somatization', *Psychoanalytic Inquiry* 17(2): 223–34.

Meares R (1998) 'The self in conversation: on narratives, chronicles and scripts', *Psychoanalytic Dialogues*, The Analytic Press, Inc., Vol. 8, No. 6, 875–91.

Meares R (1999) 'Hughlings Jackson's contribution to an understanding of dissociation.' *American Journal of Psychiatry* 156(12): 1850–5.

Meares R and Anderson J (1993) 'Intimate space: on the developmental significance of exchange', *Contemporary Psychoanalysis* 29(4): 595–612.

Meares R and Coombes T (1994) A drive to play: evolution and psychotherapeutic theory', *Australian and New Zealand Journal of Psychiatry* 28: 58–67.

Meares R and Grose D (1978) 'On depersonalization in adolescence: a consideration from the viewpoint of habituation and "identity"', *British Journal of Medical Psychology* 51: 335–42.

Meares R and Hobson R (1977) 'The persecutory therapist', *British Journal of Medical Psychology* 50: 349–59.

Meares R and Horvath T (1972) '"Acute" and "chronic" hysteria', *British Journal of Psychiatry* 121: 653–7.

Meares R and Lichtenberg J (1995) 'The form of play in the shape and unity of self', *Contemporary Psychoanalysis* 31(1): 47–64.

Meares R and Orlay W (1988) 'On self boundary: a study of the development of the concept of secrecy', *British Journal of Medical Psychology* 1: 305–16.

Meares R, Stevenson J, and Comerford A (1999a) 'Psychotherapy with borderline patients, Part I: A comparison between treated and untreated cohorts', *Australian and New Zealand Journal of Psychiatry* 33(3): 467–72.

Meares R, Stevenson J, and Gordon E (1999b) 'A Jacksonian and biopsychosocial hypothesis concerning borderline and related phenomena', *Australian and New Zealand Journal of Psychiatry* 33(6): 831–40.

Meares R, Gordon E, Haig A, and Bahramali H (1999c) 'Sensory processing in borderline patients', *Proceedings of International College of Psychosomatic Medicine Conference*, Athens.

Meares R, Penman R, Milgrom-Friedman J, and Baker K (1982) 'Some origins of the "difficult" child. The Brazelton scale and the mother's view of her newborn's character', *British Journal of Medical Psychology* 55: 77–86.

Meissner W (1980) 'A note on projective identification', *Journal of the American Psychoanalytic Association* 28: 43–67.

Meltzoff A and Moore M (1977) 'Imitation of facial and manual gestures by human neonates', *Science* 198: 75–8.

Middleton W and Butler J (1998) 'Dissociative identity disorder', *Australian and New Zealand Journal of Psychiatry* 32: 794–804.

Milgrom-Friedman J, Penman R, and Meares R (1980) 'Some pilot studies of early attachment and detachment behaviour'. In: ES Anthony and C Chailand (eds), *The Child in This Family*, Vol. 6, New York: Wiley.

Mitchell S (1988) *Relational Concepts in Psychoanalysis*, Cambridge, MA: Harvard University Press.

Monk R (1990) *Ludwig Wittgenstein*. London: Jonathan Cape, London: Vintage, 1991. Latter edition cited here.

Morris J, Öhman A, and Dolan R (1998) 'Conscious and unconscious emotional learning in the human amygdala', *Nature* 393: 467–70.

Morrison J (1989) 'Childhood sexual histories of women with somatization disorder', *American Journal of Psychiatry* 146: 239–41.

Moscovitch M (1995) 'Confabulation'. In: D Schacter (ed.), *Memory Distortion*, Cambridge, MA: Harvard University Press.

Murray H (1938) *Explorations in Personality*, New York: Oxford University Press.

Myers G (1986) *William James: His Life and Thought*, New Haven: Yale University Press.

Nelson K (1978) 'How young children represent knowledge of their world in and out of language'. In: RS Siegler (ed.), *Children's Thinking: What Develops?* Hillsdale, NJ: Erlbaum.

Nelson K (1984) 'The transition from infant to child memory'. In: M Moscovitch (ed.), *Infant Memory*, New York: Plenum.

Nelson K (ed.) (1989) *Narratives From the Crib*, Cambridge, MA: Harvard University Press.

Nelson K (1992) 'Emergence of autobiographical memory at four', *Human Development* 35: 172–7.

Nelson K and Gruendel J (1981) 'Generalized event representations: basic building blocks of cognitive development'. In: M Lamb and A Brown (eds), *Advances in Developmental Psychology*, Hillsdale, NJ: Erlbaum.

Nin A (1966) *The Diary of Anais Nin, Vol.I, 1931–4*, ed. G Stuhlmann, New York: Harvestbook, Harcourt, Brace, Jovanovich.

Nin A (1969) *The Diary of Anais Nin, Vol.III, 1939–44*, ed. G Stuhlmann, New York: Harvestbook, Harcourt, Brace, Jovanovich.

Noam G, Kohlberg L, and Snarey J (1983) 'Steps towards a model of the self'. In: B Lee and G Noam (eds), *Developmental Approaches to the self*, New York: Plenum.

Ogden T (1979) 'On projective identification', *International Journal of Psychoanalysis* 60: 357–73.

Ogden T (1982) *Projective Identification and Psychotherapeutic Technique*, Northvale, NJ: Jason Aronson.

Ogden T (1990) *Matrix of the Mind: Object Relations and the Psychoanalytic Dialogue*, Northvale, NJ: Jason Aronson.

Ogden T (1994a) 'The analytic third – working with intersubjective clinical facts', *International Journal of Psycho-Analysis* 72: 3–20.

Ogden T (1994b) *Subjects of Analysis*, Northvale, NJ: Aronson.

Ogden T (1995) 'Analysing forms of aliveness and deadness of the transference–counter transference', *International Journal of Psychoanalysis*, 76: 695–710.

Ogden T (1997a) *Reverie and Interpretation*, Northvale, NJ: Jason Aronson.

Ogden T (1997b) 'Some thoughts on the use of language in psychoanalysis', *Psychoanalytic Dialogues* 7: 1–21.

Ogden T (1997c) 'Listening: three frost poems', *Psychoanalytic Dialogues* 7: 619–39.

Ogden T (1998) 'A question of voice in poetry and psychoanalysis', *The Psychoanalytic Quarterly* 67: 426–48.

Ogden T (1999) '"The music of what happens" in poetry and psychoanalysis'. *International Journal of Psychoanalysis* (in press).

Ornstein A (1974) 'The dread to repeat and the new beginning', *The Annual of Psycho-analysis* 2: 127–49.

Ornstein A (1994) 'Trauma, memory and psychic continuity'. *Progress in Self Psychology*, Vol.10, Hillsdale, NJ: The Analytic Press.

Papousek H and Papousek M (1977) 'Mothering and the cognitive head-start: psychological considerations'. In: HR Schaffer (ed.), *Studies in Mother–Infant Interaction*, New York: Academic Press.

Parks E and Balon R (1995) 'Autobiographical memory for childhood events: Pattern of recall in psychiatric patients with a history of alleged trauma', *Psychiatry* 58: 199–208.

Partridge E (1983) *Origins: A Short Etymological Dictionary of Modern English*, New York: Greenwich House.

Passmore J (1968) *A Hundred Years of Philosophy*, Harmondsworth: Penguin.

Penman R, Meares R, and Milgrom-Friedman J (1981) 'The mother's role in the development of object competency', *Archives de Psychologie* 49: 247–65.

Perner J and Ruffman T (1995) 'Episodic memory and automatic consciousness: development evidence and a theory of childhood amnesia'. *Journal of Experimental Child Psychology* 59: 516–48.

Perner J, Leekam S, and Wimmer H (1987) 'Three-year-old's difficulty with false-belief: the case for conceptual deficit', *British Journal of Developmental Psychology* 5: 125–37.

Perry RB (1926) *A General Theory of Value*, New York: Longmans, Green & Co.

Peterson SE, Fox PT, Snyder AZ, and Raichle ME (1990) 'Activation of extra-striate and frontal cortical areas by visual words and word-like stimuli', *Science* 249: 1041–4.

Pettito L and Marentette P (1991) 'Babbling in the manual mode: evidence for the ontogeny of language', *Science* 251: 1493–6.

Piaget J (1926) *The Language and Thought of the Child*, London: Routledge & Kegan Paul. Third edition (revised), 1959. The latter edition cited here.

Piaget J (1929) *The Child's Conception of the World*, London: Routledge & Kegan Paul.

Piaget J (1951) *Play, Dreams and Imitation in Childhood*, trans. C Gattegno and F Hodgson. London: Heinemann.

Pick I (1985) 'Working through in the counter-transference'. In: E Spillius (ed.), *Melanie Klein Today, Vol 2: Mainly Practice,* London: Routledge, 1988.

Pillemer DB and White SH (1989) 'Childhood events recalled by children and adults'. In: HW Reese (ed.), *Advances in Child Development and Behavior*, New York: Academic Press.

Piper W, Azim F, Joyce S, and McCallum M (1991) 'Transference interpretations, therapeutic alliance and outcome in short-term individual psychotherapy', *Archives of General Psychiatry* 48: 946–53.

Pribor EF, Yutzy SH, Dean JT, and Wetzel RD (1993) 'Briquet's syndrome, disso-ciation and abuse', *American Journal of Psychiatry* 150: 1507–11.

Prigogine I and Stengers I (1984) *Order Out of Chaos: Man's New Dialogue With Nature*, London: Fontana.

Proust M (1951) *Remembrance of Things Past, Vol.12, Time Regained*, trans. S Hudson, London: Chatto & Windus.

Putnam FW, Guroff JJ, Silberman EK, Barban L, and Post RM (1986) 'The clinical phenomenology of multiple personality disorder: review of 100 cases', *Journal of Clinical Psychiatry* 47: 285–93.

Rank O (1914) *The Myth of the Birth of the Hero*, New York: Vintage Books, 1964. The latter edition cited here.

Rank O (1958) *Beyond Psychology*, New York: Dover.

Renik O (1993) 'Analytic interaction: conceptualization of technique in light of the analyst's irreducible subjectivity', *Psychoanalytic Quarterly* 62: 553–71.

Robinson J (1976) 'Sampling autobiographical memory', *Cognitive Psychology* 8: 578–95.

Roelfsema P, Engel A, König P, and Singer W (1997) 'Visuomotor integration is associated with zero time-lag synchronization among cortical areas', *Nature* 385: 157–61.

Rose S (1993) *The Making of Memory: From Molecules to Mind*, New York and London: Bantam.

Rosenfeld H (1952) 'Notes on the psycho-analysis of the superego conflict of an acute schizophrenic patient', *International Journal of Psycho-Analysis* 33: 111–31.

Ross CA, Norton GR, and Wozney K (1989) 'Multiple personality disorder: an analysis of 236 cases', *Canadian Journal of Psychiatry* 34: 413–18.

Ross CA, Miller SD, Bjorson L, Raegor P, Fraser GA, et al. (1991) 'Abuse histories in 102 cases of multiple personality disorder', *Canadian Journal of Psychiatry* 36: 97–101.

Rovée-Collier C (1993) 'The capacity for long-term memory in infancy', *Current Directions in Psychological Science* 2: 130–5.

Rugg M, Mark R, Walla P, Schloerscheidt A, Birch C, and Allan K (1998) 'Dissociation of the neural correlates of implicit and explicit memory', *Nature* 392: 595–8.

Russell B (1918) 'Scientific method and philosophy'. In: *Mysticism and Logic*, New York: Norton.

Russell B (1921) *The Analysis of Mind*, London: Allen and Unwin, New York: Macmillan.

Russell B (1967–9) *The Autobiography of Bertrand Russell,* Vols I, II, and III, London: Allen & Unwin, paperback, 1971. Latter edition cited here.

Rycroft (1987) 'Dissociation of the personality'. In: R Gregory (ed.), *The Oxford Companion to the Mind*, Oxford: Oxford University Press.

Ryle A (1990) *Cognitive Analytic Therapy: Active Participation in Change. A New Integration in Brief Therapy*, Chichester: Wiley.

Ryle G (1949) *The Concept of Mind*, London: Hutchinson, Harmondsworth: Penguin, 1963. The latter edition cited here.

Sadato N, Pascual-Leone A, Grafman J, Ibanez V, Deiber M-P, Dold G, and Hallett H (1996) 'Activation of the primary visual cortex by Braille reading in blind subjects', *Nature* 380: 526–8.

Sandler J (1987) 'The concept of projective identification'. In: J Sandler (ed.), *Projection, Identification, Projective Identification*, Madison, CT: International Universities Press.

Sandler J (1993) 'On communication from patient to analyst: not everything is projective identification', *International Journal of Psycho-Analysis* 74: 1097–107.

Saxe GN, Chinman G, Berkowitz R, Hall K, Lieberg G, et al. (1994) 'Somatization in patients with dissociative disorders,' *American Journal of Psychiatry* 151: 1329–34.

Schacter D (1991) 'Unawareness of deficit and unawareness of knowledge in patients with memory disorders'. In: GP Prigatano and DL Schacter (eds), *Awareness of Deficit After Brain Injury: Clinical and Theoretical Issues*, New York: Oxford University Press.

Schacter D (1992) 'Understanding implicit memory', *American Psychologist* 47: 559–69.

Schacter D (1996) *Searching for Memory: The Brain, the Mind and the Past*, New York: Basic Books.

Schacter D, Wang P, Tulving E, and Freedman M (1982) 'Functional retrograde amnesia: a quantitative case study', *Neuropsychologia* 20: 523–32.

Schacter D, Alpert NM, Savage CR, Rauch SL, and Albert MS (1996) 'Conscious recollection and the human hippocampal formation: evidence from positron emission tomography', *Proceedings of the National Academy of Sciences, USA* 93: 321–5.

Schafer R (1992) *Retelling a Life: Narration and Dialogue in Psychoanalysis*, New York: Basic Books.

Scheflen A and Brown D (1996) 'Repressed memory or dissociative amnesia: what the science says', *Journal of Psychiatry and Law* 24: 143–88.

Schenk L and Bear D (1981) 'Multiple personality and related dissociative phenomena in patients with temporal lobe epilepsy'. *American Journal of Psychiatry* 138: 1311–16.

Schore A (1994) *Affect Regulation and the Origin of Self: The Neurology of Emotional Development*, Hillsdale, NJ: Erlbaum.

Schore A (1996) 'The experience-dependent maturation of a regulating system in the orbital prefrontal cortex and the origin of developmental psychopathology', *Development and Psychopathology* 8: 59–87.

Schwaber EA (1998) 'The non-verbal dimension in psychoanalysis: "state" and its clinical vicissitudes', *International Journal of Psychoanalysis* 79: 667–80.

Schwartz MF, Saffran EM, and Marin OSM (1980) 'Fractioning the reading process in dementia: evidence for word-specific print-to-sound associations'. In: M Coltheart, K Patterson, and JC Marshal (eds), *Deep Dyslexia,* London: Routledge & Kegan Paul.

Segal H (1973) *Introduction to the Works of Melanie Klein*, New York: Basic Books.

Shalev A, Peri T, Canetti, and Schreiber S (1996) 'Predictions of PTSD in injured trauma survivors: a prospective study', *American Journal of Psychiatry* 153: 219–25.

Shallice T, Fletcher P, Frith DC, Grasby P, Frackowiak RS, and Dolan RJ (1994) 'Brain regions associated with acquisition and retrieval of verbal episodic memory', *Nature* 368: 633–5.

Shields M (1979) 'Monologue, dialogue and egocentric speech by children in schools'. In: O Garnica and M King (eds), *Language, Children and Society*, New York: Pergamon Press.

Spence D (1982) *Narrative Truth and Historical Truth: Meaning and Interpretation in Psychoanalysis*, New York: Norton.

Spiegel D (1995) 'Hypnosis and suggestion'. In: D Schacter (ed.), *Memory Distortion*, Cambridge, MA: Harvard University Press.

Sroufe LA and Wunsch JP (1972) 'The development of laughter in the first year of life', *Child Development* 43: 1326–44.

Stern D (1985) *The Interpersonal World of the Infant*, New York: Basic Books.

Stevenson J and Meares R (1992) 'An outcome study of psychotherapy in border-line personality disorder', *American Journal of Psychiatry* 149: 358–62.

Stevenson J and Meares R (1999) 'Psychotherapy with borderline patients, Part II: A preliminary cost–benefit analysis', *Australian and New Zealand Journal of Psychiatry* 33(3) 473–7.

Stolorow R (1997) 'Dynamic, dyadic, intersubjective systems: an evolving para-digm for psychoanalysis', *Psychoanalytic Psychology* 14: 337–46.

Stolorow R and Atwood G (1992) *Contexts of Being: The Intersubjective Foundations of Psychological Life*, Hillsdale, NJ: The Analytic Press.

Stolorow R and Atwood G (1997) 'Deconstructing the myth of the neutral analyst: an alternative from intersubjective systems theory', *Psychoanalytic Quarterly* 66: 431–49.

Stolorow R, Brandchaft B, and Atwood G (1987) *Psychoanalytic Treatment: an Inter-subjective Approach*, Hillsdale, NJ: The Analytic Press.

Stolum H (1996) 'River meandering a self organization process', *Science* 271: 1710–13.

Stone M (1994) 'Characterologic subtypes of the borderline personality disorder with acute or prognostic factors', *Psychiatric Clinics of North America* 17: 773–84.

Sullivan HS (1953) *The Interpersonal Theory of Psychiatry*, New York: Norton.

Suttie I (1935) *The Origins of Love and Hate*, London: Kegan Paul. Reprinted, Harmondsworth: Penguin, 1960 (this edition cited here).

Talland G (1965) *Deranged Memory: A Psychonomic Study of the Amnesic Syndrome*, New York: Academic Press.

Terr L (1981) 'Psychic trauma in children: observations following the Chowchilla school-bus kidnapping', *American Journal of Psychiatry* 138: 14–19.

Terr L (1983) 'Chowchilla revisited: the effects of psychic trauma four years after a school-bus kidnapping', *American Journal of Psychiatry* 140: 1543–50.

Terr L (1988) 'What happens to early memories of trauma?' *Journal of the American Academy of Child and Adolescent Psychiatry* 1: 96–104.

Terr L (1993) *Unchained Memories*, New York: Basic Books.

Thomä H and Kächele H (1987) *Psychoanalytic Practice: I. Principles*. Berlin, New York, London, Paris, Tokyo: Springer Verlag.

Trevarthen C (1974) 'Conversations with a two-month-old', *New Scientist* 62: 230–5.

Trevarthen C (1977) 'Descriptive analyses of infant communicative behaviour'. In: HR Schaffer (ed.), *Studies in Mother–Infant Interaction*, New York: Academic Press.

Trevarthen C (1983) 'Emotions in infancy: regulators of contacts and relationships with persons'. In: K Scherer and P Ekman (eds), *Approaches to Emotion*, Hillsdale, NJ: Lawrence Erlbaum.

Trevarthen C (1987) 'Mind in infancy'. In: R Gregory (ed.), *The Oxford Companion to the Mind*, Oxford: Oxford University Press.

Tulving E (1972) 'Episodic and semantic memory'. In: E Tulving and W Donaldson (eds), *Organization of Memory*, New York: Academic Press.

Tulving E (1983) *Elements of Episodic Memory*, Oxford: Clarendon Press, Oxford University Press.

Tulving E (1985) 'How many memory systems are there?' *American Psychologist* 40: 385–98.

Tulving E (1993a) 'What is episodic memory?' *Current Directions in Psychological Science* 2: 67–70.

Tulving E (1993b) 'The mental representation of trait and autobiographical knowledge about the self'. In: T Srull and R Wyer (eds) *Advances in Social Cognition*, Vol.V, Hillsdale, NJ: Erlbaum.

Tulving E and Schacter D (1990) 'Priming and human memory systems', *Science* 247: 301–6.

Tulving E and Thomson D (1973) 'Encoding specificity and retrieval processes in episodic memory', *Psychological Review* 80: 352–73.

Tulving E, Kapur S, Craik FI, Moscovitch M, and Houle S (1994) 'Hemispheric encoding/retrieval asymmetry in episodic memory: positron emission tomography findings', *Proceedings of the National Academy of Sciences of the United Sates of America* 91(6): 2016–20.

Urban RM (1909) *Valuation: Its Nature and Laws*, London: Allen & Unwin.

Uzgiris I (1991) 'The social context of infant imitation. In M. Lewis and S. Feinman, (eds), *Social Influences and Socialization in Infancy*, New York: Plenum.

Uzgiris I, Benson J, Kruper J, and Vasek M (1989) 'Contexual influences on imitative interactions between mothers and infants'. In: J Lockman and N Hazen (eds), *Action in Social Context Perspectives in Early Development*, New York: Plenum.

Van der Hart O and Nijenhuis E (1995) Amnesia for traumatic experiences, *Hypnos* 22: 73–86.

Van der Hart O, Brown P, and Graafland M (1999) 'Trauma-induced dissociative amnesia in World War 1 combat soldiers'. *Australian and New Zealand Journal of Psychiatry* 33: 20–9.

Van der Kolk B (1996) 'Trauma and memory'. In: B van der Kolk, A MacFarlane, and L Weisaeth (eds), *Traumatic Stress*, New York: Guilford Press.

Van der Kolk B and van der Hart O (1989) 'Pierre Janet and the breakdown of adaption in psychological trauma', *American Journal of Psychiatry* 146: 1530–40.

Van der Kolk B, Weisarth L, and van der Hart O (1996) 'History of trauma in psychiatry.' In: B van der Kolk, A Macfarlane, and L Weisaeth (eds), *Traumatic Stress*, New York: Guilford Press.

Van der Veer R and Valsiner J (1994) *The Vygotsky Reader*, Oxford: Blackwell.

Vygotsky LS (1962) *Thought and Language*, ed. and trans. E Hanfmann and G Vakar, Cambridge, MA: MIT Press.

Vygotsky L and Luria A (1994) 'Tool and symbol in child development'. In: R van der Veer and J Valsiner (eds) *The Vygotsky Reader*, Oxford: Blackwell.

Walker E, Katon W, Neraas K, Jemelka R and Massoth D (1992) 'Dissociation in women with chronic pelvic pain', *American Journal of Psychiatry* 149: 543–7.

Waller N, Putnam F, and Carlson E (1994) 'Types of dissociation and dissociative types: a taxometric analysis of dissociative experiences', *Psychological Methods* 1: 300–21.

Watkins M (1986) *Invisible Guests: The Development of Imaginal Dialogues*, Hillsdale, NJ: The Analytic Press. Paperback, Boston: Sigo Press, 1990. (The latter edition cited here.)

Wellman H (1990) *The Child's Theory of Mind*, Cambridge, MA: MIT Press, Bradford Books.

West R (1996) 'The grey men: an experience'. In: R Dalby (ed.), *Modern Ghost Stories*, New York: Barnes & Noble.

Wheeler M, Stuss D, and Tulving D (1997) 'Toward a theory of episodic memory: the frontal lobes and autonoetic consciousness', *Psychological Bulletin* 121: 331–54.

White M and Epston D (1990) *Narrative Means to Therapeutic Ends*, New York: Norton.

Whiten A (ed.) (1991) *Natural Theories of Mind*, Oxford: Blackwell.

Wilson F, Schalaidhe S, and Goldman-Rakic P (1993) 'Dissociation of object and spatial processing domains in primate prefrontal cortex', *Science* 260: 1955–8.

Winnicott DW (1953) 'Transitional objects and transitional phenomena', *International Journal of Psychoanalysis* 34: 1–9.

Winnicott DW (1960) 'Ego distinction in terms of true and false self'. In: *The Maturational Processes and the Facilitating Environment*, New York: International Universities Press, 1965.

Winnicott D (1965) *The Maturational Processes and the Facilitating Environment*, New York: International Universities Press.

Winnicott D (1967) 'Mirror-role of mother in child development'. In: *Playing and Reality*, London: Tavistock, 1971. Harmondsworth: Penguin, 1974. (Latter edition cited here.)

Winnicott D (1971) *Playing and Reality*, London: Tavistock. Harmondsworth: Penguin, 1974.

Wittgenstein L (1922) *Tractatus Logico-Philosophicus*, London: Routledge & Kegan Paul.

Wittgenstein L (1953) *Philosophical Investigations*, trans. G Anscombe, Oxford: Blackwell. Reprinted 1972. (This edition cited here.)

Wood Jones F (1924) *Unscientific Essays*, London: Arnold. Reissued 1931. (This edition cited here.)

Zanarini M (ed.) (1997) *Role of Sexual Abuse in the Etiology of Borderline Personality Disorder*, Washington, DC: American Psychiatric Press.

Zanarini M, Gunderson J, Marino M, et al. (1989) 'Childhood experiences of borderline patients', *Comprehensive Psychiatry* 30: 18–25.

Zhang Y, Suga N, and Yan J (1997) 'Corticofugal modulation of frequency processing in bat auditory system', *Nature* 387: 900–3.

Zilboorg G (1952) 'Precursors of Freud in free association. Some sidelights on free association', *International Journal of Psychoanalysis* 33: 439–49.

Author index

Subject index

abuse 56; sexual 51, 52, 56, 72, 157, 158
accommodation: pathological 21, 113–4, 134, 163–4
acting out 54
affect 81, 89–90, 97; as instinct (James) 90
affect regulation 61–2, 157
affiliation 29–30
alienation 1, 4, 24, 25, 26, 29, 56, 57, 84, 87, 88, 92, 114, 121
amygdala 103–4, 162
anoesis 102; see also unconscious
attachment 2, 21, 29–30, 99, 114, 150; & separation anxiety 76, 113
attention 157; & borderline personality 61, 62; & hysteria 61, 157; & working memory 60; 'evenly suspended' (Freud) 110, 111
attributions 73, 76–78, 80–81, 88, 89, 108, 139
attunement 17, 19
autogenous systems 114–5
automatisms 49, 66
autonoesis 102, 153, 154; see also reflection
avoidance 112–3
axiology 66

babbling 18
binding 26–8, 38, 151, 165
body feeling 11, 57, 61, 87, 92, 99–100, 124, 126
borderline personality disorder 56, 59, 61, 62, 63, 156–7, 158

'Carol' 99–100
complexity 3, 16, 23, 49, 60, 122; & resonance 124, 127–8
concomitant parallelism (Jackson) 46, 47
confabulation 78–9
constriction of consciousness (Janet) 45, 59–60
continuity: & discontinuity 11, 26–8, 44, 57–9, 67, 150–151
conversation: & 'language-games' 11, 16; chronicle-like 28, 59, 121–3; forms of 2, 3, 11, 22–31, 129, 138; in symbolic play 23, 85, 150; script-like 3, 53, 83, 98, 106, 107, 108, 130
conversational play 15–20
countertransference see projective identification

'David' 97–9
deadness & aliveness 21, 71, 114, 123, 125, 144, 145, 152, 153
depersonalization 56–7, 84
derealization 56–7
derogation 75
disjunction 116
disjunctional: anxiety 17
dissociation 1, 3, 43–54, 79, 146, 154, 155, 156; & cerebral disorganization 4, 44; & dissolution 48–50, 62; as dedoubling 43, 50; as defence 44; cardinal features 45; in imitation 84–7; recurrent 45, 52–4; vulnerability to 45, 51
dissociative identity disorder 62
dissolution (Jackson) 46, 48, 55–63, 156